Designing
and Utilizing
Evaluation
for Gifted
Program
Improvement

Designing and Utilizing Evaluation for Gifted Program Improvement

edited by
Joyce VanTassel-Baska
& Annie Xuemei Feng

PRUFROCK PRESS, INC.

Printed in the United States of America.
ISBN-13: 978-1-882664-99-3
ISBN-10: 1-882664-99-X

At the time of this book's publication, all facts and figures cited are the
most current available. All telephone numbers, addresses, and Web site
URLs are accurate and active. All publications, organizations, Web sites,
and other resources exist as described in the book, and all have been ver-
ified. The authors and Prufrock Press, Inc., make no warranty or guarantee concerning the information and materials given out by organizations
or content found at Web sites, and we are not responsible for any changes
that occur after this book's publication. If you find an error, please contact Prufrock Press, Inc. We strongly recommend to parents, teachers,
and other adults that you monitor children's use of the Internet.

PRUFROCK
PRESS INC.

Prufrock Press, Inc.
P.O. Box 8813
Waco, Texas 76714-8813
(800) 998-2208
Fax (800) 240-0333
http://www.prufrock.com

to Mary

to Lee and Ariel

 Table of Contents

 List of Tables

 # List of Figures

■■■■ Acknowledgements

The editors would like to acknowledge the help of staff and graduate students from the Center for Gifted Education in implementing the evaluation of gifted programs over the last decade that led to this text. These individuals include:

Linda Avery
Wenyu Bai
Joy Baytops
Elissa Brown
Diann Drummond
Ellen Fithian
Dennis Hall
Suzanna Henshon
Janine Lehane
Catherine Little
Lisa Rainen
Martin Reardon
Jeanne Struck
Li Zuo

We also want to thank students, teachers, administrators, and parents who have graciously agreed to be a part of our evaluation studies. We particularly want to thank the gifted program coordinators involved for their commitment to their district's gifted programs and their hospitality and support to us as external evaluators.

We greatly appreciate Chwee Quek, Julie Long, Rena Subotnik, and her colleagues Janet Soller and Sarah Hood, who shared their evaluation experiences and perspectives in the book.

A special thank you to Dawn Benson, Sarah Bundy, and Sharron Gatling for their manuscript preparation work.

Foreword (I)

In the 1990s, scholars at the Center for Gifted Education at the College of William and Mary presented the field with a substantive curriculum model for high-ability learners brought to life by multiple units in three key content areas: science, language arts, and social studies. They followed their developmental work with curriculum effectiveness studies that met the gold standard of improving student learning. Over that same period of time, the Center was involved in a series of school district and state evaluations, which culminated in this highly readable and commendable book introducing the William and Mary Eclectic Model of Gifted Program Evaluation. This new text is a gold mine of useful "how-to" information and revealing evaluation results. If we heed the message, the field will move forward.

The Joint Committee on Standards for Educational Evaluation has proposed four standards by which program evaluations should be judged: utility, feasibility, accuracy, and propriety. The first of these standards, utility, is particularly relevant to the work described in this text. Utility is the standard that suggests that evaluations should maximize the usefulness of their results for stakeholders. Evaluations do little good if they sit unused on a shelf. How does the William and Mary model fare when measured against the important standard of utility?

As the title suggests, utility is a key issue for these authors. Two chapters specifically address the use of evaluations by stakeholders. Chapter 8, "Metafindings on the Utilization of Evaluations," generalizes across local and state evaluations to discuss the ways in which evaluations are used by those who request them or participate in them. Chapter 9, "Knowledge Utilization: One School District's Experience," provides an in-depth example of local use. In addition, the importance of useful and user-friendly approaches to evaluation permeate other chapters in the book.

For example, Annie Feng's chapter focuses attention on ways to upgrade the ubiquitous stakeholder survey. If any evaluation is being done on gifted programs (VanTassel-Baska's literature review in the text indicates it is slight), it is the stakeholder survey in the threadbare clothing of a consumer satisfaction survey. Such surveys rely on questions asking what stakeholders "liked best" and "liked least" about the services provided. The results are shallow. However, in Chapter 3, "Constructing and Implementing Surveys," Feng provides examples and tips to improve stakeholder surveys and thereby increase the richness of the information generated by them. Since surveys will continue to play an important role in gifted program evaluations, the information provided in this text will help to improve them and add to their utility.

Other chapters add new tools to the gifted educator's evaluation toolbox. The chapters by Joyce VanTassel-Baska on the use of the Classroom Observation Form and by Annie Feng and Elissa Brown on focus groups provide detailed treatments of these two strategies. The reader could implement the observation form and the focus group on their own turf from the information and examples in the text. In Chapter 8, VanTassel-Baska reports that 100% of the stakeholders interviewed 6 months after their evaluations reported that the classroom observation data were useful. Again, the authors have taken care to attend to the issue of utilization through follow-up and direct inquiry. Having had the opportunity to use the Classroom Observation Form in a federally funded professional development project of my own, I can attest to the readiness with which teachers respond to its use and to the clarity of the information the form provides. In fact, our experience indicates that the William and Mary Classroom Observation Form is an avenue for continued professional development.

Designing and Utilizing Evaluation for Gifted Program Improvement does something else profoundly needed in the field: In addition to the useful explanations, how-to tips, and examples, the book also provides results from local, state, and national evaluation studies. In several individual chapters in the text and in a summary of metaevaluation findings, the authors provide us with a picture of what is really happening in programs and services for talented learners. We learn, for example, that while educators generally report that they are monitoring the achievement of their high-ability students, the achievement data are rarely available as part of the evaluation enterprise. We learn that, while teachers of talented learners are generally strong in lesson planning and clarity of teaching, they continue to employ few differentiation practices. We learn that programs and services for talented learners are seriously understaffed and lack sufficient resources to provide depth. As VanTassel–Baska reports in the final chapter, talented learners are underidentified in many school districts, given the national incidence rates of 5–15%. When they are identified, almost 40% of the districts provide limited specialized services of less than 2 hours per week. Lack of adequate staffing is evident in the evaluation findings across both state and local evaluation sites.

And yet, there are hopeful messages in the report of evaluation results, as well. These hopeful messages again come from the theme of evaluation utilization that permeates this book. Specifically, when the nature and frequency of program changes were summarized across seven separate evaluation studies, all seven reported that they now actively plan for the future of gifted education, and five of the seven reported that they now include student learning in their subsequent evaluation efforts. In other words, the Eclectic Model meets its own standard of utility. Educators used the evaluations.

My hope is that the field, like these states and districts, will heed the message and use the guidance and the results provided in this very fine book.

Ann Robinson
Center for Gifted Education
University of Arkansas at Little Rock

Foreword (II)

I t's hard enough to garner support for gifted programs during economic boom times. When budgets are lean, the challenge is that much greater. It therefore behooves us to be especially rigorous in our evidence that gifted programs are effective for the students and are a good use of public funds. This book contributes to our field's quest for evidence that we are serving gifted students and the public well.

The Center for Gifted Education at the College of William and Mary has been conducting evaluations all over the nation and around the world, and their experience is brought to bear here. Each chapter offers a double-barreled approach to subtopics in evaluation methodology. On the one hand, the authors describe the strengths and weaknesses of various components of evaluation techniques employed in gifted education. On the other, they provide examples and insights from a metaview of what they have learned from all the evaluations they have conducted.

An early chapter in the book addresses the use of stakeholder surveys in evaluation studies. They are widely used as a method of gaining an accurate picture of program effectiveness, in spite of the fact that they are deemed by most evaluation scholars as nonrigorous. Annie Feng shows us how to alleviate this problem by triangulating the data across stakeholder groups. According to Feng, the congruence of data from multiple stakeholders and other data sources speaks for the power of triangulation in enriching the confidence level of drawing conclusions from stakeholder questionnaire results.

Collecting data from various stakeholders allows the evaluators to monitor the degree of consensus that exists on key aspects of a program. This is especially important in potentially contentious areas such as admissions (selectivity and diversity), degree of separation from the general population of students, and the degree of departure from local or state academic standards and domains.

Surveys of stakeholders provide yet another important source of information. They can serve as a barometer of how knowledgeable stakeholders are about the program, how committed they are to the program, and, most importantly, how willing they are to change in regard to various aspects of the program. With a sense of these factors, the evaluators can develop recommendations that are most likely to evoke positive change. If stakeholders are not well informed or committed to the current policies, then they may not be willing to undertake constructive change.

Chapter 5 addresses the collection of classroom observation data. These methods have an honorable history as powerful indicators of classroom interaction, particularly in the literature on gender differences. As reported by the author, classroom observation data provide an excellent tool for checking on the congruence of reality and teachers' perceptions of how well they're applying models and strategies of gifted education. In this way, they provide a useful formative evaluation tool.

The author makes another important point that I'd like to repeat: Evaluation must include a discussion of inputs, such as the model of giftedness employed by the program and the quality of the teacher preparation in implementing that model. The evaluation must address the outputs, that is, the degree to which students are achieving beyond what they might have without this intervention. What surveys and classroom observation add to the mix is a good balance between the two because they provide some insight into the "why" and help explain the "what."

I would argue that classroom observation could be further employed to monitor student output. For example, data can be collected on the degree of participation of underrepresented groups in gifted classroom interaction. How often are they called on? How often are they encouraged to work through their reasoning before the teacher moves on to someone else? In heterogeneously grouped classes, one can monitor gifted students' participation and how other students respond to their gifted classmates.

Another chapter zeroes in on focus groups and their use as a data source that fills in gaps between observation and interviews. They offer a mechanism to display interaction among participants around specific questions selected by the evaluation team. As indicated, focus groups should not be used as a stand-alone variable, but they can be particularly helpful when triangulated with other data sources. In fact all of these forms of data that stand between inputs and outputs (surveys, classroom observations, and focus groups) can serve as barometers of participant knowledge, commitment, and flexibility.

As indicated by the authors, a serious problem with focus groups is that they may be affected by strong personalities or unstated political pressures. The Center has added a dimension to the process that helps to alleviate this problem: They collect anonymous individual feedback from participants to provide comparison data between what participants say publicly and what they write privately.

So many of these techniques require excellent facilitation and administration. Clearly, there is room for large amounts of training of evaluators that is sensitive to the unique characteristics of gifted programs and to the essential need to provide rigorous, evidence-based data in this era of financial and political accountability.

The utilization chapter addresses the big questions associated with evaluation: Why aren't more evaluations of gifted programs conducted on a regular basis? Why are some recommendations accepted and others not? Is the point of evaluation the appropriate implementation of a model, wherein the admission, curriculum, and assessment aspects all hang together well? Or is the bottom line that students achieve or perform beyond what could be expected from participation in regular education?

It appears as if the first reason is more frequently assessed because, as indicated by Joyce VanTassel-Baska, few evaluations include outcome measures. This can't go on!

As for what makes stakeholders comply with some recommendations and not others—this is another tough call. If you want buy-in from the program community, they need to be integrally involved in the process. On the other hand, too much involvement leads to too much self-interest. You can see this in the higher education accreditation wars, as well. Too often, program participants are just not willing to take a hard or comprehensive look at themselves.

In conclusion, in order to make evaluations work for the public, we need to incorporate outcome measures that speak to their need for program accountability. In order to make evaluations work for the stakeholders, program, school, and district leadership must ensure that positive change is supported financially and politically. The Center for Gifted Education at the College of William and Mary cannot make this difficult path easy for programs, but they provide an invaluable guidebook for those who are serious about taking this heroic journey toward program improvement.

Rena F. Subotnik
American Psychological Association
Washington, DC

Introduction to the William and Mary Eclectic Model of Gifted Program Evaluation

by Joyce VanTassel-Baska

Evaluation will contribute better information about how and when and why programs work, which will lead to better decisions, more effective action, and more effective use of resources . . . and the world will be a better place.

—Patricia J. Rogers (2001, p. 435)

The approaches used in gifted program evaluation have their origin in two central "ways of knowing" in the education world: positivist and postpositivist. This chapter will begin with these orientations to knowing and then proceed to explore evaluation models based on disparate ways of knowing. It will conclude with the evaluation model developed for specific use in gifted evaluation studies at The College of William and Mary.

Two paradigms dominate most work in educational evaluation just as they do in educational research. These paradigms may be characterized as positivist, rationalistic, and predominantly quantitative on the one hand,

and postpositivist, naturalistic, and predominantly qualitative on the other. Table 1.1 captures the essential differences between these two approaches to educational evaluation work.

The rationalistic paradigm assumes that education is a controlled enterprise. Such a mind set tends to view education as a means to an end, as producing an educated workforce or making the country more competitive. Teaching and learning are also seen as means to desired ends, as elements in a system that can, in principle, be controlled. In this worldview, teaching is regarded as a skilled craft based on technical expertise, problems with student learning can be dealt with by applying appropriate techniques, and education can be improved by a more complete mapping of cause-and-effect relationships in the teaching and learning process (Ewert, 1991).

The naturalistic paradigm assumes that education is in a state of flux and is therefore free from attempts to control its processes. Individuals who see the world of education as naturalistic acknowledge its interrelatedness and holistic realities. Teaching and learning are seen as reciprocal processes of uncovering meaning. Teaching is regarded as an art form, based on intuitive judgement about content and student and how they may best interact. In this view, education can be made more effective by a deepening understanding of individual learners and their needs and acknowledging that student growth is uneven and often unpredictable.

Most gifted program evaluations tend to combine both paradigms, rather than strictly adhere to one or the other. These paradigms emerge from the assumptions educational practitioners hold about how their world is organized and how it works. Within educational settings, these different ways of knowing are alive and well. There are educators who view their world as ordered, linear, and deliberate in moving from a written plan to its actualization in a school or classroom. Other educators know their world, not by quantitative outcomes, but by the quality of experiences provided in nurturing environments. Each type of educator inhabits school districts. Thus, an evaluation that will be credible must acknowledge both of these ways of knowing educational practice and be willing to acknowledge each role in developing strong gifted programs.

Key Evaluation Models

There is no single conceptual approach to evaluation, no more than there is a single, universally accepted philosophy of doing science. The

Table 1.1
Differences Between the Rationalistic
and Naturalistic Paradigms

Dimensions	Rationalistic Paradigm	Naturalistic Paradigm
Reality	Single, convergent,	Multiple, divergent,
Evaluator/client relationship	Independent	Interrelated
Nature of truth	Context-free generalizations	Context-bound working ideas
Role of evidence	Verify cause and effect relationships	Triangulate to identify themes and attributional shapers.
Relation to values	Value-free	Value-bound

lack of a single guiding philosophy has not prevented extensive discourse concerning philosophical assumptions about establishing truth or merit. Such debates are largely responsible for the diversity of views about educational evaluation.

Although differences in philosophy have led to alternative views of evaluation, the philosophical differences are not incompatible. Multiple approaches to describing objects of study, drawn from both objectivist and subjectivist traditions, have been used in the same evaluations to achieve important goals and purposes.

In choosing an evaluation orientation, evaluators need to consider a) the credibility of results reported to evaluation clients, b) the importance of understanding or explaining findings, c) the need to be sensitive to emerging or hidden issues during the evaluation, and d) the importance of thoroughly addressing questions posed by the client. We recognize the right of any evaluator to subscribe totally to the assumptions and premises of one particular ideology. Yet, few evaluators who succeed in a wide range of evaluation settings can afford to consider philosophical ideologies as "either/or" decisions. An evaluator should use appropriate multiple methods based on alternative epistemologies within the same evaluation. It is important to know, however, the assumptions and limitations of methods that are drawn from different worldviews about evaluation. The following evaluation models represent the ones most commonly employed in gifted program studies. They are described in respect to purpose, assumptions, and methodology.

CIPP (Context, Input, Process, Product) Evaluation Approach

If an evaluation purpose is to assess the extent to which gifted program goals have been realized, then using the Stufflebeam model (2001) or some variation of it may be useful. This model assumes that programs can be analyzed as systems, examining each aspect in turn and then rendering judgments on each facet, as well as on the whole.

This model, developed by Daniel Stufflebeam at Central Michigan University and implemented successfully in many educational evaluations, seeks to analyze components of a program and determine the relationships of those components to each other in respect to what is happening in the program versus what should be happening based on defined goals and outcomes. The resultant "discrepancy" becomes the basis for making recommendations for program improvements. Since many gifted program evaluations are shown to enhance program improvement where the target client is the program manager, this type of evaluation is often highly desirable because it yields data on program planning features and program implementation processes.

The model deliberately examines four aspects of a program: context and design, inputs, processes, and outcomes. Each aspect of the program is carefully examined with an eye toward further program planning that will address deficiency areas.

Context evaluation judges how an educational program is situated in a setting in respect to its identified needs and level of support. Design evaluation would be used to assess curricular materials and overall program design features as displayed in program manuals and other written materials. It is concerned with comprehensiveness, internal or logical consistency, relationship to need, and appropriateness for relevant audiences.

Input evaluation would be used to assess whether a program has sufficient infrastructure to function effectively, given its goals. It is concerned with the availability of resources and the extent to which program resources (money, people, materials, etc.) are available and deployed as planned.

Process evaluation would be used to assess the extent to which the program design is being implemented. It is concerned with the extent to which activities are carried out as planned, their frequency, intensity, and other qualities.

Outcome evaluation would be used to assess what happened as the result of a program being operational for a period of time. It is concerned with short-term outcomes, outcomes that are prerequisite to other outcomes, and terminal outcomes or products of the program.

Our evaluations at the College of William and Mary have tried to assess such program planning mechanisms through various strategies. They include a review of gifted program documents, using program design and curricular design criteria as the basis for such review. Resource allocations (input) are determined through budget analyses and job descriptions. Program implementation procedures (process evaluation) are revealed through questioning of relevant stakeholder groups, classroom observation, and follow-up focus group probes on key program issues. Student and program outcomes are determined by assessment data collected on students in the program and other documentation of program effects. The triangulation of these approaches provides a strong understanding of how the program is currently functioning, which in turn becomes a platform for improvement recommendations.

Table 1.2 depicts a set of questions relevant for gifted program evaluation based on Stufflebeam's (2001) componential evaluation model.

Case Study Approach

If an evaluation purpose is to understand the program deeply, then a case study approach might be an appropriate model to employ. Such a model assumes that programs can only be understood from the inside, taking into account multiple contextual layers of operation. The case study approach to evaluation has been best articulated by Robert Stake at the University of Illinois in a book called *The Art of Case Study Research* (Stake, 1995).

Case study methods have existed for many years and have been applied in such areas as anthropology, clinical psychology, law, medicine, and social work. Pioneers in applying the method to program evaluation in addition to Stake, include Campbell (1975), Lincoln and Guba (1985), and Yin (1992).

Program evaluation that is based on a case study is a focused, in-depth description, analysis, and synthesis of a particular program or other object. Investigators do not control the program in any way. Rather, they

Table 1.2

Application of Stufflebeam Model to Gifted Education Evaluation

Context (C)	1.	What are current needs of gifted students and teachers?
	2.	What is the level of support for the gifted program (internal and external)?
	3.	What general resources are available to provide support?
Design (D)	1.	How complete are program manuals and curricular materials in defining the program/curriculum?
	2.	How appropriate are the materials for the relevant audience?
	3.	How well organized are the materials?
Input (I)	1.	What gifted program strategies would best meet program objectives?
	2.	What mechanisms will be used to monitor program implementation?
Process (P)	1.	Is the gifted program operating as planned?
	2.	What program "adjustments" are occurring that facilitate/impede attainment of program objectives?
Product (P)	1.	Were program objectives attained?
	2.	What were significant interactions affecting program outcomes?
	3.	What were the unanticipated effects of the program?

look at it as it is occurring or as it occurred in the past. The study looks at the program in its geographic, cultural, organizational, and historical contexts, closely examining its internal operations and how it uses inputs and processes to produce outcomes. It examines a wide range of intended and unexpected outcomes. It looks at the program's multiple levels and also holistically at the overall program. It characterizes both central dominant themes and variations and aberrations. It defines and describes the program's intended and actual beneficiaries. It examines beneficiaries' needs and the extent to which the program effectively addressed those needs. It employs multiple methods to obtain and integrate multiple sources of information. While it breaks apart and analyzes a program along various dimensions, this model also provides an overall characterization of the program.

The case study should be keyed to the questions of most interest to the evaluation's main audiences. The evaluator must therefore identify and interact with the program's stakeholders. Along the way, stakeholders will be engaged to help plan the study and interpret findings. Ideally, the audiences include the program's administrators, staff, and beneficiaries.

Typical questions posed by some or all of the above audiences are: What is the program in concept and practice? How does it actually operate to produce outcomes? What are the shortfalls and negative side effects? What are the positive side effects? In what ways and to what degrees do various stakeholders value the program? These questions illustrate the range of questions a case study might address, yet each case study will be affected by the interests of the client and other audiences.

To conduct effective case studies, evaluators need to employ a wide range of qualitative and quantitative methods. These may include analysis of archives, collection of artifacts such as work samples, content analysis of program documents, both independent and participant observations, interviews, logical analysis of operations, focus groups, questionnaires, rating scales, and maintenance of a program database. Reports may incorporate in-depth descriptions and accounts of relevant trends, focus on critical incidents, and summarize main conclusions.

William and Mary evaluation studies typically include a case study approach, especially in the involvement of stakeholders in planning and decision making about the evaluation process itself. We also value the use of multiple data sources to understand an identified program issue or problem.

The case study approach is highly appropriate in gifted program evaluation since it requires no control of treatments and subjects and looks at programs as they naturally occur and evolve. Accuracy issues are addressed by triangulating multiple perspectives, methods, and information sources, and systematic procedures for analyzing qualitative information are outlined in each study conducted.

Utilization-Focused Approach

If the purpose of an evaluation is to lead to positive program change, then the utilization-focused approach may be highly desirable. Such an approach assumes that clients view evaluation as a part of the program development cycle naturally leading to healthy changes.

The utilization-focused approach is explicitly geared to ensure that program evaluations make an impact (Patton, 1987, 2002). It is a process for making choices about an evaluation study in collaboration with a targeted group of priority users selected from a broader set of stakeholders in order to focus effectively on intended uses of the evaluation. All aspects of a utilization-focused program evaluation are chosen and applied to help the targeted users obtain and apply evaluation findings to their intended uses and to maximize the likelihood that they will. Such studies are judged more for the difference they make in improving programs and influencing decisions and actions than for their elegance or technical excellence. No matter how good an evaluation report is, if it only sits on the shelf gathering dust, then it will not contribute positively to program improvement and accountability.

The key features of utilization-focused program evaluations are, in the abstract, the possible users and uses to be served. Working from this initial conception, the evaluator moves as directly as possible to identify in concrete terms the actual users to be served. Through a careful and thorough analysis of stakeholders, the evaluator identifies the multiple and varied perspectives and interests that should be represented in the study. The evaluator then engages this group to clarify why they need the evaluation, how they intend to apply its findings, how they think it should be conducted, and what types of reports (e.g., oral, printed, or both) should be provided. The main possible uses of evaluation findings contemplated in this approach are assessment of merit and worth, improvement, and generation of knowledge. This approach also values the evaluation process itself, seeing it as helpful in enhancing shared understandings among stakeholders, bringing support to a program, promoting participation in it, and developing and strengthening organizational capacity.

The William and Mary evaluation team sees this approach as another way to help strengthen the bases for gifted program improvement and growth. Working with stakeholders in an educative way builds program advocacy and support for substantive long-term change in a program.

Connoisseurship Approach

If the purpose of an evaluation is to gain quick insight into a program due to time and resource constraints, the connoisseurship approach may be desirable. Such a model assumes that deep expertise in an area can yield important understanding that will be credible in a given program setting, usually in a self-contained time frame.

The basis for a connoisseur-based study is the evaluator's special expertise and sensitivities. The study's purpose is to describe, critically appraise, and illuminate a particular program's merits. This approach was pioneered by Eisner (1985) and has been used in gifted program evaluations where time is limited and intense use of experts is perceived to be an effective means of obtaining direction for program improvement. The evaluation questions addressed by the criticism and connoisseur-based evaluation are determined by expert evaluators—the critics and authorities who have undertaken the evaluation. Among the major questions they can be expected to ask are: What is the program's essence and salient characteristics? What strengths and weaknesses distinguish this particular program from others of the same general type?

Understanding context also matters in this approach in terms of constructing and implementing evaluations. It is important for evaluators of gifted programs, for example, to clarify:

- the needs of program students and teachers;
- problems or barriers to meeting those needs;
- assets and opportunities that might be employed to address problems; and
- the appropriateness of program and curricular goals.

In order to gain that clarification, the evaluation team must be headed by someone with deep expertise in gifted education who could discuss the extent to which a context is facilitating or inhibiting program development and in what ways it is occurring. Such expertise, coupled with the multiple data sources of program artifacts, classroom observation, questionnaires, and focus groups provide the necessary entry points to understanding and interpreting contextual needs.

The main advantage of the criticism and connoisseur-based study is that it exploits the particular expertise and finely developed insights of people who have devoted much time and effort to the study of a precise area. Such individuals can provide an array of detailed information that an audience can then use to form a more insightful analysis than otherwise might be possible. This approach's disadvantage is that it is dependent on the expertise and qualifications of the particular expert doing the program evaluation, leaving room for much subjectivity. It also suffers from the lack of time to understand a program deeply from multiple dimensions. However, this approach to evaluation has been used in many gifted program studies. Chapter 10 on the Hunter School evaluation and Chapter 11 on the Singapore evaluation relied heavily on this approach, deliberately selecting evaluation team members for their particular type of expertise in gifted education.

Client-Centered Approach (Responsive Evaluation)

If one purpose of an evaluation is to respond to client needs, then a responsive evaluation approach may be warranted. Such an approach assumes that all evaluation work is nested in the needs, desires, and capabilities of those working in a given program; thus, the evaluation approach should be centered on these individuals.

The label *client-centered* evaluation is used here because one pervasive theme is that the evaluator must work with and for the support of a diverse client group including, for example, teachers, administrators, boards of education, and legislators. They are the clients in the sense that they support, develop, administer, or directly operate the programs under study and seek answers to improving programs. This approach charges evaluators to interact continuously with, and respond to, the evaluative needs of the various clients, as well as other stakeholders (Stake, 1991).

The client-centered study embraces local autonomy and helps people who are involved in a program to evaluate it and use the evaluation for program improvement. In a sense, the evaluator is a "handmaiden" who uses evaluation to serve the client's needs. In this approach, the program evaluation may culminate in conflicting findings and conclusions, leaving interpretation to the eyes of the beholders. Thus, it is relativistic because it seeks no final authoritative conclusion, interpreting findings against stakeholders' different and often conflicting values. It seeks to examine a program's multidimensionality and values the collection and reporting of multiple, often conflicting perspectives on the importance of a program's format, operations, and achievements. Side effects and incidental gains, as well as intended outcomes, are identified and examined.

The key features in client-centered evaluations are stakeholders' concerns about the program and the program's rationale. A representative group of stakeholders must be willing to engage in open and meaningful dialogue and deliberation at all stages of the study.

Our gifted program evaluations have used this approach as much as possible in 1) defining evaluation questions, 2) taking the temperature of various stakeholders through both focus groups and interviews, and 3) continually assessing how the evaluation process is being perceived by key stakeholders. Ongoing communication with the gifted coordinator and his or her team provides a way of keeping the client front and center in an evaluation. Involving the coordinator in reading a draft of the report for language issues, accuracy, and other concerns ensures important involvement in the evaluation process at its concluding stages.

Accreditation/Certification Approach

If the purpose of the evaluation is to document compliance with national or state standards (or both) in an area, then the accreditation approach is a good choice. Such an approach assumes that standards adequately define what a program should be and that compliance with them is a proxy for running effective programs.

Many educational institutions have periodically been the subject of an accreditation study, and many professionals, at one time or another, have had to meet certification requirements for a given position. Institutions, programs, and personnel are assessed for "goodness of fit" for specific functions and roles in society. Basically, the accreditation approach asks: Are institutions and their programs and personnel meeting minimum standards, and how can their performance be improved? The tools used in an accreditation/certification study are guidelines and criteria that some accrediting or certifying body has adopted. Accrediting agencies like the National Council for Accreditation of Teacher Education (NCATE) accredit university graduate programs; North Central and Middle States accrediting agencies perform a similar service for high schools in particular regions of the country.

In the field of gifted education, these criteria have been formulated by the National Association for Gifted Children (NAGC) in seven categories: identification, curriculum and instruction, program design, administration, professional development, guidance, and evaluation. Each of these categories have identified minimum and exemplary criteria to examine. In several of our recent evaluation studies, we have asked program coordinators to rate themselves in respect to these criteria. The evaluator and program coordinator then discuss the rating and share perspectives. A consensus view of the program is reached and a part of the evaluation report is devoted to documenting how well the district is complying with these national standards.

The William and Mary Evaluation Model

Based on the evaluation approaches just described, we have evolved an eclectic model of evaluation for working with gifted programs that incorporates the relevant features from each approach described in this chapter.

First, the evaluators at William and Mary acknowledge the importance of the use of an *accountability/discrepancy approach (CIPP)*, which seeks to uncover the discrepancy between what the program is as defined by its design, inputs, processes, and outputs and what it needs to be based on its stated goals and explicit expectations. Multiple data sources that are analyzed both quantitatively and qualitatively allow us to understand how gifted programs might move to the next level of excellence in their particular context.

The William and Mary approach also employs a *case study* orientation in its attempt to triangulate data sources to substantiate findings and in its deliberate desire to identify themes, patterns, and issues through the process of data collection. Focus group and interview analyses provide a natural venue for exploring the qualitative dimensions of a program.

Third, the William and Mary approach also is *utilization-driven*. It is important that gifted programs have a mechanism for improvement. Thus, gifted program evaluations are a critical catalyst for that improvement. The William and Mary evaluation approach engages clients in the process in order to promote ownership of the evaluation and therefore its product, the recommendations and action plan. Each evaluation lays out recommendations for easy conversion to a plan of action. A follow-up interview and questionnaire is sent 6 months after the evaluation to assess utilization practices and as a reminder for clients to continue in the ongoing use of evaluation data.

The William and Mary approach employed is also *client-centered or responsive,* engaging school district personnel in defining questions and issues in an evaluation at the first stage. Even when an RFP (request for proposal) is responded to, we still meet initially with key stakeholders to ensure how the evaluation will be shaped. Client involvement continues in many modes, including focus groups, self-assessment, and review of the preliminary report.

It also is heavily vested in a *connoisseurship* approach, using the collective expertise of a team in gifted education to penetrate issues and quickly apprehend potential solutions. The lead evaluator, for example, has 30 years of gifted program development experience that is used to full advantage in the evaluation work.

Finally, the approach also employs an *accreditation/standards approach*. Since the field of gifted education has program standards, they should be used to assess the level of any given program. Self-assessment, along with the evaluator's assessment, is employed with a discussion of each perspective occurring prior to report preparation. Recommendations are crafted with an eye to areas of noncompliance with these standards in addition to findings from other data sources. See Figure 1.1 for the graphic of the William and Mary evaluation model.

Application of the William and Mary Evaluation Model

You have been asked by the superintendent to evaluate a local gifted program in an affluent school district. According to the written information provided about the program, it begins at grade 3 and extends through high school. It includes self-contained classes for identified gifted children in language arts and math in grades 3–5. The middle school has honors classes in humanities and math. By high school, Advanced Placement (AP) and honors programs are available in a broader array of subjects. You have one year to carry out the evaluation and must report results to the school board and the parent advisory group. Parents are concerned that the program is too narrow in scope and that the challenge level is inadequate. Administrators have little investment in the program, although they see some form of program as necessary to assuage parents of gifted children. Teachers feel the program is effective and are not interested in seeing changes.

The real test of an effective evaluation is the design process itself. How one grapples with the real-world data of a program to make sense of it through the organizational structure of a design is a central challenge of the process of evaluation.

In the scenario given, the gifted program reveals itself to be limited in scope, both by grade level and subject area. There are no options for

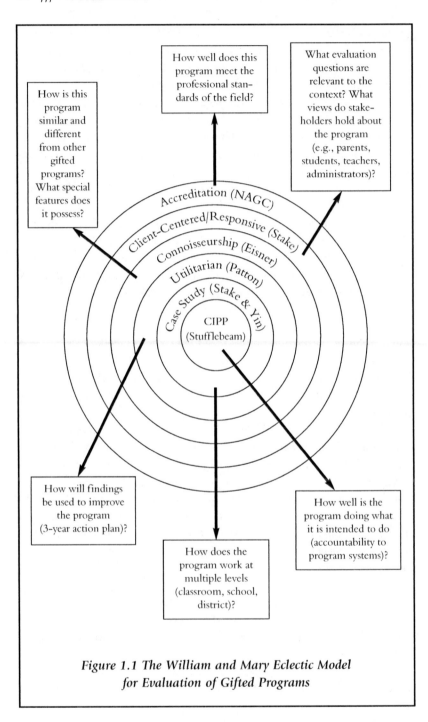

Figure 1.1 The William and Mary Eclectic Model for Evaluation of Gifted Programs

K–2 students, the focus at grades 3–8 is limited to mathematics and language arts, and high school appears to offer only Advanced Placement courses. Moreover, stakeholder groups of parents, teachers, and administrators are split in their perceptions about the program. While such a scenario is fairly typical in many school districts, it raises many real issues and questions in the process of evaluation. Overarching questions that come to mind immediately are:

1. What are the needs of this program? What is the internal and external support for the program?
2. What resources are available to provide support?
3. What does the superintendent want from this evaluation? Why is he or she seeking outside evaluation as a mechanism to find out about the program's strengths and weaknesses?
4. How can the design of the evaluation contribute to its ongoing use?
5. How does the program work at each level in the context of schools?
6. How can this program improve in ways that would address national standards?
7. What have we learned from other program evaluations that will help in understanding and helping this program move forward?

These overarching questions become a working template for investigating the program at several levels. Determining needs, support, and resources for the program will involve talking with key stakeholders, seeing the program in action, and examining program and district budget data. Interviews with the superintendent and a focus group session with the Board of Education may illuminate client motive and direction for the evaluation. Utility must be considered early so that clients are part of the process through review of instrumentation, providing formal insights through interviews, and being privy to relevant insights along the way. Uncovering how the program works will involve the same data sources as those to determine its needs, support, and resources. A formal review of standards by both the evaluator and program coordinator will clearly highlight areas for program improvement.

Other specific questions that will need to be answered about the program are:

Table 1.3

Case Scenario of Evaluation Design

Evaluation Questions/ Areas of Investigation	Data Sources	Sample	Analysis
To what extent is the program addressing and attaining its goals?	• Classroom observation data • Program data on student assessment and evaluation program • Program document review via structured review form	• Depending on size, one-third of all schools in the district sampled for classroom visits at relevant levels • All gifted student assessment data analyzed • Program procedures manual and curricular units/guides	• Comparison of expected vs. observed behaviors • Depending on data available, appropriate quantitative and/or qualitative review • Content-analysis of item checklist
What are the perceptions of stakeholder groups about the program?	• Surveys to teachers, administrators, parents, and students • Focus groups with representations of each stakeholder group	• All teachers and administrators in the district • One-third match of students and parents to schools visited • 8–12 members of each	• Descriptive statistics and correlations and tests for differences across groups • Qualitative analysis of data using content analysis techniques

		stakeholder group convened	
What are the program's strengths and weaknesses?	• Interviews • Focus groups (see above) • Questionnaire data (triangulated, see above) • Classroom observations (see above)	• Key stakeholders (superintendent, program coordinator, building principals, head of advisory committee, etc.) • Aggregated data across sources	Qualitative content analysis of primary source analyses
How well does the program meet national standards?	Review of NAGC program component criteria against knowledge of program operation via multiple data sources (eg, program documents; coordinator interview)	N/A	Quantitative and qualitative analysis of some results by NAGC program area and across areas

- What accounts for stakeholders' varying perspectives on the program?
- Why are the educators so satisfied with the program?
- What was the rationale for total focus on mathematics and language arts?
- Why are there not more program options at elementary, middle, and high school levels?
- Why are young children (K–2) not served?
- What are the specific Advanced Placement offerings? In what subject areas? What leads to AP at the high school level?
- What grouping mechanisms are employed in the program?
- What approach to ongoing professional development for educators is employed?
- How well are the program mechanisms of identification, curricula, instruction, assessment, and evaluation working?
- What is the level of communication about the program within the district?

Program-specific questions would need to be woven into the survey and interview instrumentation. Thus, surveys, focus groups, and interview protocols should contain versions of these as key questions or follow-up probes. Classroom observations and meetings with principals at their schools should also provide important insights.

After considering the landscape of the eclectic evaluation model and specific program questions, it is important to construct an evaluation design, reflecting on early discussions with the client and preliminary issues that emerged from them. A design that might be proposed for this study may be found in Table 1.3. It takes into account all the levels of questions that need to be considered in understanding and judging the program.

The process just described illustrates how the William and Mary eclectic model of evaluation is employed at the planning stage, arguably considered the most critical for ensuring integrity of the evaluation process.

Conclusion

The underlying assumptions, approaches, and methodologies employed in a gifted education evaluation matter a great deal in the degree to which both the process and product are viewed as credible. At this stage of still-nascent gifted program development and concerns in the larger environment for accountability, an eclectic approach appears most warranted. Judging the merit of a program must always be done with an eye to how it might be improved. Both qualitative and quantitative data help us to understand a program's strengths, its potential weaknesses, and areas for improvement.

Practical Tips

1. School districts need to define the purpose of an evaluation carefully. Not all purposes identified in this chapter can be satisfied within time and budget constraints.

2. Evaluation work needs to be timely for decision makers in a school district. Too-early evaluation prohibits creative trial-and-error testing of innovations. Too-late evaluation inhibits important formative data from being used to improve programs as they evolve.

3. Acknowledge that a combined use of evaluation models may respond more effectively to decision makers' desire to judge a gifted program.

4. Evaluations must be focused around a set of objectives or questions to be answered. Because no evaluation can serve all potential stakeholders' interests equally well, stakeholders representing various constituencies should come together to negotiate what issues and questions deserve priority.

5. Remember that the personal factor contributes significantly to an evaluation's effectiveness, meaning that the personal interests and commitments of those involved in an evaluation undergird utility. Thus, evaluations should be *specifically* user-oriented, aimed at the interests and information needs of clients. Careful and thoughtful stakeholder analysis should inform the identification of primary intended users, taking into account the varied and multiple interests that surround any program.

6. Focusing on intended use requires making deliberate and thoughtful choices. There are three primary uses of evaluation findings: judging

merit or worth (summative evaluation), improving programs (instrumental use), and generating knowledge (conceptual use). While uses can change and evolve over time as a program matures, most gifted programs need to focus on program improvement through the processes of shared understanding about program development mechanisms.

7. Useful evaluations must be designed and adapted situationally. Standardized recipe approaches will not work.

8. Commitment to using evaluation findings can be nurtured and enhanced by actively involving key stakeholders in making significant decisions about the evaluation. Involvement increases relevance, understanding, and ownership of the evaluation, all of which facilitate informed and appropriate use.

References

Campbell, D. T. (1975). Degree of freedom and case study. *Comparative Political Study*, 8, 178–193.

Eisner, E. W. (1985). *The art of educational evaluation*. Philadelphia, PA: Falmer Press.

Ewert, G. (1991). Habermas and education: A comprehensive overview of the influence of Habermas in educational literature. *Review of Educational Research*, 61, 345–378.

Lincoln, Y. S., & Guba, E. G. (1985). *Naturalistic inquiry*. Beverly Hills, CA: Sage.

Patton, M. Q. (Ed.). (1987). *Utilization-focused evaluation*. Beverly Hills, CA: Sage.

Patton, M. Q. (2002). *Qualitative research and evaluation methods* (3rd ed.). Thousand Oaks, CA: Sage.

Stake, R. E. (1991). Retrospective on "The Countenance of Educational Evaluation." In M. W. McLaughlin & D. C. Philips (Eds.), *Evaluation and education: At quarter century* (pp. 67–88). Chicago: University of Chicago Press.

Stake, R. E. (1995). *The art of case study research*. Thousand Oaks, CA: Sage.

Stufflebeam, D. L. (2001). Evaluation models. In G. T. Gary & J. C. Greene (Eds.), *New directions for evaluation* (pp. 7–99). San Francisco: Jossey-Bass.

Stufflebeam, D. L., Madaus, G. F., & Kellaghan, T. (Eds.). (2000). *Evaluation models: Viewpoints on educational and human services evaluation* (2nd ed.). Boston: Kluwer Academic Publishers.

Yin, R. K. (1992, November). *Evaluation: A singular craft.* Paper presented at the annual meeting of American Evaluation Association, Seattle, WA.

 **2**

The Processes
in Gifted Program Evaluation

by Joyce VanTassel-Baska

In human affairs the logical future, determined by past and present condi-tions, is less important than the willed future, which is largely brought about by deliberate choices.

— Rene Dubos

The epistemological orientation for William and Mary gifted evalu-ation studies draws heavily upon Stake's (1976) idea of "responsive evaluation," Stufflebeam's CIPP model, and Patton's utilization model. Our studies are framed by three key beliefs:

1. the fundamental role of evaluation is to provide information that can be used to improve and advance the state of the art of gifted programs;

2. evaluation research is a collaborative process among stakeholders including the state department, local school districts, and the contractor; and

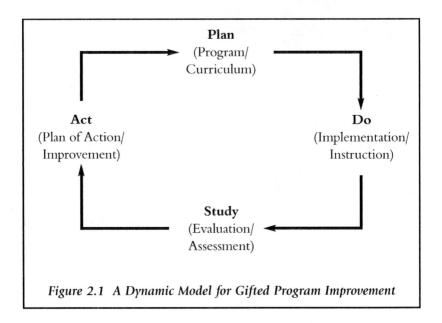

Figure 2.1 A Dynamic Model for Gifted Program Improvement

3. the use of multiple data sources helps to illuminate the complexity and salience of issues needing to be considered.

Evaluation teams also need to recognize that rational decision making is mediated by values and that the structural, social, political, and symbolic dimensions of a given context (Bolman & Deal, 1991) influence the nature and degree of change that can and will be made. Thus, conducting district- and state-level evaluations of gifted programs requires a strong emphasis on the formative process, on what is working well in a program and which areas need improvement.

Evaluation is also a part of the overall program development cycle that flows naturally out of planning and implementing programs. Moreover, it is a prelude to action planning that becomes the basis for a new cycle of program implementation. Annually, gifted programs need to experience the process of evaluation and learn from its results. Programs for gifted learners will not improve until evaluation is incorporated as a logical part of this program development process. Figure 2.1 depicts this important interplay.

At the classroom level, evaluation is concerned with the curricular goals and outcomes of a program, the instructional delivery system, and outcomes for students. Understanding the relationship of these variables

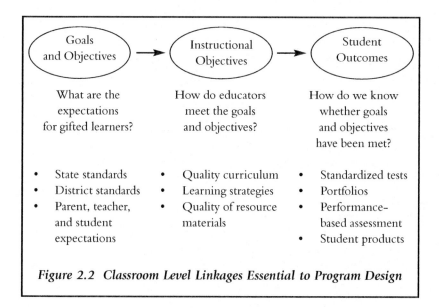

Figure 2.2 Classroom Level Linkages Essential to Program Design

is essential in conducting evaluations of gifted programs (see Figure 2.2), for the linkages among these elements provide an important argument for the presence or absence of quality in gifted education.

Review of Relevant Literature

In a review of 70 evaluation reports of gifted programs, Hunsaker and Callahan (1993) found a paucity of student outcome data, although some of the local evaluations used multiple methodologies and data sources to provide useful formative data for program improvement purposes.

Since one of the problems in evaluating student outcomes is associated with the nature of the assessment itself, Baker, O'Neill, and Linn (1994) argued for the use of performance-based assessments in gifted programs even as they acknowledged the technical inadequacy of many of the available measures. Because gifted students exhibit characteristics similar to expert performers in many domains, their performance might serve as higher benchmarks for overall student performance (Baker & Schacter, 1996).

Processes for the evaluation of available materials has been the subject of two articles in the field. Johnson, Boyce, and VanTassel-Baska (1995) described the process for evaluating science curricula for gifted learners, noting the efficacy of selected modular curricula in science and the inefficacy of basal materials for the gifted population. The review delineated specific criteria for judging science curricula, based on general curricular criteria, content-based criteria, and differentiation for gifted considerations. More recently, Purcell, Burns, Tomlinson, Imbeau, and Martin (2002) shared the criteria by which the National Association for Gifted Children (NAGC) curriculum committee has reviewed curricula in the field, noting broad categories for considering design, development, and implementation.

Some evaluation studies have focused on the effectiveness of particular curricular approaches. Assessing the effectiveness of the Integrated Curriculum Model (ICM) within targeted curricular units of study has been the central focus of several studies (VanTassel-Baska, Bass, Ries, Poland, & Avery, 1998; VanTassel-Baska, Johnson, Hughes, & Boyce 1996; VanTassel-Baska, Zuo, Avery, & Little, 2002). Evaluating the impact of these curricular units on schools and school districts has also been the subject of one qualitative study (VanTassel-Baska, Avery, Little, & Hughes, 2000). A mixed-design evaluation study examined the impact of the Schoolwide Enrichment Model (SEM) on student attitudes toward learning (Olenchak, 1990), finding that it had a strong effect as perceived by multiple stakeholders. Long-term effects of the Purdue Three-Stage model were studied by interviewing students and parents, with findings supporting the efficacy of program goals in promoting the use of higher level and independent learning (Moon, Feldhusen, & Dillon, 1994). The DISCOVER model was evaluated in respect to the degree of implementation of problem-solving stages. Findings suggested that a significant relationship existed between the level of implementation of the stages of problem solving and positive changes in student performance in mathematics (Maker, Rogers, Nielson, & Bauerle, 1996).

Program evaluation data have documented a number of interesting findings about gifted programs. One set of findings has suggested that teachers of the gifted use significantly more critical thinking and problem-solving behaviors in their work than regular classroom teachers (Avery, VanTassel-Baska, & O'Neill, 1997). Another set of findings suggests that even limited teacher training impacts positively on teacher performance in the classroom in respect to these same behaviors (VanTassel-Baska & Feng, 2002). Another study found that internal barriers such as lack of infrastructure, lack of clients' political sophistication, and personnel changes impact negatively on the potential for an evaluation to be utilized (Avery & VanTassel-Baska, 2001).

These few evaluation studies in the last decade reveal the need for deep gifted program development with curricular interventions that demonstrate both fidelity of implementation and evidence of student learning. Future studies will need to focus more sharply on these issues if the field is to move forward.

For the past 5 years, I have served as a principal investigator on five local, two state, one special school, and one international evaluation of gifted programs. These experiences have led me to reflect on important understandings that educators must have about the process and the common core of findings that emerge from evaluation work.

Standards for Judging Evaluation Work

School districts need to know that a set of clearly defined standards should guide the work of any evaluation team. These standards include: utility, feasibility, propriety, and accuracy. The *utility standards* are intended to ensure that an evaluation will serve the information needs of attended users. The *feasibility standards* are intended to ensure that an evaluation will be realistic, prudent, diplomatic, and frugal. The *propriety standards* are intended to ensure that an evaluation will be conducted legally, ethically, and with due regard for the welfare of those involved in the evaluation, as well as those affected by its results. The *accuracy standards* are intended to ensure that an evaluation will reveal and ensure technically adequate information about the features that determine worth or merit of the program being evaluated.

These standards were developed by a joint committee on standards for educational evaluation in 1981 and updated in 1994 through the participation of several organizations, including the American Psychological Association, the American Educational Research Association, and the National Council on Measurement in Education, to ensure ethical practice in the conduct of educational evaluations. Each of the standards addresses important concerns about the underlying structure of evaluation contracts, the procedures to be followed, the utilization purposes to be employed, and the safeguards of both human subjects and the accuracy of information attained (see Appendix A for a complete summary of these standards).

The role of the standards in any school district evaluation should be at all stages: planning, implementation, and reporting. An evaluation checklist, such as the one in Figure 2.3, challenges both the evaluation team and the contractor to adhere to these standards in respect to various aspects of the evaluation process. Moreover, each evaluation model described in Chapter 1, if implemented well, meets these evaluation standards well or very well according to an external analysis performed (Stufflebeam, 2001).

In order for an effective evaluation of gifted programs to occur, it is essential to consider a set of important steps that need to be carefully planned at various stages of the process.

Step 1: Determining Evaluation Purposes and Questions

A first important stage for any evaluation of gifted programs is determining why it is being done and what answers an educational agency wants about a program. Usually a representative group from the district or state is a good body to determine the right focus for an evaluation. Most evaluations are done with an eye to program improvement as a part of a larger district or state initiative to upgrade all programs and services. Some may be done if the key individuals running these programs are leaving the system, whether through retirement or for other reasons. Sometimes, problems are so visible in the program that an evaluation is absolutely necessary. Some sample stated purposes or objectives of evaluations are:

1. to identify the effectiveness of gifted services within and across levels of the system;
2. to identify strengths, weaknesses, and make recommendations regarding the most appropriate (best) delivery model for the program; and
3. to make recommendations for gifted program improvement and for further development of each program model and service within existing resources.

Additional common questions that may be answered by evaluations include the following:

1. To what extent are the stated mission and goals of the gifted program fulfilled in their actual operation?
2. To what extent is the gifted program meeting the needs of identified students as perceived by relevant groups?

(1) Basic Considerations
___ Purpose of the evaluation
___ Stakeholders
___ Authorized evaluator(s)
___ Guiding values and criteria
___ Standards for judging the evaluation (i.e., utility, feasibility, propriety, accuracy)
___ Contractual questions

(2) Information
___ Information sources
___ Participant selection
___ Data collection procedures
___ Data collection instruments and protocols
___ Provisions to obtain needed permissions to collect data

(3) Protocol
___ Contact persons
___ Rules for contacting program personnel
___ Communication channels and assistance

(4) Evaluation Management
___ Time line for evaluation work of both clients and evaluators
___ Assignment of evaluation responsibilities

(5) Contractor Responsibilities
___ Access to testing and assessment information
___ Personnel access for interviews and focus groups
___ Program-relevant data and documents
___ Transportation assistance

(6) Evaluation Budget
___ Payment amounts and dates
___ Conditions for payment, including delivery of required reports
___ Agreed-upon indirect/overhead rates

(7) Analysis
___ Procedures for analyzing quantitative information
___ Procedures for analyzing qualitative information

(8) Reports
___ Deliverables and due dates
___ Final report format, content, length, audiences, and methods of delivery

(9) Review and Control of the Evaluation
___ Contract amendment and cancellation provisions
___ Provision for evaluating the evaluation against professional standards of sound evaluation (ie., utility, feasibility, propriety, accuracy)
___ Restrictions/permissions to publish information from the evaluation

Preparer _____

Date _____

Use this checklist to ensure that each item is either addressed in the evaluator proposal, or negotiated in writing at the first planning meeting.

Figure 2.3 Evaluation Contract Checklist

3. What evidence exists to document positive student performance trends for students participating in the gifted program?
4. What are the program strengths and weaknesses in relation to the state of the art or best practices in gifted education?

A goal-based evaluation is almost always a major consideration and approach, driven by the question of the discrepancy between stated program goals and evidence of implementation of those goals through various data sources.

Step 2: Creating an Evaluation Design

Once evaluation questions, objectives, or both have been articulated, it is important to decide on approaches to evaluating them. These strategies can range from research designs that are experimental or quasi-experimental in nature, where one compares the performance of teachers in the gifted program to those not in the program on a common observation scale (e.g., to assess important differences in instructional delivery), to interviews with key stakeholders. The approaches to evaluation are solidified by using multiple strategies and matching the strategy to the question in an appropriate way. Evaluation designs should include key questions of interest, data sources to be used in answering them, instruments to be used, procedures for data collection, people responsible, and a timeline for completion of key facets of the work.

Step 3: Creating or Tailoring Instrumentation

Another phase of creating the evaluation design is deciding how to operationalize the evaluation approach with respect to instrumentation. Typically, in an evaluation, some instruments are created, others are tailored to the requirements of a particular context, and others are reused for multiple evaluations based on relevance and technical adequacy considerations. Stakeholder groups who will complete or experience the instruments of choice must be considered in their design. Common instruments employed in the conduct of evaluations include the following types:

Survey Questionnaires. This type of instrument typically would contain multiple-choice and Likert items, with one or two open-ended questions.

It should be limited to approximately 30 items and designed for electronic scanning. It should parallel best practices emphases in identification and assessment, curriculum and instruction, organizational arrangements (i.e., grouping), evaluation, and administration. In addition, it should probe staff development and personnel qualifications and parent communication. Tailored versions of such a survey should be developed for teachers, administrators, and parents, and a modified version with more targeted questions should be created for students.

Classroom Observation Form (COF). This specific instrument has been developed by the Center for Gifted Education at the College of William and Mary and used in a variety of program evaluation and research projects. It involves using trained observers to script an observation and then confirm the presence or absence of 40 behavioral indicators grouped into nine categories. These indicators focus on general teaching practice, elements of educational reform, and differentiation for gifted learners. The content validity of the instrument was established by expert review and calculated at .97, and the interrater reliability using Cohen's Kappa was calculated at .82 (Feng, 2001), although the use of a team strengthens this psychometric property even more.

Administrator Interview Form. This structured interview form is used to gather specific data about the features of a local gifted program and the context for on-site data collection. It supplements and verifies the information received on the local district survey. It also probes more deeply the interviewee's sense of program development and resource impact. Typically, it is employed with program coordinators, principals, and superintendents.

Focus Group Protocol. The focus group protocol typically involves five to seven open-ended questions tailored to participants' perceptions of their endemic situation. A small group of individuals, usually 8 to 12, would be invited to participate in each focus group (Morgan, 1998). The facilitator hands out note cards and asks participants to respond to the first question. After everyone has had an opportunity to respond, the facilitator records group responses on a flip chart. The process is repeated for each question. Participants are asked to build on the conversation that unfolds, rather than sequentially sharing their own written responses. Students are grouped separately from adults in order to promote more open communication. Guidelines are provided to the district about representative selection for focus group participation of teachers, students, and parents.

Document Review Form. This form is used to ascertain the extent and quality of program documentation. Separate forms are used for policy or administrative documents and curricular documents. These forms provide narrative and (in the case of the curricular unit reviews) quantitative data on the nature of the written material. Document review is primarily used to confirm or support perceptual data provided by stakeholders and classroom observation data.

These data sources are essential for understanding how well gifted programs work in a given setting. However, sometimes evaluations are also concerned about the way programs work for special populations. In order to ensure that adequate attention is given to questions of interest about how disadvantaged or at-risk learners fare in programs for the gifted, the following guidelines may be useful to consider as a checklist (House & Lappan, 1994):

- Students are identified by nontraditional procedures that are appropriate to the particular types of students and the program.
- Critical components of the program have been adequately described in the evaluation, including descriptions of the actual classroom teaching.
- Higher level thought processes, creativity, and other particularly appropriate outcomes for gifted students, depending on the particular program, have been examined by appropriate means other than standardized tests.
- Multiple measures have been employed.
- Possible negative side effects of the program have been examined.
- Other unanticipated effects on students, teachers, parents, and the community have been examined.
- The program contains culturally relevant material for culturally different students and recognizes and respects their particular cultural identity.
- The program displays sensitivity to females and includes materials with female role models.

Step 4: Implementing the Evaluation Design Through Data Collection

The decision about data sources and relevant instruments to be used in an evaluation leads to the necessary data collection strategies to be employed. Typically, data collection will involve the client in important ways, such as mailing surveys, organizing focus groups, and setting up interviews. Data collection procedures for each instrument or approach must be clearly defined and implemented accordingly. Mailing procedures should include considerations for follow-up. Scheduling of focus groups and interviews needs to be done collaboratively with both client and evaluator input.

Step 5: Analyzing and Triangulating the Data

Once the design of the evaluation is solidified and implemented through a series of on-site visits to schools and off-site assessment of program documents, the evaluation must carry through with data analysis techniques appropriate to the instruments employed. A quantitative analysis is conducted on all test score data, questionnaires, and observations. A qualitative analysis is conducted for all interviews, focus groups, and open-ended questions or written surveys. Content analysis of program documents is also conducted, and sets of data are then analyzed individually.

At the next stage of analysis, the evaluator engages in a cross-checking process to see how the separate findings begin to coalesce across data sources. This process, called *triangulation*, allows one to discuss "patterns of understanding" that are revealed through multiple data sources (Yin, 1989). It is preferable to treat findings that emerge from two or more data sets as more important or relevant for program improvement than those findings that emerge from only one source. However, the issue of varied stakeholders who share a common perspective coupled with strong reactions to particular program dynamics may occasionally lead evaluators to violate that rule in favor of a strong unitary finding that may emerge. Table 2.1 shows three themes that emerged from an evaluation and the triangulation of data sources that documented their importance.

Step 6: Answering the Evaluation Questions

Once all the data have been analyzed and triangulated and the themes identified, it is imperative to return to the core evaluation questions and

Table 2.1

Themes Derived From Triangulated Findings: An Example

Themes	Supportive Data Sources
There is a lack of equity and consistency in programs and services across buildings within one district, as well as across districts within the state.	Surveys, focus groups, document review
Gifted students are underidentified in the majority of school districts given the national incidence rates of 5–15%.	Interviews, document review
Curricular emphases are derived from individual teacher preferences, with the majority of emphasis areas being project work and critical or creative thinking.	Classroom observation, document review, surveys

construct a response that incorporates the derived themes and "layers" them appropriately in light of the questions asked. Frequently, evaluation questions require disaggregating the data sources in order to respond appropriately. For example, appropriately answering a question on how key stakeholders perceive the program would require focusing on the results of questionnaire, interview, and focus group data by stakeholder groups and across stakeholder groups. A question on student learning impacts might focus on data collected on student performance, modulated with stakeholder perceptions of learning benefits derived.

Step 7: Framing Recommendations

A critical stage of any evaluation is the end game. What recommendations will be left with program personnel and how should they use them? It is a best practice to consolidate the number of recommendations to a manageable number so that action planning can move forward expeditiously. Across all evaluations, there are some common weaknesses we have found in gifted programs, regardless of the state or district involved. These general weaknesses include the following areas:

- lack of attention to the curricular structure of the program, such that curricular frameworks and scope and sequence elements are nonexistent;
- lack of a strong curricular base being used in the program (teacher-developed units are limited, and, many times, the curriculum employed is neither sufficiently differentiated nor accelerated for gifted learners);
- lack of attention to assessment of student learning as a direct outcome of the gifted program (there appears to be little systematic collection of student product data or program-specific student assessment data that can demonstrate program effects); and
- lack of a systematic counseling and guidance program that supports and nurtures the development of gifted learners over the K–12 years of schooling.

These weaknesses are also revealed when program coordinators complete a self-assessment using the NAGC program standards as a guideline for best practice.

Step 8: Communicating Results

The results of the evaluation should be made available in written and oral form to all audiences that participated in data collection efforts. In many contexts, a series of meetings are scheduled to provide different audiences access to the results, and the evaluator presents the study and answers questions from the audience. Typically, there is also a final presentation to local and state boards. This oral and written communication process is a central part of ensuring that clients understand the findings and recommendations in light of their own experiences, thus preparing them to become part of a representative task force to move the recommendations forward.

Step 9: Developing a Plan of Action

The more successful the evaluation, the more likely the client will immediately utilize the recommendations for effective program improvement. Too frequently, evaluation data are underutilized in program improvement (Avery & VanTassel-Baska, 2001). The best way to ensure strong utilization is for the evaluator to sit down with a planning group and help them develop a plan of action for the next few years based on the recommendations received. A sample set of curricular recommendations that have been worked into such a plan at the local level is included in Table 2.2.

Conclusion

Gifted program evaluations are central to the continued development and evolution of the field. Without access to good data for making program decisions, we can fall further behind in our efforts to expand and deepen program opportunities for gifted students. Because gifted programs are seriously underfunded and underresourced everywhere, there is a real need to leverage evaluation findings to gain a stronger position within educational contexts for continued and stronger support. In an era of educational accountability, we must be proactive in our efforts to enhance program services on behalf of gifted learners.

Practical Tips

1. Evaluators and clients should be clear about the belief systems that undergird an evaluation because they impact design, data collection, findings, and recommendations in profound ways.

2. The spirit of evaluation as a tool for enhanced program development must be clearly understood and communicated by clients. Otherwise, it may be perceived as "harsh judgment" of the world of practicing educators.

3. National evaluation standards should guide the process of evaluation in an overt way. The use of a prepared checklist can facilitate this process.

4. The framing of evaluation questions completed with an appreciation for issues about the program in a context are essential starting points for any gifted program evaluation.

Table 2.2

Sample of Action Steps Derived
From Recommendations in the Evaluation

Recommendations	Anticipated Action Plans
1. Continued differentiation of curricula and instructional processes in both gifted classrooms and regular classrooms for gifted learners.	1.1 Elementary Level: Provide staff development for classroom teachers on teaching gifted students in the regular classroom. 1.2 Continue to revise/modify curricula to include more hands-on activities. 1.3 Continue to modify curricula to offer more alternatives in assignments, etc. 1.4 Middle School Level: Continue process of bringing curricula into alignment with state content area standards 1.5 Study the content areas used in the middle school model to determine if changes need to be made. 1.6 Encourage all middle school teachers to take gifted course. 1.7 Provide staff development for middle school teachers on the learning needs of high-ability students. 1.8 Both Levels: Train all teachers in a critical thinking model.
2. Continued refinement and development of existing gifted curricular units of study.	2.1 Continue summer curriculum development for gifted teachers. 2.2 Conduct staff development for gifted teachers on using state standards at higher, more complex levels of thinking.
3. Evaluate student impact data annually to assess the nature and extent of learning in gifted at each level.	3.1 Establish a longitudinal database that can easily access all data on gifted students, including all test scores, grades, high school courses, etc. 3.2 Use off-level performance-based and portfolio-based assessment approaches for classes. Collect data annually.

5. Using multiple data sources to answer each evaluation question increases the validity of the findings.

6. Recommendations need to be framed in such a way that they can be easily converted into a plan of action.

7. Action planning should occur very closely in time to the conclusion of the evaluation process to ensure movement toward program improvement.

References

Avery, L. D., & VanTassel-Baska, J. (2001). Investigating the impact of gifted education evaluation at state and local levels: Problems with traction. *Journal for the Education of the Gifted, 25*, 153–176.

Avery, L. D., VanTassel-Baska, J., & O'Neill, B. (1997) Making evaluation work: One school district's experience. *Gifted Child Quarterly, 41*, 124–132.

Baker, E. L., O'Neill, J. R., & Linn, R. L. (1994). Policy and validity prospects for performance-based assessment. *Journal for the Education of the Gifted, 17*, 332–353.

Baker, E. L., & Schacter, J. (1996). Expert benchmarks for student academic performance: The case for gifted children. *Gifted Child Quarterly, 40*, 61–65.

Bolman, L. G., & Deal, T. E. (1991). *Reframing organizations: Artistry, choice, and leadership*. San Francisco: Jossey-Bass.

Feng, X. A. (2001). *Technical report on inter-rater reliability of the classroom observation scale*. Williamsburg, VA: Center for Gifted Education, College of William and Mary.

House, E. R., & Lappan, S. (1994). Evaluation of programs for disadvantaged gifted students. *Journal for the Education of the Gifted, 17*, 441–466.

Hunsaker, S. L., & Callahan, C. M. (1993). Evaluation of gifted programs: Current practices. *Journal for the Education of the Gifted, 16*, 190–200.

Johnson, D. T., Boyce, L. N., & VanTassel-Baska, J. (1995). Science curriculum review: Evaluating materials for high-ability learners. *Gifted Child Quarterly, 39*, 36–43.

Maker, C. J., Rogers, J. A., Nielson, A. B., & Bauerle, P. R. (1996). Multiple intelligences, problem solving, and diversity in the general classroom. *Journal for the Education of the Gifted, 19*, 437–460,

Moon, S. M., Feldhusen, J. F., & Dillon, D. R. (1994). Long-term effects of an enrichment program based on the Purdue three-stage model. *Gifted Child Quarterly, 38*, 38–48.

Morgan, D. L. (1998). *The focus group guidebook.* Thousand Oaks, CA: Sage.

Olenchak, F. R. (1990). School change through gifted education: Effects on elementary students' attitudes toward learning. *Journal for the Education of the Gifted, 13*, 66–78.

Purcell, J. H. , Burns, D. E. , Tomlinson, C. A., Imbeau, M., & Martin, J. L. (2002). Bridging the gap: A tool and technique to analyze and evaluate gifted education curricular units. *Gifted Child Quarterly, 46*, 306–321.

Stake, R. E. (1976). A theoretical statement of responsive evaluation. *Studies in Educational Evaluation, 2*(1), 19–22.

Stufflebeam, D. L. (2001). Evaluation models. In G. T. Gary, & J. C. Greene (Eds.), *New directions for evaluation* (pp. 7–99). San Francisco: Jossey-Bass.

VanTassel-Baska, J., Avery, L. D., Little, C., & Hughes, C. (2000). An evaluation of the implementation of curriculum innovation: The impact of the William and Mary units on schools. *Journal for the Education of the Gifted, 23*, 244–270.

VanTassel-Baska, J., Bass, G., Ries, R., Poland, D., & Avery, L. D. (1998). A national study of science curriculum effectiveness with high-ability students. *Gifted Child Quarterly, 42*, 200–211.

VanTassel-Baska, J., & Feng, A. X. (2002). An evaluation of the Idaho state gifted program: A lesson on teacher training as a lever for program development. *NAGC Research Briefs, 16,* 99–104.

VanTassel-Baska, J., Johnson, D., Hughes, C., & Boyce, L. N. (1996). A study of language arts effectiveness with gifted learners. *Journal for the Education of the Gifted, 19*, 461–480.

VanTassel-Baska, J., Zuo, L., Avery, L., & Little, C. (2002). A curriculum study of gifted-student learning in the language arts. *Gifted Child Quarterly, 46*, 30–44.

Yin, R. (1989). *Case study research: Design and methods.* Newbury Park, CA: Sage.

 3

Constructing
and Implementing Surveys

by Annie Xuemei Feng

Good evaluation is good social science; it embraces the gallant aims of precision in articulation of theory, rigor in empirical testing, confederation in lines of inquiry, and cumulation in the body of findings.
— Ray Pawson & Nick Tilley (2001, p. 324)

A stakeholder survey is one of the data collection strategies used in a typical program evaluation. It is obvious that a stakeholder questionnaire is an instrument designed to ask stakeholders questions about their perceptions and opinions about a program in which they are involved. Yet, who are the constituencies of the stakeholders? Why do we choose them to answer the questions? What questions do we ask and how should we ask those questions in order to get accurate replies? This chapter will deal with these issues in a typical gifted program evaluation.

Who Are the Stakeholders?

As simple as this question sounds, which stakeholders to choose for gathering questionnaire data is indeed contextually determined. Typically, in a gifted program evaluation, gifted students, teachers of the gifted, building and program administrators, and parents of the gifted comprise the stakeholder groups. Yet, it also depends on the dynamics of stakeholder groups that a state or local program agency specifies in its request for proposals, particularly when a group, such as charter school parents, may hold perceptions about the program important to administrators running it.

For example, in one program evaluation, the sponsor was also interested in knowing why some students who were eligible for their district's gifted program chose programs in other districts or attended charter schools or private schools instead. To the evaluator, it was interesting to examine the motive of these groups of students and parents in leaving the available gifted program the district provided. They constituted stakeholder groups whose perceptions of the gifted program helped the evaluator to interpret the dynamics of the gifted program being evaluated. Thus, it is important to keep in mind that stakeholders also include people who are not directly involved in the gifted program; these stakeholders might not be accountable for any part of the program, but their existence and their perceptions partly explain the program's success or failure.

What Questions to Ask and How to Ask Questions

Fowler (1995) stated in his book on survey questions, "In the social sciences, and increasingly in medical sciences as well, important measurements are based on a question-and-answer process" (p. 1). While it is important to derive reliable and valid instruments in conducting experimental and quasi-experimental research, it is equally crucial for the evaluators to develop survey questions that stakeholders will answer consistently (reliability) and that respondents' answers to the questions reflect what the evaluators are asking (validity).

Demographic Questions

In constructing questions for a gifted program evaluation, we intend to ask several questions regarding the demographic characteristics of the

1. Role: (choose **one**)

   ❏ regular classroom teacher ❏ gifted program teacher

2. The grade level you currently teach:

   ❏ 3rd   ❏ 4th   ❏ 5th   ❏ 6th   ❏ 7th   ❏ 8th   ❏ other

3. Your years of teaching:

   ❏ 1–5   ❏ 6–10   ❏ 11–15   ❏ 16–20   ❏ 21 and above

4. Your years of teaching the gifted (if applicable):

   ❏ 1–3   ❏ 4–6   ❏ 7–9   ❏ 10 and above

5. Your background in gifted education (choose **one**):

   ❏ No formal training
   ❏ At least 6 hours of coursework and working toward endorsement
   ❏ State endorsement in gifted education
   ❏ Master's degree with a concentration in gifted education
   ❏ Doctoral degree with a concentration in gifted education

Figure 3.1 Sample Demographic Section of Teacher Questionnaire

respondents. The purpose of building demographic questions is not for the sake of the characteristics of the respondents themselves. Rather, we ask these questions mainly for two purposes: 1) to determine if there is any pattern of answers associated with respondents of different characteristics; and 2) to conduct subsample analysis because sometimes the evaluator or the local agent is particularly interested in the perceptions of a special group within the same stakeholder category.

Figure 3.1 is an example of the demographic section of an educator questionnaire used in one gifted program evaluation. These questions were designed to derive the role information of the respondents, their representativeness with respect to the grade levels they taught, and their teaching experiences and gifted-related training background. Questions 1 and 2 will help the evaluators to determine if there is any relationship between respondents' perceptions of the current gifted program practices and their role status and if the sample is well represented in terms of their role and grade distribution in the general population. Both questions will also serve to distinguish the sample into subgroups for subsample analysis (e.g., elementary vs. middle school teacher; teachers of the gifted vs. regular classroom teachers). The teaching experiences and gifted-related training background questions (Questions 3–5) provide the evaluators some baseline for checking the accuracy of data obtained regarding particular questions since the accuracy of the self-reported answers, to a certain extent, depends on respondents' knowledge of gifted education. Thus, these demographic questions enable the evaluators to examine the subsamples, check against the representativeness of the sample together with a response rate, and detect any pattern related to the demographic characteristics of the respondents.

The Content of Questions

In designing survey questions, we must understand the objectives behind the set of questions we ask. In a gifted program evaluation, we want to know the stakeholders' perceptions of the gifted program and how they view the program. A good start to constructing questions is to align the questions with different components of the best practice standards for gifted programs. In the following sections, sample questions were selected from a teacher questionnaire. Examples of problematic questions will be provided to illustrate why they are flawed. An improved version of the problematic question will be presented, and the rationale for improvement is discussed. We will use these selected questions in this survey as examples to illustrate how to write good survey questions. The principles apply equally to surveys of other stakeholder groups.

Correspondence of Question Content to Best Practice Standards

In constructing a stakeholder survey, we should first determine what components of a gifted program we would like to write in the questionnaire. The best practice standards of the National Association for Gifted Children (NAGC) are a good template for doing this. These components of a gifted program include identification and assessment, curriculum and instruction, program evaluation, program management and administration, organizational arrangement, staff development, and parent communication. Questions soliciting stakeholders' perceptions of each of the above dimensions of a gifted program need to be outlined, although the number of questions and question emphasis within each program component depend on the major purposes of an evaluation.

Using the identification and assessment component as an example, we will illustrate how to write specific questions and the rationale behind them. While we could review the guidelines and policies and instrument of identification for a gifted program through the examination of documents in place, we have to assess stakeholders' perceptions of the relevant aspects of the process. In a stakeholder survey, we would like to know stakeholders' perceptions of the fairness of the identification process and to what extent the identification criteria match the services the program offers. A sensitive issue in identification procedures is whether special student populations like minority groups, ESL students, and low-SES students are overlooked. In Figure 3.2, Questions 9–12 serve these purposes.

It is important to include a question about respondents' familiarity with the identification process. Such a question is called the screening question. Only those who answer "yes" are eligible for reporting the next three questions accurately. For the analysis purpose, such a question serves as a filter to exclude invalid answers provided by people who are not familiar with the issue.

Similarly, questions on other program components and the proposed evaluation questions can all be drafted in such a fashion, with the question emphasis aligned with the best practice standards for a particular component.

Align Question Content to Program Goals and Objectives

Every gifted program has its specific program goals and objectives. Constructing a question on program benefits that aligns with these goals and objectives will help examine stakeholders' perceptions on the degree to which these goals and objectives have been achieved. Alternatively, a question related to program improvement will help to examine the weaknesses of the program and provide directions for further improvement. Question 25 and 26 in Figure 3.3 are examples of questions for such purposes.

How to Derive Response Categories

Several types of response categories are frequently employed in constructing a question. The response categories are mainly derived from

9. Are you familiar with the identification process to select students for the gifted program in your district?

    ❏ Yes   ❏ No

10. If "Yes," which statement best describes your perception of the identification criteria (choose **one** only)?

    ❏ The criteria are fair.
    ❏ The criteria are too broad.
    ❏ The criteria are too narrow.
    ❏ Other (Please specify)

11. Which statement best reflects your opinion (choose **one** only)?

    The identification criteria . . .
    ❏ are congruent with the services the program offers.
    ❏ do not match with the services the program offers.
    ❏ No opinion
    ❏ Other (Please specify)

12. Are there any populations that you think do not have equitable access to gifted education in your district because of the identification process (choose **all** that apply)?

    ❏ Economically disadvantaged students
    ❏ Minority students
    ❏ Students for whom English is a second language
    ❏ Learning-disabled students
    ❏ Underachieving students
    ❏ ADD/ADHD
    ❏ Other (Please specify)

Figure 3.2 Sample Survey Questions
on Identification and Assessment

25. What do you think are the important benefits of the gifted program to identified students (choose **all** that apply)?

❑ Mastery of core areas of learning at appropriate pace and depth
❑ Better understanding of the concepts, themes, and issues
❑ Emphasis on interdisciplinary learning
❑ Emphasis on critical and creative thinking skills
❑ Emphasis on research and problem-solving skills
❑ Emphasis on independent learning skills
❑ Emphasis on creative expression and aesthetic values
❑ Expectation for high-quality products
❑ Opportunities to learn with students of similar abilities and interests
❑ Enhanced self-esteem
❑ Better knowledge of one's strengths and limitations

26. If you could change up to three things about the gifted program in your school, what would they be (choose **up to three**)?

❑ Goals and mission statement
❑ Identification and selection
❑ Organizational structures
❑ Program options
❑ Curricula and instruction
❑ Student evaluation methods
❑ Parent communication and involvement
❑ Staff development
❑ Other (please specify)

27. Please describe the nature of change you would like to see:

1) _____

2) _____

3) _____

Figure 3.3 Sample Questions
to Align Program Goals and Objectives

four sources: 1) the research literature on questions (variables of interest), 2) best practice standards, 3) program goals and objectives, and 4) brainstormed ideas and suggestions from experts in the field and local program evaluation committee members. In the above examples, the response category in question 25 was derived from a combination of research literature and the program goals of the district. The areas for change options were constructed based on the critical program components documented in the best practice standards.

The "Other" Option as a Response Category

Except for the exhaustive responding categories for a question (e.g., question 3 and 4 in Figure 3.1), we usually include an "other" option as one of the response categories. This is important for building future questionnaires, as it is crucial to recognize that the selected response categories do not always exhaust all the possible options. Thus, the option of "other" provides respondents an opportunity to express different opinions or add alternatives.

To Have an Open-Ended Question or Not

It is still controversial among survey research methodologists whether open-ended questions should be included in a survey. It is argued that many respondents choose not to answer the narrative form of a question, and this will affect the validity of the question. The handwriting of the respondents also creates a problem for coding and interpretation of the data. Yet, researchers seem to agree that a question such as asking for additional comments at the end of a survey should not create any problems for the analysis of the whole data set (Fowler, 1993, 1995; Mangione, 1995). Psychologically, it makes the respondents feel good when they have the chance to give their own ideas or opinions. As a result, it might increase the sample size for returned questionnaires. Dillman (2000) described such a process as a trust-building process in social exchange, which he argued is a healthy practice in constructing a questionnaire.

Our evaluation experiences using the stakeholder survey strategy appeared to support such an orientation. It helps the evaluator to understand better what a respondent means by selecting a choice (see Question 27 about the nature of change following the closed-ended

Question 26). The open-ended question can also help cross-check the validity of a respondent's answer to parallel close-ended questions. Additionally, Fowler (1995) and Mangione (1995) have suggested that open-ended questions can best be used as a data collection strategy when responding categories for a question might be unpredictable or rarely cited in the research literature. Such questions are best described as exploratory in nature. However, several survey researchers have suggested using pilot testing results to transfer open-ended questions to the close-ended format.

How to Ask/Write Good Questions

In order to ask/write good questions, we must define what a good question is and what its characteristics are. Fowler (1995) stated that "a good question is one that produces answers that are reliable and valid measures of something we want to describe" (p. 2). This means that respondents understand the question in the same way as the researcher and answer the questions consistently. Moreover, the respondents' answers provide what the researchers are interested in knowing. Fowler (1995) summarized five criteria for a good survey question:

1. The questions need to be consistently understood.
2. The questions need to be consistently administered or communicated to respondents.
3. What constitutes an adequate answer should be consistently communicated.
4. Unless measuring knowledge is the goal of the question, all respondents should have access to the information needed to answer the question accurately.
5. Respondents must be willing to provide the answers called for in the question. (p. 4)

Principles in Writing Good Survey Questions

1. *Write brief questions.* According to Armstrong and Overton (1971, cited in Mangione, 1995), brief questions are more valid because of their ease of reading and less likelihood for extraneous influences through qualifying phrases that characterize long sentences. Indeed, a long sentence question often asks more than one question, thus violating the uni-

dimensionality principle of a good survey question. The best way to improve it is to break the long question into small parts based on the concept that the question conveys. In Figure 3.2, question 12 is a long sentence question that can be improved by splitting it into two as shown in Figure 3.4.

2. *Write understandable questions.* While we are constructing survey questions, we should always keep in mind our audience. For a student questionnaire, the survey designer must be sensitive to the reading and comprehension level of the student respondents even though the respondents are identified as gifted. This is particularly important if the respondents are primary school students. However, this principle is equally important for the adult stakeholder groups. While the questionnaire designer may take for granted some terms (e.g., curriculum compacting, telescoping, acceleration, etc.) and build them as categorical choices for a question, the respondents might not necessarily be clear about what these terms mean. Even for the educator questionnaire, these terms might sound like jargon to some of the teacher respondents, let alone parents of the gifted or administrators who have not had many experiences with gifted education. It is helpful to include a glossary of specific terms to minimize the measurement error caused when respondents misunderstand terms used in the survey. On the other hand, if the evaluator is an external evaluation agency, it also creates challenges for the evaluator to understand and acquire the terminology used in a local district. Mutual exchange of ideas and trials of draft questionnaires becomes an indispensable step before the final draft of an instrument. In such a way, the evaluator can write questions that are clear to the local respondents.

3. *Ask relevant people relevant questions.* In the process of constructing questionnaires, the designer should be alert to the relevance of a particular question for the sampled respondents. Sometimes, not everyone in the sample is expected to know the answer to a question; that depends on the respondents' experiences and involvement with a gifted program. When such a subsample is expected, yet a question is particularly important to ask, a screening question should be built into the survey. Respondents who are able to provide valid answers should be distinguished from those who are probably not. The subgroup who cannot answer particular questions should be guided to skip to the next answerable question (e.g., questions 12a and 12b in Figure 3.4).

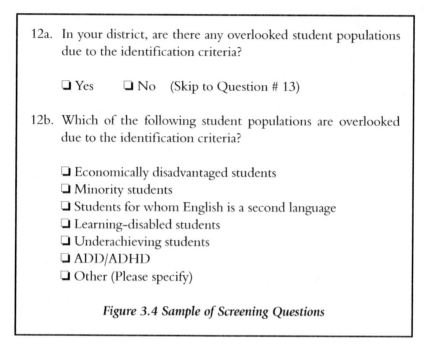

12a. In your district, are there any overlooked student populations due to the identification criteria?

❏ Yes ❏ No (Skip to Question # 13)

12b. Which of the following student populations are overlooked due to the identification criteria?

❏ Economically disadvantaged students
❏ Minority students
❏ Students for whom English is a second language
❏ Learning-disabled students
❏ Underachieving students
❏ ADD/ADHD
❏ Other (Please specify)

Figure 3.4 Sample of Screening Questions

4. *Write unidimensional questions.* In writing a question, one should keep in mind that each question should address only one objective (or concept). Sometimes, we may unintentionally ask at least two things in one question. This creates a burden for the respondents because they must decide which aspects of the question they should answer, and, as a result, the data obtained are vulnerable to validity problems and become difficult to interpret. For example, consider the following question: "Which statement best describes your perception of the screening process and identification criteria of your district's gifted program?" The screening process and the identification criteria are two aspects of the identification process, and a respondent may know one, but not the other. Yet, the evaluator will not be able to distinguish and determine which aspect of the identification process a respondent is answering. Such multidimensional questions create irreparable measurement error that jeopardizes the evaluation.

5. *Write unidimensional categories.* Just as writing unidimensional questions helps to increase the validity of the measurement, so does writing unidimensional categories. Figure 3.5 is a communication question with

such problematic response categories; three alternatives were included for revision and improvement. The five response categories are indeed connoting two dimensions of judgment: adequacy and consistency. It is true that a rating of "excellent" might indicate the consistency of the communication, but such options lead respondents to think and recall different aspects of the communication between the responding teacher and parents and may yield a result with confusing conclusions. This scale can be improved by using only one scalar dimension each time. The revisions in Figure 3.5 (Questions 19a, 19b, 19c) are intended to cover one aspect of the judgmental category. All three versions can be built into the questionnaire, or only one of them can be used, depending on the focus of the question.

6. *Write mutually exclusive categories.* Mutlidimensional categorical responses is one of the examples of overlapping response categories. In the above example (Question 19), "poor" and "inconsistent" are overlapping, which creates another source of measurement error in addition to the multidimensionality of the categories. The other frequently committed error with regard to mutual exclusivity is related to the frequency of numbers as alternatives for choices. For example, the response category for frequently held activities might be written as such: 1–5, 5–10, 10–15, 15 and above. Such a response category seems neat at first sight, but the respondents whose experiences are at the point of 5, 10, and 15 will yield random answers to the specified categories, and it shouldn't be a surprise if some respondents leave the question blank.

7. *Avoid writing loaded questions.* A loaded question is a biased or slanted question (Mangione, 1995). The manner in which a question is worded oftentimes influences how the respondents answer it. An example in respect to asking people's opinion on abortion might be worded like this: "Should the state ignore the principles of the Bible, which is the law of God, and morality by legalizing murder by abortion?" (cited in Mangione, 1995, p. 21).

To avoid loaded questions, we can place a screening question before the intended question. Instead of asking, "Are there any populations that you think do not have equitable access to gifted education in your district because of the identification process?," we can first examine the stance or belief of the respondents with the question, "In your district, are there any overlooked student populations due to the identification criteria?"

19. How do you evaluate the communication between yourself and parents of gifted students?

❏ The communication is excellent.
❏ The communication is adequate.
❏ The communication is poor.
❏ The communication is inconsistent.
❏ I generally do not communicate with parents
   unless their children have a problem.

19a. How do you evaluate the communication between yourself and parents of gifted students?

❏ The communication is outstanding.
❏ The communication is very good.
❏ The communication is good.
❏ The communication is fairly good.
❏ The communication is poor.

19b. How do you evaluate the communication between yourself and parents of gifted students?

❏ The communication is adequate.
❏ The communication is somewhat adequate.
❏ The communication is somewhat inadequate.
❏ The communication is inadequate.

19c. How do you evaluate the communication between yourself and parents of gifted students?

❏ The communication is consistent.
❏ The communication is somewhat consistent.
❏ The communication is somewhat inconsistent.
❏ The communication is inconsistent.

Figure 3.5 Sample of Unidimensional Response Categories

Then proceed to elicit the stakeholders' perceived distribution of various overlooked populations (see Figure 3.4).

8. *Use scalar responding format wherever possible.* After the surveyor obtains a list of responding categories, it is important to choose a responding format for maximum data. The choices become crucial for a question with more than one answer. Typically, the response categories are listed and respondents are asked to "choose all that apply," instructing them to check one of the bubbles beside each item in a survey instrument (see Question 25). Those items that are not checked by the respondents are interpreted as nonbeneficial, which is not necessarily true. Several strategies can be used to improve such a question: 1) ask respondents to rank the top three benefits; 2) add a scale of yes/no after each item to judge the accuracy of the report; 3) use a scale such as 1 to 5, with 1 being "to a small extent" and 5 being "to a large extent." With the third approach, the distribution of respondents' perceptions on each response item can be calculated, and the data will provide richer information about stakeholders' perceptions.

Question Evaluation

After a draft questionnaire is completed, the questions need to be evaluated. Four types of questionnaire evaluation are involved: developer-evaluation, in-house questionnaire evaluation, local personnel evaluation, and pretest. For developer-evaluation, it is most critical to ask yourself (the survey designer): Did I cover the components of a gifted program sufficiently? What is the objective of each question? Which proposed evaluation questions will be helpful to address? Are there any redundant questions? What statistical techniques will be used for analyzing the data?

Both in-house evaluation and local personnel questionnaire evaluation serve the same purpose: to ask colleagues and local school district personnel who are involved in the gifted program about the clarity of instructions, question wording and structure, if the questions are understandable to the targeted stakeholder groups, and if the questions are worded in a way that respondents will be willing to answer (see also Fowler, 1995; Mangione, 1995). It is particularly important to ask local personnel to point out any unfamiliar terms they feel uncomfortable with, as well as any special terms typically used in their district or state's gifted program. In a state gifted program evaluation we conducted, we used the phrase "gifted facilitator" to describe "the teacher of gifted students," a phrase commonly used elsewhere. In one local personnel evaluation of the survey, we found that "EPGY" was a more familiar term in the region than "Stanford Math Program"; thus, a follow-up revision was conducted to update the terminology.

Pretesting has been approved as an important way to derive a reliable and valid instrument (Dillman, 2000; Fowler, 1993; Mangione, 1995). This is particularly important when a new instrument is developed from scratch. However, in reality, time and budget usually limit the use of pretesting. For novices in gifted program evaluation, we suggest adapting an available instrument to the specific situation, rather than starting each question from scratch.

Developing a Sampling Plan

Although it is ideal to know all stakeholders' perceptions and attitudes about a gifted program in which they are involved, it is often unrealistic given time, budget, and human resource limitations. Results from a well-represented sample will render equally valid conclusions given a high response rate (75%) and well-developed instrument.

A well-developed sampling plan becomes an indispensable part of an evaluation project. There is a large set of literature on sampling (Fowler, 1993; Henry, 1990; Mangione, 1995; Jaeger, 1984). For the purpose of this chapter, we will give a brief introduction to the basics of sampling theory and the five commonly used probability sampling techniques. Some sampling caveats will also be shared in respect to gifted program evaluation.

Three components build the cornerstone of sampling theory: sampling frame, sampling units, and probability sampling procedures. According to Jaeger (1984), a *sampling frame* refers to a list of people, objects, or institutions from which a sample is selected. Ideally, a sampling frame is equal to an ordered population to which results from a study of its sample will be generalized. The elements that comprise a population are called *sampling units* (Fowler, 1993). The sampling units could be students, teachers, or parents for stakeholder survey sampling, or schools or school districts for the purpose of sampling for on-site visitation in a gifted program evaluation. *Probability sampling procedures* refer to the various techniques in selecting a sample from a sampling frame.

There are five basic probability sampling procedures: simple random sampling, systematic random sampling, stratified sampling, cluster sampling, and multistage sampling. Henry (1990) summarized the definition of each sampling design and conducted a detailed discussion of the benefits and costs of each. In gifted program evaluation, we typically use stratified and cluster sampling strategies in selecting schools or school districts for on-site visits and stakeholders for survey implementation. Simple random sampling and systematic random sampling design have rarely been used alone; instead, the procedures are often incorporated into the other sampling processes. Due to its liability of increased sampling error and complexity of computation, multistage sampling is not frequently used. Table 3.1 presents the definitions and pros and cons of each sampling technique, as well as applications of these techniques in gifted program evaluations.

There are some caveats in the sampling process in gifted program evaluation. One is that sometimes the evaluator has to conform to the reality of a particular gifted program. In an evaluation of state gifted programs, we developed a stratified sampling plan to select 12 school districts for on-site visitation using three strata: SES level, district size, and geographical location. However, when using the geographical region as a stratum, not every district within each stratum had an equal probability of being selected. The criteria had to be compromised by selecting those districts that were within driving distance of the four preselected urban districts, given the limitation of completing the planned task for each visit in one week. Secondly, not every selected district or school agreed to participate in the study. An alternative list was needed to substitute those who turned down an invitation for cooperation. Although the substituted districts were similar to the replaced districts with regard to the three strata, the program coordinator's referral of a district in the substituted list often made cooperation easy. However, even though a soundly developed sampling plan was in place, the implementation process often introduced selection bias, depending on the extent to which the designated personnel implemented the survey distribution according to the instructions provided.

Probability sampling is a process that requires sophisticated skills, thus it should be designated to people who have expertise to ensure that a sound sampling plan is developed for an evaluation study.

Survey Implementation

There are three typical methods of survey administration: mail/self-administered survey, telephone survey, and personal interview survey. In gifted program evaluation, we often employ the mode of self-administration for collecting data from students, teachers, administrators, parents, and other stakeholder groups. The advantages of mail/self-administered surveys compared to the other modes of data collection are 1) time efficiency, 2) realistic budget, and 3) sampling. Moreover, self-administered surveys allow participants more time to reflect on the questions, offer privacy for answering questions, and have room to accommodate more questions. An extension of the self-administered type of data collection is a group-administered strategy, where stakeholders (e.g., gifted students) complete the survey at a particular time and place.

How to Implement Stakeholder Surveys

We have used different approaches to implement stakeholder surveys depending on specific situations. For student surveys, group-administration proved to be most efficient. The evaluator mailed the student surveys to the program coordinator with detailed instructions on sample size for each school and specific descriptions of the administration procedures (see Figure 3.6 for a sample instruction). All designated teachers were supposed to bring the completed survey to the program coordinator, who, in turn, sent the data to the evaluator. A tracking list of schools indicating the return status should also be provided beforehand. While some methodologists argue that in-class group administration might produce bias among students because of the presence of their instructional teacher, our experiences and analyses of students' responses have not validated such a claim. Instead, group administration has proven to be the most efficient way to obtain a high response rate in gifted program evaluation (see Chapter 4).

For adult stakeholder groups, we usually use the self-administration strategy. Ideally, the evaluator prepares a set of questionnaires for each sampled respondent (including a cover letter, a copy of the survey, and a prepaid self-addressed envelope) and mails the instrument to the sample. However, in reality, conducting a gifted program evaluation is different from a household survey or medical survey, where the surveyor is able to get a mailing address for the population and mail the survey to that list. The list of adult stakeholders to be sampled is not under the evaluator's control.

Table 3.1

Probability Sampling Strategies: Definitions and Applications in Gifted Program Evaluation

Sampling Techniques	Selection Strategy[a]	Advantages[b]	Disadvantages[b]	Application in Gifted
Simple random	Each member of the study population has an equal probability of being selected.	Straightforward; self-weighting; easy for analysis and generalization.	Hard to get an updated and complete list of sampling frame; nonsampling bias is likely to occur; geographical dispersal characteristics of the sample may make on-site visitation difficult.	Program evaluation often used as a part of stratified sampling strategy for stakeholder surveys (e.g., the amount of training grant as a stratum for sampling educators in districts across the state).
Systematic	Each member of the study population is either assembled or listed, a random start is designated, then members of the population are selected at equal intervals.	Similar to simple random sampling in statistical properties; ease of selection (e.g., does not require random number table or generator; less-trained staff can select number if given the interval and the starting number).	The sampling frame must be well-mixed; an unintended cyclical list with the same interval of selection will create a biased sample; costly in terms of geographical dispersal of locations for on-site visits.	Similar to the application of simple random sampling strategy, but used less frequently since a list of sampling units (e.g., schools or districts) by designated numbers often implies a systematic order within a certain district or state.

Stratified	Each member of the study population is assigned to a group or stratum, then a simple random sample is selected from each stratum.	Increasing precision of estimates; improved sampling efficiency; feasible for conducting subpopulation analysis.	Weighting is needed if disproportionate stratification is applied; costly for more information to stratify.	Most frequently used in selecting sampling schools or districts for on-site visitation.
Cluster	Each member of the study population is assigned to a group or cluster; then clusters are selected at random and all members of a selected cluster are included in the sample.	Only list of clusters is needed; cost-effectiveness for concentrated travel time.	Increasing sampling error (i.e., the precision of estimates is reduced).	Can be used in sampling stakeholders for survey implementation (e.g., students in selected classes within a sampled school are selected for student survey questionnaire).
Multistage	Clusters are selected as in the cluster sample, then sample members are selected from the cluster members by simple random sampling. Clustering may be done at more than one stage.	Similar to cluster sampling strategy, but more efficient.	Reduces the precision of estimates; needs complex computation procedure for sampling error.	Due to its complexity, this strategy is less frequently used than either stratified or cluster sampling.

Note.

[a] Henry, 1990, p. 27

[b] These pros and cons of different probability sampling strategies are based on Henry's (1990, pp. 95–116) discussions on the benefits and costs of each.

We must depend on district personnel (most often, the program coordinator) to administer the survey to the sampled number of stakeholders. Even with a well-developed sampling plan, not every teacher, parent, or administrator has an equal chance of being selected for survey administration.

However, some questions in the demographic section of the survey can be helpful in assessing the extent to which the responding subjects are representative of the selected demographic characteristics. For example, in a teacher questionnaire, a question on grade level serves such a purpose. Similarly, in a parent questionnaire, a question about the grade level in which their identified gifted child is currently enrolled will help to check how well the responding parents are represented. In other words, the stakeholders' responses to selected demographic questions will help to determine the extent to which the respondents' demographic distribution is reflective of the overall population they represent.

Sometimes, the evaluator implements the survey. This happens in a gifted program evaluation when an available list for sampling (sampling frame) can be accessed by the evaluator. For example, in two of the state-level gifted program evaluations we conducted, a district gifted program coordinator survey was administered. The evaluator was provided a complete list of the districts and the relevant contact information. The evaluator was thus able to administer the survey to each of the sampled subjects. Direct mail surveys afford the evaluator more leverage in tracking the sample and the response rate; yet, the disadvantage is that they often yield a lower response rate due to the external orientation of the evaluator. However, a systematic monitoring mechanism and good survey design will help in ensuring a reasonably high response rate.

Survey Monitoring and Time Management

How long does a mailing cycle take? And how many waves of mailing are needed to reach a reasonable response rate? Research literature suggests that it takes about 8 to 10 weeks for a survey mailing cycle to be completed; and four waves of mailings, including two reminders, should be employed (Dillman, 2000; Fowler, 1993; Mangione, 1995). Using patterns of returns obtained from survey studies of work-related alcohol policies and problems in six companies, Mangione suggested the following guidelines for monitoring the four waves of mailings (see Table 3.2). He found that about 14 days after each previous mailing, the return significantly dropped; therefore, he suggested that the surveyor

Dear Ms. [Program Coordinator]:

A critical component of the evaluation design is to derive stakehold-ers' perceptions of the effectiveness of the gifted program. We would like you to help us with the administration of the [stakeholder sur-vey questionnaire]. The survey is anonymous, thus confidentiality is guaranteed. Below are directions that need to be followed in the process of survey administration.

1. The [stakeholder] questionnaire has two sheets. The first sheet is printed on both sides. Be sure to remind [stakeholders] to complete both sides of the first sheet.
2. Please select [stakeholders] randomly in each sampled school based on the number of classes (cluster) provided in the sampling plan.
3. Each sheet of the [stakeholder] questionnaire has a serial # block on it. Please tell participants to write down and bubble their school code in the last two digit columns. The code for each school is listed in the cover letter.
4. Please be sure to check that participants fill in their school code in the serial # block because that will be the information source used for sorting data and subsequent analyses.
5. The coordinator may use the number labels to double confirm the school information after the completed questionnaires are received.
6. Please track the status of survey return for each sampled school and complete the survey administration in all sampled schools.
7. Please collect the completed questionnaires and mail them back to the Center for Gifted Education, the College of William and Mary.

Many thanks for your help in this data collection process.

Sincerely,

Annie Feng
Research and Evaluation Coordinator
Center for Gifted Education, College of William and Mary

Figure 3.6 Sample Instruction
for [Stakeholder] Questionnaire Administration

send the follow-up mailing at such a time so that the subjects will receive the new mailing around 14 days after the previous one. Another interesting pattern is that the return rate of each of the following mailings is about half of that obtained during the previous one. In such a way, four waves of mailing systematically tracked can reach a response rate of 75%. It is also suggested that a different focus be emphasized with each mailing.

It should be noted that such a procedure of mailing and time tracking was based on a pattern derived from surveys in the business world. The mailing time cycle also depends on the distance between the location of the gifted program and that of the evaluator. A mailing during holiday seasons will often prolong the mailing cycle and should therefore be avoided. It also depends on what type of mail service was used, especially if the budget is limited. Nevertheless, our experiences with gifted program evaluation suggest that the four-mailing approach is an efficient strategy, although the mailing interval for sending reminders might be longer or shorter depending on specific evaluation situations.

In addition, a privilege that a gifted program evaluator often enjoys is good contacts in the targeted evaluation site (e.g., the program coordinator or the evaluation committee members). Also, there is yet another strategy to reach a better response rate: call the sampled subject if the mailings did not achieve an expected response rate. A sincere call to the attention of the respondent regarding the uncompleted survey usually results in a positive and prompt response. In one evaluation where we used a four-mailing strategy and follow-up phone calls, we not only reached a response rate of 75%, but also got responses from all of the districts that were sampled for on-site case studies. The participation of all such districts in the survey provided a quantitative baseline for comparison with the qualitative data obtained during the on-site visitations.

Increasing the Response Rate

A good response rate from a survey is what an evaluator struggles to obtain since it is directly related to the generalizations that can be made to the whole population of stakeholders represented. A response rate of 70% or above is considered highly desirable in a survey design study (Mangione, 1995). Although there seem to be no foolproof statistical or methodological techniques to guarantee an increased response rate,

Table 3.2

Monitoring and Timing of Four Mailings

	Mailing Time	Response Rate	Emphasis
1st mailing	Dated in contract	40%	Complete packet; thorough; cover letter with clear purpose and procedure statement
1st reminder	14 days	20%	A post-card reminder; be gentle and friendly; emphasis on reminding
2nd mailing	14 days	10%	Complete packet; emphasize confidentiality and importance of good return
2nd reminder	14 days	5%	Post-card reminder; the last call; set specific deadline and encourage people to send in questionnaire so that their views be represented

Note. This table was tabulated according to Mangione's (1995) discussion on getting a good response rate.

researchers who have conducted surveys in different disciplines have found a number of helpful techniques:

1. Write a cordial and professional respondent letter.
2. Provide maximum convenience to respondents.
3. Ensure confidentiality/anonymity.
4. Design a good instrument (e.g., brief and clear questions, friendly lay-out).
5. Fulfill the four-mailing cycle.
6. Make phone calls as a last resort.

The above principles apply to the situation where the mailed self-administration is the only available method. If group administration is a feasible option, there is a better possibility of reaching a high response rate. However, it might evoke social desirability among the respondents, causing them to answer the questions in a way they think will leave a good impression on the evaluator. However, with a reasonably large response rate, the bias might be off-set to some extent; the anonymous character- istic of the survey design will also minimize such a tendency. In addition, other techniques—such as choosing a friendly color (e.g., yellow) for questionnaire printing, using a personalized letter, and indicating the authority of sponsorship through letter stationery—can also be employed to increase the response rate.

The Response Rate of Parents

Based on our experience, parent questionnaires typically receive the lowest response rate among all adult stakeholder surveys in gifted pro- gram evaluation. A typical response rate of a parent survey is about 35% (J. VanTassel-Baska, personal communication, February 2002), which often makes the interpretation of the results vulnerable. No research lit- erature specifically discussed the reasons and remedies for the problem. From our experiences with gifted program evaluations, we can rarely control parental responses. In some cases, the administration of parent questionnaires is conducted via teachers of gifted students at a particular sampled school; in others, the questionnaires are mailed out by the school districts directly. Some parents may have never received the questionnaire by any of the sequences for administration. As one of the adult stake- holder groups, the parent group might represent the highest variability end of a scale with respect to all kinds of demographic characteristics, which makes it even harder to find the sources of nonresponse. Persistent contact with the teachers of students whose parents were sampled is one follow-up approach, along with encouraging the district to conduct a sec- ond mailing.

We suggest that the local gifted program coordinators lobby for a sec- tion in districtwide parent surveys that most school systems already have. In addition, it is highly recommended that a question asking "if any of your children are in the gifted programs the district provide" be built into the demographic section of the survey so that a multiyear data set (although a very small number of questions) will be available for both internal and external evaluators to track, analyze, and compare.

Conclusion

The process of constructing and implementing survey questionnaires for gifted program evaluation is a tension-filled process among survey design theory, the reality of survey implementation, and the competence of the evaluator in balancing such a dynamic process. While following the principles of good survey design and standard practice of survey implementation, evaluators also need to keep in mind the reality and deviations that will occur. To make the instrumentation as reliable and valid as possible is the priority. Triangulating the data derived using other methodologies will also strengthen the results and interpretations obtained from the stakeholder survey design.

Practical Tips for Survey Construction and Implementation

Following are some practical tips on constructing and implementing self-administered surveys. However, given the complexity of questionnaire design, it is suggested that novices in the field solicit help from an expert or adapt available authentic surveys (reliable and valid) and tailor them to their particular settings. The following tips will help both novice and experienced gifted program evaluators in questionnaire construction and implementation. Also included are criteria for selecting surveys to use for tailoring purposes.

Tips on Questionnaire Construction

1. Design demographic questions for subanalysis.

2. Align question content with the best practice standards to cover fully the critical components of a gifted program.

3. Align program benefits and change questions with program goals and objectives to examine perceived degree of program implementation and direction for improvement.

4. Employ multiple sources to create contextual response categories.

5. Write good questions.

Tips on Survey Implementation

1. Develop a sound sampling plan.

2. Prioritize group administration over mailed administration if possible.

3. Establish a good rapport with relevant local educators to increase support for enhancing the response rate.

References

Dillman, D. A. (2000). *Mail and Internet surveys: The tailored design method* (2nd ed.). New York: Wiley.

Fowler, F. J. (1993). *Survey research methods* (2nd ed.). Newbury Park, CA: Sage.

Fowler, F. J. (1995). *Improvising survey questions.* Thousand Oaks, CA: Sage.

Henry, G. T. (1990). *Practical sampling.* Newbury Park, CA: Sage.

Jaeger, R. M. (1984). *Sampling in education and the social sciences.* New York: Longman.

Mangione, T. W. (1995). *Mail surveys: Improving the quality.* Thousand Oaks, CA: Sage.

Pawson, R., & Tilley, N. (2001). Realistic evaluation bloodlines. *American Journal of Evaluation, 22,* 317–324.

A Metaevaluation of Survey Results of Stakeholder Perceptions of Gifted Programs

by Annie Xuemei Feng

The field of evaluation has been developed to assist, support, and extend natural human abilities to observe, understand, and make judgments about policies and program.
—Melvin M. Mark, Gary T. Henry, & George Julnes (2000, p. 5)

Self-reported behaviors have been criticized as an inadequate method of inquiry due to their lack of accuracy in obtaining data and too much reliance on memory for recalling information. The approach has been criticized by cognitive psychologists and language comprehension experts as a vulnerable methodology in deriving desirably accurate and reliable information (Schwarz & Oyserman, 2001). Nevertheless, self-reported behaviors have been one of the most consistently employed methods in social science research and program evaluation. Their use seems to be increasing, even with the acknowledgment of their limitations. Thus, methodologists in all areas have been working to derive strategies for combating shortcomings to self-report and providing constructive ways for obtaining desirable data through such means.

In the past decade, the Center for Gifted Education at the College of William and Mary has conducted numerous evaluations on gifted programs at both the local and state levels. One of the typical strategies used in these evaluation studies has been to survey stakeholders' perceptions of important dimensions of the gifted program. In this chapter, we have aggregated stakeholders' perceptual data from six separate gifted program evaluations (four local, two state) and analyzed the composite data. Using this accumulated empirical evidence, we will both demonstrate how surveys may be useful in gifted program evaluation and showcase a general picture of stakeholder perceptions of current gifted program practice.

Methods

Selection of Survey Data

We selected survey data from six evaluations of gifted programs, including four at the local level and two at the state level. The selection was based on recency and continuity, stakeholder representation, and the comparability of the questions across surveys within each site, as well as across sites. The time range of these evaluations was from 1995 to 2002, with up to 3-year intervals between two consecutive studies. The stakeholders were comprised of students, educators (including regular teachers, gifted teachers, and administrators), parents, and district program coordinators for the two state-level evaluations.

Table 4.1 shows the number of participants for each survey and the respective response rate where applicable for the six selected gifted program evaluation studies (the capital letters A through F are consistently used in this chapter to represent the six evaluation sites). The response rate for the student survey was the highest; the parent survey had the lowest. While site E received the highest response rate (65%) for the parent questionnaire, it should be noted that this survey was administered on-site where special meetings were held for parents and community members; therefore, the parent sample was a convenient sample of those who showed up at the meetings, with no systematic sampling procedures involved.

Table 4.1
Stakeholder Survey Data Sources:
Participants and Response Rate

	95		97		00		00		01		02	
	A		B		C		D		E		F	
Student	–	–	–	–	1848	86%	1833	90%	–	–	465	93%
Educator	255	–	–	–	401	87%	366	50%	582	58%	293	65%
Parents	374	58%	–	–	658	37%	735	36%	97	65%	183	26%
Coord.	–	–	344	56%	–	–	–	–	77	75%	–	–

Composition of Stakeholder Questionnaires

The stakeholder questionnaires contained mostly close-ended questions and one or two open-ended questions. It was suggested that the number of questions be limited to approximately 30 items, hoping for a high response rate and for the convenience of electronic scanning where appropriate. The questions probed the presence or absence of best gifted program practices in identification and assessment, curricula and instruction, organizational arrangements (e.g., grouping), evaluation, and administration. In addition, questions on staff development, personnel qualifications, and parent communication were typically included, as well as any other questions solicited from the request for proposal or the local evaluation planning team. Tailored versions were developed for different stakeholder groups.

Procedures

Questionnaire data were aggregated for each stakeholder group across sites chronologically based on the same or similar questions. Only when there were at least two sites that had available data on a question addressing a particular dimension of gifted programs were they included for the secondary analyses. Based on these selection criteria, data from the following sites were compared for each stakeholder group: sites C and F for comparative analysis of student perceptual data; sites A, C, D, E, and F for comparative analysis of educator questionnaire data; sites A, D, and F for comparative analysis of parent questionnaire data; and sites B and E (state sites) for comparative analysis of the local district program coordinator questionnaire data.

Characteristics of Selected Stakeholder Survey Respondents

Educator questionnaires. A majority of the educator respondents were regular teachers (56–79%) except for one evaluation site where a majority of respondents were teachers of the gifted. The rest of the educator respondents included administrators; teachers of arts, music, or physical education; guidance counselors; and psychologists. There was a balanced representation among four of the districts' educator participants with respect to their years of teaching experience (no teaching background information was provided in site D's teacher questionnaire). A majority of the educator participants had limited coursework in gifted education (66–71%), 14 to 28% of them had a minimum of 6 hours of coursework toward endorsement, and a minority of them (5–12%) had a state endorsement in gifted education. However, teachers of the gifted had a much better training background; more than 80% of them had at least 6 hours of coursework in gifted education, among which 25 to 60% held a state endorsement. Those who held a master's degree in gifted education consisted of only 3 to 6% of the gifted teacher population across sites except for one district (site F), where 17% of gifted teachers had a high level of gifted education background.

Parent questionnaires. The parent questionnaire in three sites (A, D, and F) had parallel questions similar to their respective educator questionnaires. The site C parent questionnaire was administered using a telephone survey (voice poll); the parent questionnaire at site E was administered on-site. These two surveys had more variations in questions due to the methods and goals of data collection; thus, a majority of the comparative analyses on parent questionnaire data were based on three school districts' parent survey data (sites A, D, and F), while selected items were compared across all evaluation sites where appropriate.

Student questionnaires. Students' perceptual data from two local school districts (C and F) were compared because of the similarities in question items and the scale used.

District program coordinator surveys. For the two state-level gifted program evaluations (sites B and E), we also administered a district gifted

program coordinator survey. These coordinator surveys were characterized by a fuller coverage of gifted program components and a K–12 span
of program services. State B, which is located in the Midwest, had 344
coordinators responding to the questionnaires, yielding a response rate of
63%. In State E, which is located in the Northwest, 77 district coordinators responded, with the response rate being 75%. The Midwest state has
a diversified student population; however, the Northwest state is much
less diverse. Despite the significant size differences and the population
diversity between the two states, the reasonable responding rate from
both sites made the evaluation results well represented within each state,
thus making the comparison between the two gifted programs both feasible and interpretable.

Because the local district program coordinator surveys are unique to
the two state gifted programs, the comparative results were reported separately from the other stakeholder survey analyses.

Cross-Site Stakeholder Results: District Level

Identification Process

The cross-site educator questionnaire results suggested that educators had uneven opinions about the fairness of the identification criteria
and the congruity with the services provided. Such a trend seemed to be
related to the flexibility of the identification process that a local district
could exercise. The two sites (C and E) that received higher proportions
of positive ratings (60% and 65%, respectively) had an identification system with more flexibility with regard to local discretion on identification
criteria cutoffs, whereas the other three sites (A, D, and F) enjoyed less
such control. The disparity of educators' perceptions of the congruity
between identification and the services provided concurred with the
flexibility the local district enjoyed. Ranging from 38 to 78% positive
ratings, the site that received the highest congruity rating (site E) was one
of the state gifted programs where local districts enjoyed the most flexible decision making in identification, whereas the site (F) receiving the
lowest rating had strict state standardized identification procedures.

Parents across the sites had a similar perceptual pattern regarding the
fairness of the identification criteria, as well as service congruity. More than
half of the parents (50–58%) felt that the identification criteria were fair

enough to select students for purposes of the gifted program. Between 20 and 27% of the parents felt the identification criteria were either too broad or too narrow; however, about 20% of the parents at sites D and F revealed that they were not familiar with the identification process. Similarly, a slight majority of the responding parents (53–62%) believed that the identification was congruent with the services provided for gifted students; a little over 10% of them noted a mismatch. Between 28 and 36% of the parents in sites D and F, however, had no opinion on this question.

The Overlooked Special Student Populations

The ESL students (English as a Second Language) were consistently rated by both educators and parents as the most overlooked special-needs gifted student population due to the identification criteria employed. The other populations perceived as "disadvantaged" varied from site to site; these included economically disadvantaged, minority, underachieving, and learning-disabled students. None of the special population options received more than one-third of ratings by the educators in these evaluations, and they were rated by even fewer parents (less than 15%). The consistent ranking and low ratings on these options suggested that 1) the "overlooked" populations were not perceived as a salient problem in the gifted program at each site; 2) the question did not yield accurate data due to the way it was constructed (i.e., a screening question might have yielded more clarity; and 3) the low to medium response rate from some evaluation sites (see Table 4.1) might have affected the interpretation of the results. Nonetheless, as Fowler (1993) pointed out, a consistent rating pattern derived from stakeholder surveys might be indicative of problems. It is suggested that the perceptual ranking needs to be checked against other data sources. However, we did not have such information available except at one evaluation site (F). At this site, the district record on the minority representation in the gifted student population was examined, and it concurred with stakeholders' perceptions of the issue.

Salient Instructional Emphasis in Gifted Programs

Four major instructional approaches were identified as typically used with gifted students: higher order questions, individual and group project work, student discussions, and inquiry-based problem-solving activities. At least two-thirds of the educators across sites noted their use of these approaches with gifted students. Other less-frequently cited approaches included cooperative learning, facilitation of learning, and direct instruction. These data suggested that educators perceived themselves as using a variety of high-level instructional approaches with their gifted students.

Differentiation Strategies With Gifted Students

The top three differentiation strategies reported by the educators (62–93%) across sites included: 1) emphasizing higher order thinking skills, 2) engaging students in problem-solving activities, and 3) developing students' research skills. Other differentiated methods were also reported as being employed by 39 to 71% of the educators, including the use of different materials and resources, employing independent study, teaching skills for autonomous learning, using quality products, and compacting for acceleration, with emphases fluctuating depending on specific program goals and operational models.

Parents from two evaluation sites (D, 60%; F, 73%) cited the emphasis of higher order thinking skills as a prominent differentiation strategy used with gifted students. Using different materials and resources was also consistently noted (41–59%). Some parents also cited that teachers differentiated through adapting the core curriculum and providing depth in topics explored (40–57%). Independent study and research, as well as providing specific curricula for gifted students, were also noted by more than 60% of the parents at respective sites.

Interestingly, both educators and parents noted the emphasis on higher order thinking skills as a salient differentiation strategy employed with gifted students. Both stakeholder groups also rated the emphasis on research skills as another frequently used approach. Despite the differences among these gifted programs, the consistent rating across sites and stakeholder groups appeared to indicate the typicality of the two methods of differentiation for gifted students.

Communication and Parental Involvement

A majority of the educators favorably rated their communication with parents of the gifted students (62–87%). Educators' dissatisfaction with their communication with parents fluctuated site by site, ranging from 6 to 29%. Some educators confessed that they did not communicate with parents of gifted students unless problems appeared. These data suggested that, across sites, the majority of educators were satisfied with their level of communication with parents of the gifted.

However, parents rated the communication with their child's gifted program teachers modestly as compared to educators' more favorable perceptions. While 40 to 76% of the parents rated the communication favorably across five evaluation sites, 21 to 60% of them rated it as inadequate or poor. Overall, parents had a lower rating of the communication scale than educators did, suggesting problems in this area.

Staff Development: High Demand vs. Inadequate Training Opportunities

Close to half of the educators at three sites (C, D, and F) noted that the gifted-related staff-development activities in their districts were adequate, while fewer educators rated them as excellent. A range of 33 to 51% of educators complained about the inadequacy of the training provided by their districts. These data suggested that gifted-related staff development was a weak area in these districts. The lack of sufficient and high-quality training opportunities conflicted with the demanding nature of a gifted program, where well-trained teachers are the essential cornerstone.

Program Benefits and Impact

Data on important program benefits to gifted students were available from educator questionnaires at three sites (C, E, and F). The following benefits were most frequently cited across sites: 1) accelerated and challenging learning, 2) opportunities to learn with students of similar abilities and interests, 3) the program's emphasis on critical and creative thinking skills, and 4) emphasis on problem-solving and research skills. The other benefits were cited by fewer than 10% of the educators in each evaluation.

Students across two sites (C and F) highly complimented their gifted programs. The programs appeared to have a positive impact on students cognitively, affectively, and socially. A strong majority of the students (mean percentage point 92.2% and 91.5% for the two sites, respectively) found that being in a gifted program was enjoyable, and they were motivated, encouraged, and held to high expectations by their teachers. They noted they could learn advanced content at a faster and more comfortable pace and further stretch their critical and creative thinking skills and problem-solving competence (mean percentage point 89% and 92%, respectively). Furthermore, students expressed the view that participation in gifted programs provided them the opportunity to interact with other students of similar abilities and nurtured their social and communication skills (mean percentage point 89% and 91%, respectively). All these results corroborated the benefits noted by educators through the educator survey.

Interdisciplinary learning was also cited as a program benefit by a majority of students at both sites. Both student questionnaires also queried the possible negative impact of the gifted program with regard to the challenge level, instructional pace, and social needs. Only a small percentage of students indicated problems in these dimensions (mean percentage point 12% and 10%, respectively).

Perceived Areas for Change

Educators across sites (A, C, E, and F) consistently felt that the identification and selection of gifted students was an area needing to be changed. However, the nature of the needed changes depended on specific programs, expecting either broader or narrower criteria, and including more teacher input in the process. Program options, curricula and instruction, and staff development were the three areas that were alternatively considered as the second or third priority area for change. The consistency of the survey results, despite a span of 8 years and a wide range of geographical locations, suggested that these problems in gifted programs have not been solved and that the top priorities for change need to be directed toward these issues.

Parents' perceptions of areas for change fluctuated site by site; no consistent pattern was evident. As was mentioned earlier in this chapter, the low response rate of parent questionnaires called for caution in interpreting their results.

Cross-Site Gifted Program Coordinator Survey Results: State Level

Identification

The identification questions in the two district program coordinator surveys were used in the state evaluations for understanding a general picture of the identification process and policies on ensuring cultural diversity.

Ensuring cultural diversity. The top three strategies district program coordinators in both states reported using to promote cultural diversity during the identification and selection process were nominations (60–73%), use of student sample products (21–37%), and use of creativity measures (23.3–34.2%). Nominations appeared to be employed most frequently in both states. For the smaller state (E), about one-third of the districts also reported using multiple measures and peer or self-nominations. However, these categories were not listed as the options in the larger state evaluation (B) that was conducted earlier; thus, no data were available for comparison in these categories. Due to the relatively high nonminority homogeneity of the smaller state population, close to 40% of the district coordinators indicated that this question was irrelevant to their districts. The data also suggested that some districts in both states had employed a combination of several methods to address the cultural diversity issue.

Identifying twice-exceptional children. The two states appeared to have a different distribution of districts that had identification policies in accommodating twice-exceptional students. While a lower proportion of site B districts (40%) made adaptations to the existing identification process to accommodate such students, a higher proportion of the districts in state B had routine procedures to identify them. Given the size differences of the two states and the characteristics of the population structure, these data suggested that the larger state (site B) was more sensitive to twice-exceptional students and tended to have specific guidelines to identify them.

Organizational Arrangements

There was a similar grouping pattern of K–12 gifted program services in the two states. The comparative results showed that regular classroom with pull-out model operated predominantly at the elementary level (74% vs. 62%), but decreased as the grade level increased at the middle school level (40% and 33%) and high school level (5% vs. 6%) for the larger and smaller states, respectively. By contrast, ability grouping in specific subjects was used more and more as the grade level increased, from an average of one-quarter of the districts at the elementary level, to about 40% at the middle school level, to more than 45% at the high school level. However, more than half (53.4%) of the smaller state districts consistently rated regular heterogeneous classrooms as the typical grouping model across grade levels versus an average of 16% of the district coordinators in the large state. Such a difference suggested that gifted program services are more diffused in the smaller state as compared to those in the larger state. The results also indicated that none of the states had extensively employed full-time self-contained gifted classes or a special school for gifted students (less than 3% in site B and none in site E).

Program Differentiation for Special Populations of Gifted Learners

Overall, the larger state's gifted programs appeared to be more sensitive to the special populations of gifted learners, such as minority groups, ESL students, and low-SES students. Even so, results indicated that less than a majority of districts addressed these needs directly. Using multicultural materials (34%) and addressing multicultural perspectives (25%) were two major differentiation strategies employed by school districts in the larger state. The two states were similar in that about equal percentages of the districts cited classroom adaptations as an approach to accommodate the needs of special population students in the program, despite a lower proportion of usage in both states (18% vs. 15%). The other strategies such as counseling, mentoring, tutoring, and special "bridging" programs were rarely employed (10% or less in both states).

High School Options for Gifted Learners

Gifted learners at the high school level had opportunities to stretch their talents through more rigorous Advanced Placement (AP) coursework and International Baccalaureate (IB) programs. Higher proportions of districts in both the larger state (site B, 55%) and smaller state (site E, 40%) offered one to five such courses, while fewer districts had an offering of more than six (17% vs. 15% in the larger and smaller state, respectively). A much higher percentage of the smaller state's districts had no offerings of AP courses (45%). Dual enrollment at high school and college appeared to be another viable option for gifted learners at the high school level; 76% of districts in the larger state (site B) and 59% of districts in the smaller state (site E) provided dual-enrollment options for their juniors and seniors. Given that the evaluation for the larger state was conducted 4 years earlier, it can be assumed that the discrepancy might be even larger now.

Technology Impact on Gifted Program Development

Information on the long-distance options for high school credit placement reflected the degree to which technological resources were employed for gifted program development. Sixteen percent of the school districts in the larger state (site B) and 56% of those in the smaller state (site E) were able to provide college correspondence courses. Smaller state districts also benefited more from interactive video coursework. While 52% of the districts in the larger state did not have any long-distance options in 1997, 30% of the smaller state districts were facing such limited options in 2002. These data suggested that the faster pace of technological development might have benefited gifted programs tremendously. It should also be noted that many districts in the smaller state were located in mountain areas, which made such long-distance options a stronger necessity.

The positive impact of technology became more obvious when comparing the technology resources for use in gifted classrooms between these two states. While 41% of the districts in the larger state had Internet access in 1997, 96% of the smaller state's school districts had access by 2002. These significant differences were also reflected in the ownership of classroom computers and use of CD-ROM and multimedia, e-mail, and Web sites. The laser disc and interactive disc of an earlier generation of technology have been replaced by the more advanced technologies of today.

Assessing Gifted Students

The two states were similar in reporting the kinds of assessment tools employed for measuring gifted students' learning in the program. Data from both states suggested that content mastery in language arts, math, science, and social studies have been the priority domains for assessment. Both states' gifted programs appeared to measure gifted students' learning in areas such as the development of critical and creative thinking skills, metacognitive skills, students' self-awareness, and their conceptual understanding level and interdisciplinary connections. The two states differed in assessment for gifted students in that the larger state had consistently high ratings in the development of a series of thinking skills, whereas the smaller state had a consistently higher rating in the mastery of content areas. These percentage differences may reveal the emphasis of each state's gifted programs, with one content-oriented and the other more skills-focused. The instruments used by both states in evaluating gifted students' performance were composed of observations; norm- and criteria-referenced tests; performance-based instruments with rubrics, portfolios, and products with rubrics; and observation, which was the most frequently employed tool reported in both states. These perceptual data stand in sharp contrast to the lack of actual student impact data available in either state, indicating that assessment practices with gifted students are classroom-based at best and not aggregated at district or state levels.

Program Management

The program management status of gifted programs in these two states was assessed through their mechanism for evaluation and monitoring of program implementation. The larger state had a better evaluation system implemented by 45% of the districts annually, almost double that of the smaller state. The major approaches for conducting evaluations in the two states were similar, including classroom observations, student performance data analysis, and stakeholder questionnaires, with the larger state having higher ratings for all these approaches; focus groups were employed by a minority of the districts in both states. These data show that the larger state had an evaluation system in place for more of its districts than the smaller state, suggesting that its gifted education programs operate at a more formal level.

The typical program monitoring methods the coordinators used in both states included visiting classrooms on an informal basis (83% and 70%) and meeting with teachers regularly (75% and 51%) to discuss program implementation. However, a sharp drop occurred for districts that used structured forms for observations (29% and 34%), formal consultation with the building principals (23% and 39%), and systematically conducting videotape analyses of gifted classes (0% and 3.2%). These data revealed that, for the two states, gifted program supervision was still limited and that enhanced and more rigorous guidance in this area needed to be put in place.

Parental Involvement and Education

Four types of parental involvement were enjoyed by more than half of the districts in both states: volunteers on field trips, volunteers in classes, parent conferences, and survey instruments. A little over one-quarter of the school districts in both states had a formal advisory group in place to advise, advocate, or monitor their gifted programs.

However, a majority of the district coordinators in both states noted that they did not have a formal parent education program available. For those districts that had such educational programs in place (37% and 22% for the larger and smaller state, respectively), orientation was the most typical feature of the program. Affective needs of gifted students also received some attention. Some districts in both states offered parental education programs on topics of academic preparation, college planning, and out-of-school activities, with a higher percentage of the districts in the smaller state featuring these topics (43–75% vs. 22–37%).

Staff Development

A substantial percentage of districts in the larger (48%) and the smaller (60%) state reported having one to two staff-development activities annually. However, staff-development activities were more frequently and regularly held in the larger state than in the smaller state (45% vs. 32%). The smaller state provided staff development more frequently through conference participation, regional in-service, and college coursework, while the larger state provided the services more often through regular in-district and school-based services. Such a discrepancy between staff-development features in the two states was most probably related to size and resource allocations. The smaller state also had a targeted statewide emphasis on training that called for more teachers involvement in summer institutes. Table 4.2 presents a summary of cross-site stakeholders' perceptions of dimensions of gifted programs.

Discussion

By analyzing data obtained from stakeholder surveys across six evaluation sites, we can derive a general picture of gifted program practice in several dimensions. The consistent findings document problems and provide directions for further gifted program development in these and other similar local and state program agencies.

The prominent issue in identification and assessment lies in the fairness of the selection process and congruity of the services with the selection focus. The cross-site analyses suggested that, while a slight majority of educators and parents were satisfied with the identification process and felt the criteria were a fair measurement in identifying gifted students, close to half of the two stakeholder groups felt just the opposite. The split of pros and cons on the issue of identification fairness seemed to be related to the extent of local discretion on cutoff scores that a district could exercise and stakeholders' knowledge about the process. The more such flexibility a local district enjoyed, the more likely that stakeholders were satisfied with the identification criteria. For those stakeholders who perceived the unfairness of the criteria, the split between those who wanted them to be more broad and those who wanted them to be more narrow could possibly be attributed to the philosophical understanding of what giftedness is within each stakeholder group and lack of communication about the actual state or local process used.

Another aspect of the fairness of the identification measurement is cultural sensitivity to students of special populations such as ESL, minority, low-SES, underachieving, learning-disabled, and twice-exceptional students. One of the most consistent findings across stakeholder groups and across sites was that ESL students were perceived as the most overlooked student population for gifted services due to the identification criteria. The best practice standards (National Association for Gifted Children, 1998) in identification stipulated that "identification instruments must measure the capabilities of students fairly in such a way that the tools with students' most fluent language needs to be available" and the instrument needs to be "culturally fair," as well. The data suggested that such a standard is far from being met in gifted programs. As was suggested in the district coordinator survey results, nomination was the dominant approach used in identifying cultural diversity in 2001 just as it was in 1996. Not much change has occurred in practice, and culturally and linguistically fair identification tools are still underutilized.

The congruity between the services provided and the identification focus appeared to present a similar pattern across sites and stakeholder groups as that of perceived fairness of the identification criteria. The flexibility that a local district could exercise was congruent with the degree that stakeholders felt a match between the services and the criteria.

From the results obtained using the aggregated data, we found a diverse range of curricula used with gifted students over these years. Some programs used the same curriculum with gifted students, but provided a series of enrichment activities to enhance it. Other programs adapted the core curriculum to provide in-depth topics through themes and concepts. And still other programs employed completely new curricula for their gifted students. An issue raised from the overall data analysis was the extent of the relationship between the regular curriculum and the curriculum for the gifted. There seemed to be a disintegration between the two material sources in most of the evaluation sites, with the problem being more prominent at the elementary level. In addition, an analysis of the two state-level programs

Table 4.2

A Summary of Cross-Site Stakeholders' Perceptions of Gifted Programs

	Educators	Parents	Students	Coordinators
Identification	• uneven perceptions of the fairness of the ID criteria and congruity with services • local flexibility appeared to affect ratings • current ID practice disadvantaged special student populations, with ESL students affected the most	• uneven perceptions of the fairness of the ID criteria and congruity with services • local flexibility appeared to affect ratings • ESL students, low–SES students, minority students, and under-achievers were disadvantaged by the ID criteria	N/A*	• Some strategies have been used to ensure cultural diversity in the ID process; yet, few cultur-ally sensitive ID tools have been employed • Policies in addressing twice-exceptional children varies

Curriculum, Instruction, and Assessment	• employ high-level instructional approaches
	  – higher order questions
	  – project work
	  – student discussions
	  – inquiry-based problem-solving activities
	• Top 3 differentiation strategies
	  – higher order thinking skills
	  – problem solving
	  – research skills
		The top three differentiation strate-gies perceived to be used:
		  – higher order thinking skills
		  – research skills
		  – specific curriculum with gifted learners
			N/A	• The availability of AP and IB options provide opportunity for gifted students to stretch their academic strengths at high school
				• Technological resources increasingly used in gifted classrooms
				• Classroom–based assessment practice dominates the trend of assessment

Communication and Parental Involvement	• Favorable rating of communica-tion with parents of gifted students • Less dissatisfaction with the cur-rent status of communication	• Modest rating of communication with teachers of gifted students • Higher percentage of parents expressed dissatisfaction with the communication with teachers	N/A	• The type of parental involve-ment does not exceed that expected for a regular class-room • Lack of formal advisory group

Staff Development	A majority of educators cited the inadequacy of the training opportunities	N/A	N/A	• Lack of formal parent education program • Low frequency of staff-development activities • The staff-development activities were budget confined
Organizational Arrangement	No comparable cross-site data for analysis	N/A	No comparable cross-site data for analysis	• Transit from pull-out model to ability grouping in specific subjects as grade level increases • Lack of self-contained gifted classes or a special school
Program Management/ Evaluation	N/A	N/A	N/A	• Lack of formal and regular evaluation mechanism at both states
Program Benefits and Impact	• Accelerated and challenging learning • Positive peer group influence • Critical and creative thinking skills • Problem-solving and research skills	N/A	Positive program impact on their cognitive, affective, and social development	
Areas for Change	• Need a fairer ID process • Need more program options • Curriculum and instruction • Staff development	No consistent perceptions cross the evaluation sites.	N/A	

Note. *N/A: A particular question was not asked for a stakeholder group, or no comparable data were available for cross-site analysis for that particular stakeholder group.

suggested that not many local districts used multicultural materials to accommodate the cognitive and affective needs of minority gifted students.

While there was an uneven picture of curricula use across gifted programs in different geographical locations, there seemed to be a consistent pattern of instructional approaches employed for differentiation. Common to these gifted programs were teachers who emphasized higher order thinking skills, nurtured independent research skills, and encouraged inquiry-based problem-solving skills in their instructional practices. The lack of coherent curriculum use and the harmonious picture of differentiation strategies in instruction across sites suggested a lack of a well-defined and planned curricular framework for gifted learners across sites, indicating a weak component at the program structure level.

The assessment of gifted students' learning as reflected in the two states' coordinator survey appeared to be consistent with the program emphasis, either in mastery of advanced content or a series of thinking skills at the classroom level. However, a systematic assessment mechanism that corresponds to curricular goals and objectives had yet to be established at both the local and state levels.

In the area of professional development, data from both local and state levels presented a similar picture of the current status quo of training in gifted education. Across the sites, there seemed to be few (one to two) regularly scheduled staff-development activities related to gifted education annually. However, such activities in most instances seemed to be open to and used by teachers of gifted students only; regular teachers were not optimally involved, except in one of the state-level gifted programs, where a state training grant was provided that targeted both teachers of the gifted students and regular teachers. Not surprisingly, over two-thirds of the educator respondents reported in the survey that they had limited or no formal training in gifted education. It can be inferred that school and district administrators might be even less trained in the relevant topics. These results suggest that a comprehensive staff-development plan is needed. It is not only teachers who are directly involved in the instructional process of gifted students who need sustained training, but also the program support staff, including administrators, so that gifted students will maximally benefit from the program.

Despite the fact that more teachers and parents favorably perceived the teacher-parent communication within each respective stakeholder group, higher proportions of teachers were satisfied with the communication across sites. Such a perceptual difference between stakeholder groups indicated a concern for communication overall. The data also suggested that regularly scheduled information exchange between parents and teachers of the gifted rarely occurred. Some districts did survey parental satisfaction about the gifted program. However, such surveys were conducted at most on a yearly basis, and there was no well-structured educational programs in place for parents of gifted students in these districts.

Conclusion

The consistent and inconsistent perceptual patterns of stakeholders over these evaluations were affected by the following three conflicts:

1. Managing gifted programs is such a value-laden enterprise that stakeholders' philosophy about gifted education directly affected their perceptions of a particular program policy such as identification and assessment.
2. There is a clash between the traditional definition of giftedness (intelligence, well-rounded quantitative and verbal ability) with the demands of accommodating students who have high aptitude in a particular academic or nonacademic area. The discrepant opinions of stakeholder groups on the congruity of services with the selection process might have been affected by such a foundational misunderstanding of program purpose.
3. A gifted program itself suffers from the vulnerability of being labeled as elitist in U.S. society.
4. The multicultural characteristics of the gifted population call for a culturally and politically sensitive program. However, effective change to meet such a need has yet to come. Assessment tools, curricular framework, and program differentiation need to be reformed to accommodate such a demand.

Probably the most noticeable change in gifted program development over the years of these evaluations was the impact of technology, which brought more opportunities to gifted students through long-distance options, interactive videos, accumulated information, and numerous ways of doing research. Moreover, the power of human resources as reflected in the motivation, enthusiasm, and expertise of many local and state gifted program coordinators holds promise for the field developing in a healthy and promising direction.

Practical Tips for Evaluators

Based on the results obtained through aggregated survey data, the following section summarizes several suggestions for personnel conducting evaluations.

1. Use surveys with multiple stakeholder groups.

2. Establish and maintain an evaluation survey database; develop a systematic coding mechanism.

3. Triangulate survey findings across stakeholder groups, across sites, and across time to enhance credibility of findings and results and recommendations.

References

Dillman, D. A. (2000). *Mail and Internet surveys: The tailored design method* (2nd ed.). New York: Wiley.

Fowler, F. J. (1993). *Survey research methods* (2nd ed.). Newbury Park, CA: Sage.

Mangione, T. W. (1995). *Mail surveys: Improving the quality*. Thousand Oaks, CA: Sage.

Mark, M. M., Henry, G. T., & Julnes, G. (2000). *An integrated framework for understanding, guiding, and improving policies and programs*. San Francisco: Josey-Bass.

Miller, D. C., & Salkind, N. J. (2002). *Handbook of research design and social measurement* (6th ed.). Thousand Oaks, CA: Sage.

National Association for Gifted Children. (1998). *Best standards of gifted education programs*. Retrieved August 18, 2003, from http://www.nagc.org/webprek12.htm.

Schwarz, N., & Oyserman, D. (2001). Asking questions about behavior: Cognition, communication, and questionnaire construction. *American Journal of Evaluation, 22*, 127–160.

 **5**

Assessing Classroom Practice: The Use of a Structured Observation Form

by Joyce VanTassel-Baska

For me, the fundamental mandate of school reform is to examine every decision, practice, and policy, and ask the question: "What, if anything, is anyone learning as a consequence of this?" Whether we are called teachers, principals, or parents, our primary responsibility is to promote learning in others and in ourselves. That's what it means to be an educator.
                                                                —Roland Barth

If "teaching matters" is a key premise of educational reform, then teaching high–ability learner matters, as well. However, the research base on the implementation of best instructional practices in classrooms serving gifted students is fairly scant. Westberg, Archambault, Dobyns, and Salvin (1993) documented that no curricular or instructional adaptations were made for gifted learners in heterogeneous classrooms in 84% of their instructional activities, a finding that led to sounding the clarion call for differentiation again. Avery and VanTassel-Baska (2003) found that the use of a high-powered curricular intervention in social studies, coupled with staff development on its implementation, led to increases in instructional behaviors tied to elements of educational reform. Few other studies have sought to provide empirical evidence of the nature of teaching practices with academically advanced learners against the landscape of the reform agenda.

During the past several years, I had the opportunity to conduct multiple local site evaluations of elementary and middle school gifted education programs. The organizational models used to deliver services across these districts included cluster grouping in the regular classroom, self-contained center-based classes, special classes, and pull-out programs. These 16 districts, covering geographical regions in the northwest and southeast areas of the country, represented a diverse range of socioeconomic levels for rural, urban, and suburban schools.

We were able to use the same Classroom Observation Form (COF) in each evaluation and thereby establish an incipient database on the nature of classroom practice in multiple settings serving high-ability learners across different models at different levels of the system. Most recently, we have begun to explore the specification of a benchmark for what constitutes acceptable classroom practice at the gifted program level.

Purpose

The purpose of this chapter is to share the instrument, the Classroom Observation Form (COF), used to conduct these classroom observations and the analysis of the database created by its application in multiple instructional contexts. This analysis allows us to examine differences in instructional behaviors seen in different organizational arrangements. We would also like to share our emerging efforts to establish a quantitative threshold for what is considered an acceptable level of practice in gifted education program contexts, using the COF database to illustrate viability.

Theoretical Framework

Over the past several years, there has been considerable evidence from different areas suggesting that the ways in which teachers behave in the classroom and the instructional approaches they employ significantly affect the degree to which students learn. Sanders and Rivers (1996) reported that the effects of ineffective teachers over 3 years had a depressed effect on student achievement in math by as much as 54% regardless of the ability of the learner. Wenglinsky (2000) found positive effects of using key practices such as critical thinking and metacognition on student learning in math and science across elementary and middle school levels. The literature in gifted education suggests that teacher behavior is the link to differentiated programs and services for this special population. Studies consistently suggest that regular classrooms have limited differentiated activities (see Westberg et al., 1993). Moreover gifted and talented teacher behaviors are not systematically monitored. In 5 years of evaluation work, only 2 out of 16 districts indicated that they monitored classroom implementation.

Classroom reform is highly dependent on positive teacher behavioral change in key areas. Thus, the professional development literature is instructive on how best to effect these changes. A study of math and science programs found that teachers will use strategies linked to content that show results with students (Kennedy, 1999). Collegiality and support have also been found to be necessary for change to occur (Garet, Porter, Desimone, Birman, & Yoon, 2001). Another study has shown that the use of higher level reform behavior takes 2 or more years of intensive training to demonstrate results (Borko, Mayfield, Marion, Flexer & Cumbo, 1993). Based on these findings, it is clear that attention to classroom-level instruction must be carefully monitored in order to improve teaching.

Yet, the use of teacher evaluation alone or disconnected from ongoing professional development appears to be unsuccessful as a catalyst for teacher change. A recent study of teacher evaluation practices in three districts in Wisconsin (Kimball, 2002) found that few teachers reported substantial changes in their instructional practice as a result of their evaluation experiences, and the large majority of teachers did not see the evaluation process as an incentive to seek out professional development opportunities. Untenured teachers were more likely than more experienced teachers to report improvements in their instruction based on feedback received during their evaluations. Some explanations for this finding might be that untenured teachers were often novices with little classroom teaching experience, struggling with the most basic aspects of teaching. Principals and other evaluators were often able to draw on their prior teaching experience and their work as instructional leaders to provide constructive feedback on these practices that novice teachers could put to immediate use. Second, evaluators were required to spend more time with untenured teachers, observing more of their classroom sessions and conducting more pre- and postobservation conferences. The additional time evaluators devoted to assessing untenured teachers gave these teachers more opportunity for direct and ongoing feedback. Kimball also found that evaluators' own content backgrounds affected their ability to make informed inferences about the quality of teachers' instruction on specific content and to provide deep feedback.

Gifted education practice has had an uneasy alliance with key facets of educational reform (VanTassel-Baska, 1993), supporting the need for challenging standards, but questioning the impact of inclusion on talent development. To its credit, the field is recognized for advancing the introduction of innovative instructional practices into the classroom, such as inquiry learning, critical and creative thinking skills, higher order questioning strategies, metacognition, and the use of rich and varied curricular materials, rather than sole reliance on textbooks (Tomlinson & Callahan, 1992). Most recently, the introduction of content-based curricula tied to state and national standards and evaluated on student learning gains (VanTassel-Baska, Bass, Ries, Poland, & Avery, 1998; VanTassel-Baska, Zuo, Avery, & Little, 2002) has again positioned the field in the forefront of curricular reform, with the emphasis on "going through the standards and not around them" to achieve instructional impact.

In spite of such advances, there is little evidence that gifted education programs systematically assess student gains using appropriate learning measures (Avery & VanTassel-Baska, 2001). In the absence of student impact data, evaluators must often rely on the quality of the instructional experience as a proxy method for investigating program effectiveness. In fact, teacher effectiveness has been shown to be the main determinant of student progress (Sanders & Horn, 1998). Classroom observation provides a nexus between the input variables of the teacher and his or her students and the process of instruction itself, a process that combines instructional intent (goals and objectives), curricular resources and materials, instructional and assessment strategies, and classroom management skills within a delimited period of time. In meeting the needs of the gifted learner, the observer must focus on three dimensions of practice: good teaching in general, key elements of educational reform, and differentiation for high-ability learners.

Assumptions About the Act of Teaching

There are certain assumptions made about the act of teaching that underlie the use of any observation tool, especially one like the COF, which is extensive and in-depth in respect to behaviors.

Teaching is a complex social activity requiring the capacity to split attention by student, area of the room, and activity. It requires making multiple decisions during a teaching episode by instructional regulation, strategies, use of time, and lesson emphasis. Moreover, teachers must think in complex ways in order to implement many behaviors simultaneously. For example, one type of thinking that teachers must employ relates to following the lesson plan, responding to pacing, modulating student-teacher interaction and ensuring a variety of stimuli. A second type of thinking required of teachers is awareness of teaching to multiple objectives, such as teaching a concept at the same time as they are teaching content and skills and at the same time they are attending to the teaching of group dynamics. A third way of thinking involves orchestrating feedback strategies and responses, flexibility in grouping patterns, and questioning and activity choices. Planning, monitoring, and assessing both group and individual learning is another level of thinking that teachers must employ *en medias res*. Finally, teachers need to think about sequencing their lessons. How does the current lesson relate to yesterday's and how will it link to tomorrow's?

Teaching has traditionally been a solitary activity; thus, teachers are not socialized to external observations of their work. Just as doctors would not be comfortable with overseers in the midst of an operation, so teachers oftentimes are uncomfortable with the observation process. Yet, improvement in teaching clearly requires a change in teacher behaviors that promotes learning in students. Such improvement appears to imply the use of higher order thinking, problem solving, and metacognitive approaches. In order to ensure that teachers are employing such strategies, some form of monitoring of their teaching behaviors must occur. Such monitoring is also essential to effective program evaluations.

The Role of Classroom Observation in Program Evaluation

Classroom observation is a seminal part of program evaluation. It affords an opportunity to access the actual instructional experience that is at the heart of teaching and learning. It provides a nexus between the input variables of the teacher and his or her students and the process of instruction itself. It is the one part of a program evaluation process that allows the critical pieces to come together in an authentic opportunity for insight and knowledge about the quality of the learning experiences that are delivered.

One way of thinking about the classroom observation component of an evaluation is to see it as a performance-based assessment of the teacher within the context of the learning environment. This allows for many of the same features afforded by performance-based assessment of students, but with the teacher as the unit of focus. For instance, it is a relatively open-ended experience, with teachers exercising much control over the selection of the lesson to be taught. It allows for the demonstration of complex and higher order behaviors, recognizing that good teaching derives from a sophisticated set of skills that unfold in an integrated way. It also allows for self-assessment, providing a metacognitive dimension to the experience. Most importantly, by using a structured form, it provides a benchmark against which the teaching process can be assessed based on expectations derived from best practices in the field of gifted education.

However, it is important to distinguish between program and teacher evaluation in terms of the parameters used in the classroom observation process. In our work, the focus is on program evaluation, which targets the collective whole. Teacher behavior is sampled through the classroom observation process, and the intent is to allow teachers to prepare for the observation period in order to reduce the level of threat that permeates this current school climate of accountability. By aggregating data across classrooms, a snap-shot of instructional practice is created that helps inform our understanding of program quality.

Direct observation is also an important component of a teacher (or staff) evaluation process, but deeper sampling of the individual being assessed must occur when used for this purpose. Also, teacher evaluation should involve some opportunity for unplanned visits to the classroom to assess the consistency of instructional performance. While the two uses of classroom observation (program and teacher evaluation) can complement one another, it is important to acknowledge that the limited sampling template used for program evaluation is not sufficient to make inferences regarding individual staff performance tied to retention or promotion decisions.

Methods

Researchers collected data on 228 gifted classrooms across 16 school districts with trained observers using the Classroom Observation Form (COF; VanTassel-Baska & Avery, 2003; Avery, VanTassel-Baska, & O'Neill, 1998). This form has 40 items grouped into nine categories of behavior. Teams of trained observers, drawn from within the relevant districts and the Center for Gifted Education, conducted each observation, first completing the checklist independently, then conferring on their final assessment. The content validity, established by expert review, was found to be .97. The interrater reliability of the instrument had previously been calculated at .63 (Avery & VanTassel-Baska, 2001). For this study, the reliability using Cohen's Kappa was found to be .82 (Feng, 2001). Interrater reliability was further enhanced by using a team consensus model for final determination of scores. Observations were conducted during the relevant school year, and each lasted approximately 35 to 45 minutes. Elementary and middle school classrooms were included, with representation from four different organizational models serving gifted learners. Visitations were scheduled, and teachers were notified in advance of the purpose of the observation (see Appendix B for a copy of the COF.)

The data collected for this study have been analyzed using means and percentages with comparisons among different content areas, school levels, and organizational models presented graphically. Analyses of variance (ANOVAs) were conducted to test for categorical mean differences by level, content area, program type, and gifted versus regular classrooms. Chi-square statistics were calculated for distribution differences by item in subgroup analyses.

Results

Whole Sample Analysis

Classroom observations were conducted across grades 2–12, with the highest frequency occurring at grades 3–8, where 16–42 observations were conducted at each grade level. More language arts ($N = 62$) and math ($N = 41$) lessons were observed than either science ($N = 37$) or social studies ($N = 17$). Frequency of observations varied across the districts, ranging from 51–68 (or 25–58 gifted classes).

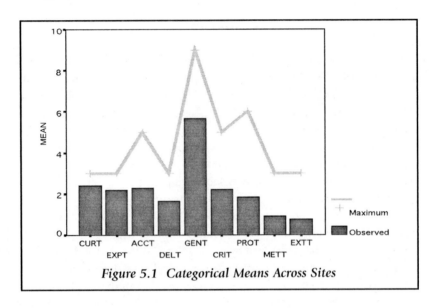

Figure 5.1 Categorical Means Across Sites

Figure 5.1 reflects the differences between observed behaviors and optimal performance in all nine categories of teaching performance. The overall differences by category between observed and optimal behavior reflected important differences in the key areas of accommodation to individual differences, critical thinking, problem solving, metacognition, and classroom extensions. An analysis by teams using the form suggested items within categories necessary to be observed in order to infer acceptable behavior in that category. Such determination varied by categories based on number of items and the nature of the category itself. For example, acceptability in employing critical thinking would require three out of the five items in that category to be observed. The reality of limited observation time also affected judgments of acceptability. Using this schema, a total score of 21 was required for judging the teacher behaviors at an acceptable level. This level was validated by a team of external experts who also concurred on its acceptability as a minimum threshold score. Results across the data set using this benchmark suggested that less than half of the teachers met acceptable levels of performance. External expert validation also suggested that 30 observed behaviors were necessary for teachers to be judged exemplary.

Table 5.1 reflects the presence or absence of teaching behaviors by item across all district gifted classrooms. Several behavioral terms ($N = 5$) on the scale were infrequently observed in over one-third of classrooms. Other

Table 5.1
Overall Classroom Observation Results (*N* = 228)

Area	The Teacher . . .	Obs.	Not Obs.
Curriculum Planning	1. had a written lesson plan linked to course objectives.	200 (87.7%)	28 (12.3%)
	2. communicated the purpose/objectives of the lesson to students.	154 (67.5%)	74 (32.5%)
	3. adhered to the basic framework of the lesson as originally intended.	217 (95.2%)	11 (4.8%)
Expectations for Learners	4. was clear in giving directions and discussing activities and assignments.	215 (94.3%)	13 (5.7%)
	5. set high expectations for student performance in the classroom.	146 (64.0%)	82 (36.0%)
	6. provided clear and consistent feedback on student performance.	155 (68.0%)	73 (32.0%)
Accommodation to Individual Differences	7. presented content that challenged students.	157 (68.9%)	71 (31.1%)
	8. accommodated individual or subgroup differences through material selection or task assignments.	64 (28.1%)	164 (71.9%)
	9. incorporated multicultural perspectives or knowledge, reflecting at least two cultures.	38 (16.7%)	190 (83.3%)
	10. addressed at least two different modes of learning (e.g. visual, auditory, kinesthetic).	215 (94.3%)	13 (5.7%)
	11. allowed students individually or in small groups to move through basic materials more rapidly.	62 (27.2%)	166 (72.8%)
Curriculum Delivery Features	12. emphasized depth in learning.	146 (64.0%)	82 (36.0%)
	13. taught according to key concepts and ideas relevant to content area being addressed.	184 (80.7%)	44 (19.3%)
	14. encouraged or indicated interdisciplinary connections.	80 (35.1%)	148 (64.9%)

continued on the next page

Table 5.1 continued

Area	The Teacher ...	Obs.	Not obs.
General Teaching Strategies	15. used flexible patterns of grouping to deliver the lesson.	127 (55.7%)	101 (44.3%)
	16. used more than one instructional strategy to deliver the lesson.	186 (81.6%)	42 (18.4%)
	17. provided activities in which students applied new learning.	186 (81.6%)	42 (18.4%)
	18. provided the opportunity for the students to use technology.	72 (31.6%)	156 (68.4%)
	19. kept all or most of the students on task.	222 (97.4%)	6 (2.6%)
	20. used hands-on approaches, including such things as journaling, manipulatives, experiments, etc.	186 (81.6%)	42 (18.4%)
	21. used cooperative or collaborative learning strategies.	139 (61.0%)	89 (39.0%)
	22. allowed students to discover central ideas on their own through structured activities and/or questions.	140 (61.4%)	88 (38.6%)
	23. emphasized higher level thinking strategies/skills.	150 (65.8%)	78 (34.2%)
Critical Thinking Strategies	used activities or questions that enabled students:		
	24. to make judgments or evaluate situations, problems, or issues.	167 (73.2%)	61 (26.8%)
	25. to compare and contrast.	144 (63.2%)	84 (36.8%)
	26. to generalize from specific data to the abstract.	107 (46.9%)	121 (53.1%)
	27. to synthesize or summarize information within or across the disciplines.	93 (40.8%)	135 (59.2%)
	28. to debate points of view or develop arguments to support ideas.	53 (23.2%)	175 (76.8%)
Problem-Solving Strategies	used activities or questions that encouraged students:		
	29. to brainstorm ideas or alternatives.	121 (53.1%)	107 (46.9%)

Area	The Teacher ...	Obs.	Not obs.
	30. to define problems (to go from a "mess" to a well-defined problem statement).	52 (22.8%)	176 (77.2%)
	31. to select and implement solutions to problems.	80 (35.1%)	148 (64.9%)
	32. to explore multiple interpretations.	94 (41.2%)	134 (58.8%)
	33. allowed students to use alternative, rather than single, modes of expression for class/homework activities/ products (e.g. charts, graphics, videos, journals, etc.).	77 (33.8%)	151 (66.2%)
	34. allowed students to self-select topics for further investigation.	53 (23.2%)	175 (76.8%)
Meta-cognition	35. modeled metacognitive strategies such as planning, monitoring, self-reflection, or self-appraisal.	80 (35.1%)	148 (64.9%)
	36. provided opportunities for students to think about their own thinking.	77 (33.8%)	151 (66.2%)
	37. had students reflect on their own performance.	67 (29.4%)	161 (70.6%)
	38. reinforced or expanded the lesson by assigning homework.	119 (52.2%)	109 (47.8%)
Classroom Extensions	39. provided follow-up ideas of special projects for students to pursue.	36 (15.8%)	192 (84.2%)
	40. identified people or materials that could be used to supplement student learning.	41 (18.0%)	187 (82.0%)

behaviors ($N = 8$) were even less frequently observed (i.e., in less than half of the classrooms), while a sizable set of behaviors ($N = 9$) were not observed in the vast majority of classrooms (less than 70%). These behaviors clustered in the categories of accommodation to individual differences, critical thinking, problem solving, metacognition, and learning extensions. The general teaching strategies of technology employment and the curricu-

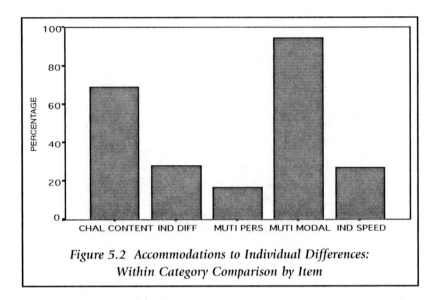

***Figure 5.2 Accommodations to Individual Differences:
Within Category Comparison by Item***

lum delivery feature of interdisciplinary connections were also infrequently employed. Figure 5.1 provides the graphic portrayal of these findings.

Figures 5.2, 5.3, and 5.4 reflect the proportion of observed behaviors within the category of accommodation to individual differences, critical thinking, and problem-solving strategies—three critical components of differentiation expected for teachers of the gifted. These graphs illustrate the degree and locale of the inadequate employment of differentiation strategies in gifted classrooms. In these classrooms, limited attention was dedicated to flexible grouping and material selections; neither were multicultural perspectives appreciably used to accommodate program students' individual needs. Three out of five critical thinking strategies—generalization, synthesis, and debate for different point of views—were observed in less than half of the gifted classes. Only one of the five problem-solving strategies was observed in more than half of the classes, that being the strategy of brainstorming.

Results by Subject Area

An ANOVA analysis revealed one significantly different strategy use by subject area ($p < .05$). This difference occurred in the category of "extensions," where differences were detected between math and science, favoring the use of extensions by math teachers over science teachers.

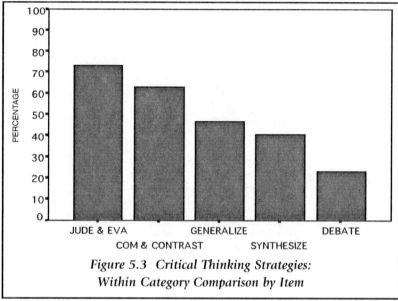

Figure 5.3 Critical Thinking Strategies:
Within Category Comparison by Item

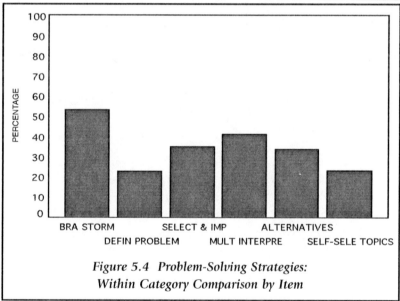

Figure 5.4 Problem-Solving Strategies:
Within Category Comparison by Item

Other subject area differences affected strategy use, as well, but not at the level of statistical significance. Consistent use of more flexible strategies was evident in language arts classrooms, while social studies classrooms

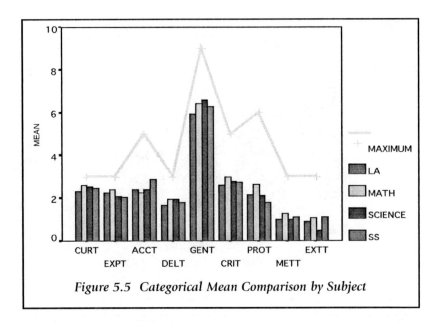

Figure 5.5 Categorical Mean Comparison by Subject

employed multicultural perspectives far more frequently than any other content area. Clarity in lesson purpose, higher level thinking, problem solving, and metacognition were more apparent in mathematics classrooms than in other content areas. Homework was also more consistently employed as a strategy for learning in math classrooms (see Figure 5.5).

Results by Grade Level

An ANOVA analysis revealed several significant differences in strategy use by level of schooling. Significant differences ($p < .05$) were reflected in the use of reform–based strategies, favoring middle school classrooms over elementary; general strategies, favoring both elementary and middle school classrooms over high school; problem-solving strategies, favoring middle schools over high schools; and use of extensions, favoring high school over elementary school (see Table 5.2)

Results by Program Grouping Model

Type of gifted program grouping was analyzed for differences using ANOVA, yielding no significant categorical differences among models, but a numerical difference favoring center-based programs. In general,

Table 5.2
ANOVA on Nine Categorical Means by School Level

Area	N	df	F
Curriculum Planning	228	2	2.57
Expectations for Learners	228	2	.22
Accommodation to Individual Differences	228	2	.56
Curriculum Delivery	228	2	3.70*
Post Hoc mean			
Difference			
ES-MS = -.30*			
General Strategies	228	2	7.33**
Post Hoc mean difference			
ES-HS = 1.79*			
MS-HS = 1.83*			
Critical Thinking	228	2	2.74
Problem Solving	228	2	3.68*
Post Hoc mean differences			
MS-HS = 1.01*			
Metacognition	228	2	.12
Extension	228	2	12.14**
Post Hoc mean differences			
ES-HS =-.61*			

Note. $*\ p < .05; **\ p < .01$

teachers in self-contained center-based programs employed more differentiation behaviors than did teachers whose classrooms were organized under the other models. More specifically, they were stronger in using critical thinking, problem solving, and metacognitive behaviors (see Figure 5.6). Using the chi square index, pull-out programs were strong in communicating purpose to students ($\chi^2 = 19.84$, $p < .01$). Except for the special class model, programs operating under the other three models were strong in addressing students' learning styles ($\chi^2 = 10.11$, $p < .05$), using multiple instructional strategies ($\chi^2 = 8.62$, $p < .05$), and providing application activities ($\chi^2 = 16.18$, $p < .01$). Regular in-class cluster-grouped classrooms evidenced strong accommodation to task and motivational differences for subgroups ($\chi^2 = 9.97$, $p < .05$) and were equally as strong as the Center-based program in providing opportunities for students to reflect upon their own thinking ($\chi^2 = 10.55$, $p < .05$).

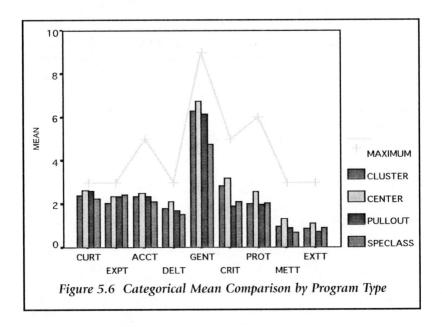

Figure 5.6 Categorical Mean Comparison by Program Type

Results by Designated Gifted vs. Regular Classrooms

In two selected evaluation sites, we also collected observation data in regular classrooms. When an ANOVA analysis was performed on the classroom observation data according to designated regular ($N = 68$) versus gifted classrooms ($N = 228$), more statistically significantly behaviors by category ($p < .01$) were observed in gifted classrooms in all but three categories (curriculum planning, accommodation to individual differences, and extensions). Particularly noted were the differences in general strategy use, critical thinking, and problem solving, where gifted classrooms excelled strongly over regular classrooms (see Figure 5. 7).

Discussion

This exploratory study has begun to shape an inquiry into the question of what constitutes "practice" in classrooms serving gifted learners. We cannot afford to ignore what theory and research have found about teacher behaviors that contribute to improved teaching effectiveness. This study has begun to lay the groundwork for assessing individual teacher performance in response to high–ability learners. If, in fact, classroom

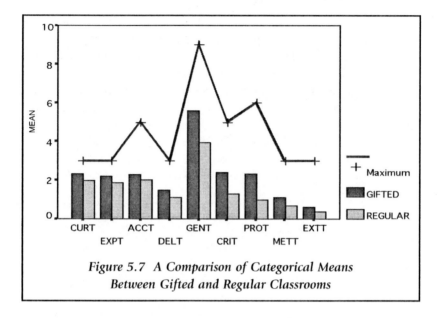

*Figure 5.7 A Comparison of Categorical Means
Between Gifted and Regular Classrooms*

practice for the high-ability learner requires differentiated services, then how is this criterion translated into expectations for teacher performance and accountability? This study contributes to providing a mechanism for using quantitative parameters to answer that question.

Furthermore, this study of teacher behaviors provides a snapshot look at teachers who work with high-ability learners in various types and levels of classrooms and evidences important understandings about the prevalence of differentiated behaviors thought to evoke stronger learning in this population. The following issues are relevant to consider in light of the findings.

While teachers of the gifted appeared strong in many categories of good teaching, they fell short in many categories that examined differentiation practices. Although educators of the gifted pride themselves on the use of higher level thinking models, these models were less in use than might be expected in classrooms when gifted learners form a critical mass of the student body. Very little emphasis was placed on accelerative strategies in gifted programs. Rate differences between gifted learners were not routinely attended to by classroom teachers, even those trained in gifted education.

Models that explore different types of thinking and problem-solving behaviors were not routinely employed in gifted program classrooms.

The most prevalent problem-solving behavior observed was brainstorming, many times used in isolation of more fulsome models that examined a broader array of problem-solving behaviors. Use of "compare-and-contrast" and evaluation activities were the most prevalent critical thinking approaches employed. Although metacognition is seen as a strategy central to curricular reform and also frequently promoted as a strategy for the gifted, little evidence of its use in gifted classrooms was observed. Moreover, little emphasis of out-of-class learning was found in observed teachers of the gifted classrooms as judged by their lack of providing extended activities. Secondary math teachers were more likely to employ such behaviors than elementary teachers.

Conclusion

This study of teacher behaviors across school districts suggests that teaching of the gifted employs fewer higher level strategies than anticipated, given the nature of teacher training emphases at state and national levels in the field. Individualizing for differences within the gifted population, critical thinking, and problem solving were found to be underutilized in most observed classrooms. Core teaching behaviors like lesson planning and clarity in providing directions were more routinely observed. Curricular reform elements were in evidence unevenly, with greater prevalence of concept teaching than other behaviors. However, in comparison to regular classrooms, classrooms of teachers of the gifted evidenced significantly more behaviors associated with promoting student learning.

Implications

There are several implications for professional development practices that emerge from this study. Staff development plans must take into account the evolving skills of teachers such that workshops are more tightly focused on needed skills as opposed to desired areas of interest. Gifted programs need to consider the sophistication of using higher level skills effectively and the need for teachers to develop these skills over time through appropriate methods. The tendency to have these teachers in-service others without having mastered the techniques themselves is not a wise deployment of program resources, although it constitutes a relatively common practice.

The Classroom Observation Form may prove useful in charting overall growth in desirable teacher behaviors by school or district as has been found in other checklists with self-monitoring capabilities (Hague & Walker, 1996). Diagnoses of individual teacher skills needed to work effectively with gifted learners can also easily occur through the use of such a tool. Videotape analysis of teaching can employ self-assessment using the instrument, as well as using external observers. Working effectively with gifted learners implies greater use of individualization techniques to accommodate vast differences within the population. Thus, gifted programs must provide strategies for teachers to apply such techniques routinely in classroom settings.

Teaching is a performance art. Therefore, the test of success is demonstrating mastery of relevant techniques. The use of monitoring approaches, including coaching, structured observation, and videotape analysis, increases the chance that teachers will improve in important ways the behaviors that optimize learning for our best students.

This study has pinpointed a need for more extensive staff development work with teachers of the gifted that is well planned and ongoing. Future research should be conducted on the relationship between teacher behaviors and the professional development opportunities they are afforded in schools, especially those that provide systematic follow-through to the level of demonstrated impact on student learning (Guskey, 2000).

A study of differential teaching behaviors based on content emphasis would also be interesting and might suggest behavioral adaptations relevant to one domain, but not to others. Moreover, a comparative study of teachers trained specifically to work with other special needs populations may also yield important understandings about the relationship between teacher behavior and perceived student characteristics.

Practical Tips

1. All gifted program evaluations should include classroom observation as a check on program document claims and stakeholder perceptions.

2. The use of a credible observation tool that acknowledges good general teaching and gifted pedagogy enhances the evaluation effort.

3. A team approach to classroom observation enhances its credibility as a process.

4. The use of classroom observation procedures in an evaluation provides a model for district leaders to continue to employ for program improvement.

5. Classroom observation should be used as a needs assessment tool for staff development, not as an evaluation of teachers.

6. Trend analysis of teacher behaviors over time provides a database for administrators to document instructional improvement within the gifted program and across all teachers' classrooms.

References

Avery, L. D., & VanTassel-Baska, J. (2003). *Changing teacher behavior: The struggle to provide gifted-level instruction in the greater classroom.* Unpublished manuscript under review.

Avery, L. D., & VanTassel-Baska, J. (2001). Investigating the impact of gifted education evaluation at state and local levels: Problems with traction. *Journal for the Education of the Gifted, 25,* 153–176.

Avery, L. D., VanTassel-Baska, J., & O'Neill, B. (1998). Making evaluation work: One district's experience. *Gifted Child Quarterly, 41,* 124–132.

Borko, H., Mayfield, V., Marion, S., Flexer, R., & Cumbo, K. (1993). Teachers developing ideas and practices about mathematics performance assessment: Successes, stumbling blocks, and implications for professional development. *Teaching and Teacher Education, 13,* 259–278.

Feng, A. X. (2001). *Technical report on inter-rater reliability of the Classroom Observation Scale.* Williamsburg, VA: Center for Gifted Education, College of William and Mary.

Garet, M. S., Porter, A. C., Desimone, L., Birman, B. F., & Yoon, K. S. (2001). What makes professional development effective: Results from a national sample of teachers. *American Research Journal, 38,* 915–945.

Guskey, T. R. (2000). *Evaluating professional development.* Thousand Oaks, CA: Corwin Press.

Hague, S. A., & Walker, C. (1996). *Creating powerful learning opportunities for all children: The development and use of a self-monitoring checklist for teachers.* (ERIC document #ED396844)

Kennedy, M. (1999). Form and substance in mathematics and science professional development. *NISE Brief, 3*(2), 1–7.

Kimball, S. M. (2002). *Analysis of feedback, enabling conditions, and fairness perceptions.* Madison: University of Wisconsin, Wisconsin Center for Education Research, Consortium for Policy Research in Education.

Sanders, W. L., & Horn, S. P. (1998). Research findings from the Tennessee value-added assessment system (TVASS) database: Implications for educational research and evaluation. *Journal of Personnel Evaluation in Education, 12,* 247–189.

Sanders, W. I., & Rivers, J. C. (1996). *Cumulative and residual effects of teachers on future students' academic achievement.* Knoxville: University of Tennessee Value-Added Research and Assessment Center.

Tomlinson, C. A., & Callahan, C. M. (1992). Contributions of gifted education to general education in a time of change. *Gifted Child Quarterly, 36,* 183–189.

VanTassel-Baska, J. (1993). Linking curriculum development for the gifted to school reform and restructuring. *Gifted Child Quarterly, 16,* 34–37.

VanTassel-Baska, J., Bass, G. M., Ries, R. R., Poland, D. L., & Avery, L. D. (1998). A national pilot study of science curriculum effectiveness for high-ability students. *Gifted Child Quarterly, 42,* 200–211.

VanTassel-Baska, J., Zuo, L., Avery, L. D., & Little, C. A. (2002). A curriculum study of gifted student learning in the language arts. *Gifted Child Quarterly, 46,* 30–44.

Wenglinsky, H. (2000). *How teaching matters.* Princeton, NY: Educational Testing Service.

Westberg, K. L., Archambault, F., Dobyns, S., & Salvin, T. (1993). The classroom practices observation study. *Journal for the Education of the Gifted, 16,* 120–146.

Using Focus Groups in Gifted Program Evaluation

by Annie Xuemei Feng & Elissa Brown

The social practice of evaluation helps to shape and constitute the socio-political institutions and political discourse to which it is designed to contribute. It is time for evaluators to claim this responsibility . . . and to position our work as not an observer of but rather a constitutive part of collective human struggles to improve ourselves and our societies.
— Jennifer C. Greene (2001, p. 400)

ocus group interviews have been increasingly employed by social science and evaluation researchers in recent years (Morgan, 1988; Morgan & Krueger, 1993). They have been used as a self-contained qualitative research methodology and jointly with other methods, including participant observations, individual interviews, survey, and experimental research in investigating various topics in anthropology, sociology, marketing, health and medicine, policy research, and education (Morgan; Stewart, & Shamdasani, 1990). Focus groups have also been extensively employed in evaluating social programs (Krueger, 1988).

In the past several years, we have used focus group interviews as one data collection source in gifted program evaluations, accumulating focus group data from 195 stakeholder groups involving 1,804 participants. The purpose of this chapter is to share the process of constructing focus group sessions for use in gifted program evaluations, as well as the rationale and implementation accompanying it. Concrete examples will be used to illustrate selected procedures of focus group interviews. Caveats in conducting focus group interviews will be discussed, as will suggestions on how to utilize focus groups effectively in gifted program evaluations.

What is a Focus Group?

A simple but straightforward definition of a *focus group* is "an interview style designed for small groups" (Berg, 1998, p. 100). It is one qualitative research tool used for meaning construction from group participants on a particular topic of interest to the researcher. According to Stewart & Shamdasani (1990), "Focus groups are an exercise in group dynamics, and the conduct of a group—as well as the interpretation of results obtained—must be understood within the context of group interaction" (p. 7). Morgan (1988) defined it as a qualitative tool between participant observation and individual interview and noted that "The hallmark of focus group is the explicit group interaction to produce data and insights that would be less accessible without the interaction found in the group" (p. 12).

Five Components of a Focus Group Interview

Five components are essential in a focus group session: facilitator/moderator, participants, location/setting, facilities, and focus group protocol.

A *facilitator/moderator* is the person who facilitates the focus group session. It can be the researcher him- or herself, a research team member, or a skillful professional who is hired by the sponsor of a research project. An effective facilitator has a good combination of both individual and situational factors, so that he or she is able to balance sensitivity and objectivity, empathy and detachment. He or she is able to facilitate group discussions and keep the conversation ball rolling while also managing the dominant speaker, leaving opportunities for other members (Stewart &

Shamdasani, 1990). It is crucial for the moderator to clarify participants' ambiguous contributions and be alert to new themes not addressed by the interview questions. In gifted program evaluations, trained evaluation team members typically serve as the facilitators.

Participants are the sources on which researchers have to depend for collecting data and investigating targeted research questions. In gifted program evaluations, we conduct focus group interviews with different stakeholder groups, including students, teachers of the gifted, regular teachers, administrators, program personnel, parents, and any other groups that we deem to be relevant in providing important information for answering evaluation questions.

The *location/setting* of a focus group session can be a room in a community center, a local library, or a school, depending on the research topic, time, and budget. It is suggested that the setting be comfortable and relaxing to the participants, who should be seated in a roundtable manner so that no order of status is evident, but maximum opportunity for eye contact among participants and moderator may be attained (Morgan, 1988; Stewart & Shamdasani, 1990). Since gifted program evaluation is often conducted in a school setting, the focus group session is usually held in a library or a conference room at the presampled school; sometimes, the group interviews are conducted in a faculty lounge or the cafeteria. Despite the desirable circular seating arrangement, flexibility is the rule to be honored because it is most often the gifted program coordinator who negotiates the selection of participants, as well as the location for the focus group interview. It is his or her effort and rapport with various sampled schools that will determine the degree of optimal setting arrangements.

The *facilities* in a focus group session in gifted program evaluation include a flip chart on which the note taker records comments, index cards and pencils for participants to write down their responses, and an easel folder citing the interview questions as a reminder. While it is not an unusual practice for a social science researcher or marketing researcher to videotape or audiotape a focus group session, it was not a common practice in the gifted program evaluations conducted by the College of William and Mary due to restrictions in permission to record in some schools and the time burden involved in analyzing transcripts.

A focus group protocol, together with the facilitator, are the instrumentation of focus group research. The protocol consists of a detailed guide to the facilitator on both the prestructured questions and possible probes where appropriate under each question. In gifted program evaluation, the focus group protocol consists of two sections: demographic characteristics of the participants and the interview questions. The demographic section allows the evaluation team members to check the participants' representation in terms of their grade, role status, ethnicity, gender, and other variables that are important in analyzing data; these variables can also be used for checking the extent to which the participant composition deviates from that specified in the sampling plan. The question section typically consists of four to eight semistructured questions on important dimensions of a gifted program. The development of these probes is discussed later in this chapter.

Advantages and Disadvantages of Focus Group Interviews

Focus group researchers have compared and contrasted the focus group with other research methods, including participant observation, individual interviews, and surveys, and have elaborated on both advantages and disadvantages of focus group interviews (see Fern, 2001; Morgan, 1988; Morgan & Krueger, 1993; Stewart & Shamdasani, 1990).

The advantages of focus group may be summarized as follows:

1. It takes a shorter period of time to conduct an interview with a group of people, which significantly reduces the personnel and time costs compared to an individual interview.
2. It is easier to collect information from a group of preidentified participants than in other methods, such as participant observations, where the researcher has no control over the consistency of the informants' participation.
3. It allows for the interaction between moderator and respondents, through which clarification of responses and follow-up probes for emerging themes or issues becomes feasible.
4. Group dynamism features the unique characteristics of focus group interviews, which one cannot find with other methods.
5. The focus group interview is flexible in that the number of participants can range from 8 to 12, and the presence and absence of one or two respondents to a session will not affect the results to a large extent.
6. The open-response format allows for understanding the topic of interest at a deeper level with a contextual background.

7. The verbal and nonverbal reaction of group members in a session will provide much richer information to the researchers in reporting the results.

However, there are disadvantages with focus group interviews, too. The criticism of focus group as an evaluation tool rests with the following:

1. the small number of respondents and the convenience nature of the sample;
2. the moderator effect, where participants' responses might be affected by the moderator's unconscious cues;
3. the side effect of group member interaction by which hostile communication might be evoked and defensive debate of one's own ideas may occur; and
4. the results of a focus group interview might only represent the opinion of a selected dominant speaker of the group.

Functions of Focus Group Interviews

Despite these limitations, the use of focus group interview is advantageous in several research situations, such as exploring new themes and issues and triangulating findings from other data sources. A review of the research literature shows that focus groups are mainly used for four major purposes in a range of research or evaluation settings: exploratory, confirmatory, triangulation and as a self-contained tool (Fern, 2001; Morgan, 1988; Morgan & Krueger, 1993; Stewart & Shamdasani, 1990).

Exploratory Purpose

Focus groups have been a preferred research tool when very little about the phenomenon of interest is known. Marketing researchers and social scientists have employed it extensively to meet such an objective. It has also been used frequently in the process of survey construction. In gifted program evaluations, this latter case occurs quite often during a preliminary visit to the contracted school district; the evaluator usually calls for an exploratory focus group session with stakeholders, comprising key figures of a local gifted program, and solicits ideas about prominent program issues, which are used for developing stakeholder survey questionnaires, as well as to finalize evaluation questions.

Confirmatory Purpose

Jointly used with survey instruments, focus groups have also been frequently utilized to confirm or disconfirm survey findings, as well as to refine survey instruments by clarifying participants' comprehension of the questions. After a large-scale quantitative survey, researchers some-times conduct follow-up focus group interviews to seek valid evidence through an in-depth discussion to confirm findings resulting from the survey data and to provide contextual explanations for divergent findings. Importantly, by asking selected respondents to read aloud what they think when they are filling out the survey, the researcher is able to increase the validity of the survey instrument by confirmation or revision.

Triangulation Purpose

A more frequent use of focus group interviews in gifted program eval-uations is for the purpose of triangulation. The focus group sessions are conducted at about the same time as stakeholder surveys as a complemen-tary design through which mutual enhancement of analysis and under-standing of each component is expected and the ability and confidence to draw conclusions from findings is increased (Wolff, Knodel, & Sittitrai, 1993). In the gifted program evaluations we have conducted, focus group findings were triangulated with survey findings and findings from class-room observations and individual interviews where appropriate so that the validity of the findings was increased and we were more confident in drawing conclusions and providing suggestions for plans of action.

Self-Contained Research Tool

Focus group interviews have also been used as an independent/self-contained qualitative research tool in a range of research settings (Morgan, 1988; Knodel, 1993). Fern (2001) argued that, "under certain conditions, focus group research has the same scientific status as quanti-tative research (i.e., surveys and experiments)" (p. 141). Nevertheless focus groups are consistently regarded as best used jointly with other research methodologies in research and evaluation settings.

The Political and Human Dimension of Focus Group Interviews

Gifted program coordinators typically have to convince decision makers that their gifted programs are necessary and make a difference in the lives of gifted students. This becomes increasingly difficult in times of fiscal constraints, when school boards are required to trim their budgets. Gifted programs are often targeted for budget cuts because, in some instances, they are regarded as educational frills (Clark, 2002). Proponents of gifted education are often required to defend gifted children's need for differentiated education through gifted programs in order to reach their potential and meet their unique academic and socioemotional needs. Unless program coordinators routinely monitor the program components along the way, the program will lack coherence in instruction, delivery, assessment, and student outcomes.

Thus, the focus group approach allows participants to share their knowledge and experiences framed around a problem or issue to be solved, ensuring that the resulting evaluation will reflect participants' thinking *in situ*, as opposed to an externally imposed model. Conducting focus group sessions with a variety of stakeholder groups as part of a larger educational evaluation not only promotes accountability in response to administrative concerns, but also makes sound pedagogical and political sense. Focus group sessions are a valuable aspect of conducting an evaluation in gifted education because they allow stakeholder participation, promote shared collaboration, are action-oriented, and can clarify a shared political agenda.

Stakeholder Participation

Each focus group session is about gathering information to help people make decisions, thus representing a definition of educational evaluation in general (Shula & Cousins, 1997). Having equal participation in a semistructured environment allows participants the opportunity for engaging with ideas within a psychologically safe context. The session is an egalitarian one; it levels the playing field. Each participant, regardless of his or her role in the school system or community, comes to the session as an equal voice, which encourages a spirit of fairness and openness. In our experience of conducting over 200 focus group sessions, comments from a variety of individuals have reflected that they felt the session was "fair" and participants were treated "equally." One way to ensure that equal participation occurs is for the facilitator to limit the number of participants involved in a focus group session and employ strategies to both restrain conversation monopolizers and encourage reluctant speakers.

Collaborative Process

One of the key assumptions framed in Stake's (1995) idea of "responsive evaluation" is that evaluation research is a collaborative process among stakeholders, including the state department, local school districts, and the contractor. Presumably, focus group participants bring to the session personal assumptions about gifted students and the services or programs employed in their district, but the facilitator makes certain that all stakeholders in the session are working from the same frame of reference, responding to the same sets of questions, and given an equal amount of time to respond. The group works collaboratively to assist the school or school system in making decisions. The outcomes of the focus group session are the sum result of all the comments, not just particularized to one or two members. The method is a conduit for capitalizing on various stakeholders' familiarity with the gifted program by recognizing that no one person has the full range of experience with all aspects of the program's functions. Conducting a focus group session framed by a collaborative process fosters respect, active listening, and an appreciation of diverse opinions.

Action-Oriented

Each member in a focus group represents a stakeholder (e.g., student, parent, teacher, school board member, administrator, counselor, etc.). Their participation not only strengthens the outcome of the evaluation, but signals to others that this is an important project. People like to see achievements, to know that "something" is being done. Being part of a focus group builds a common understanding of the importance of the program under study, in this case, the gifted program. It also acknowledges the fluidity of change in a given context and engages individuals in influencing the nature and degree of changes that can occur within their system (Fullan, 2001). The facilitator works to focus the discussion with an action orientation in order to support the idea of program improvement.

Sharing a Political Agenda

Evaluations are political. They can be used to determine allocation of resources, build (or destroy) reputations, respond to constituent concerns, and establish new emphases. They can also be used to improve programs, reward teaching excellence, and communicate to parents how well their children are doing. Gifted program coordinators must recognize that, even though conducting a focus group session as part of the evaluation process is a technical procedure, it has a political dimension. Each participant brings to the session a political agenda, and evaluators must recognize these agendas in order to balance them productively. Gifted program coordinators need to understand that the evaluation process provides a lever for positive change that should not be squandered (Avery & VanTassel-Baska, 2001). The gifted program coordinator advocates the program and documents its benefits through the evaluation. Moreover, he or she has a responsibility to persuade educational decision makers that the results are useful, a task made more difficult in times of scarce resources (Gallagher, 1998).

Because gifted programs are traditionally underfunded, there is a real need to leverage the evaluation findings to gain stronger support in the school system. Conducting focus group sessions as part of a gifted evaluation by involving key decision makers can garner desperately needed political support and ultimately enhance program services for the gifted students in the district.

Planning for Focus Group Interviews

Planning for focus group interviews should be nested in an overall evaluation design. Since we typically conduct stakeholder focus group sessions during a 4–5-day on-site visit, we need to schedule ahead each component of the case study, including the number of classrooms to observe, individual interviews to be conducted, as well as the number of focus group sessions to be held. Within an 8-hour working day, we typically conduct focus group sessions with at least three stakeholder groups within a school building, including students, classroom teachers, and parents, and cross-building sessions with building administrators, gifted program teachers, and district program personnel and administrators. Depending on the intensity of evaluation objectives and time constraints for a particular evaluation project, the number of stakeholder focus groups conducted ranges from 12 to 56 during a maximum 5-day visit.

Determining the Number of Groups

The number of groups relates to the complexity of the research or evaluation project, the range and type of variables in which a researcher is interested, and the purpose of the focus group interview. According to Fern (2001), fewer than five groups is adequate for most focus groups with exploratory purposes; more groups are needed, however, if experiential tasks are involved where shared perspectives of group members is the purpose of the research. In addition, the number of groups also has to depend on the group characteristics and number of issues in the interview guide. Knodel (1993) suggested that two groups per characteristic be used to create homogeneous groups. Typically, the more issues that need to be addressed, the greater the number of groups needed. Fern documented that some researchers have employed quite a large number of focus group sessions, ranging from 24 to 76 groups.

Evaluators need to keep two factors in mind when determining the number of focus group sessions at the planning stage: time constraints and evaluation questions. In a local district gifted program evaluation, for example, the rule of thumb is to involve at least one separate focus group for each stakeholder group, including students, regular teachers, parents, building administrators, and gifted program teachers and personnel. These stakeholder groups should parallel those targeted in the survey component of the evaluation design. Since each group has a unique role or perspective in the school system, these focus group sessions need to be conducted separately. Time-wise, we usually recruit gifted program teachers, program personnel, and building administrators across schools for a focus group session. With these factors in mind, the number of groups we interview at each evaluation site has varied.

Homogeneity and Heterogeneity of Participants

Although focus group samples do not follow the same rigorous sampling procedure as a survey does, the selection of group members is a well-intended process. Within-group homogeneity and cross-group heterogeneity are the two rules to be followed in selecting participants and designating group membership.

The *homogeneity rule* refers to the fact that the group membership should be as homogeneous as possible; for example, the teacher focus group should comprise only regular teachers, not the administrators or gifted program teachers. Group dynamism research suggests that a homogeneous group has the potential to elicit interactions among participants and avoid conflicts rising from the different role status of group members (Morgan, 1988; Morgan, & Kruger, 1993; Stewart, & Shamdasani, 1990). Thus, homogeneous group membership will make it easier for participants to contribute their opinions and share experiences by building upon other participants' discussions.

The *heterogeneity principle* relates to group members' representation in the population in terms of crucial demographic variables such as gender, ethnicity, and grade level for student groups and role status, educational background, working or teaching experiences, and level of involvement in gifted program evaluation for the adult stakeholder groups.

Determining the Size of the Group

While there is no overall consensus in the literature on the size of the group, Morgan (1988) has suggested six to eight people as a reasonable sample. Stewart & Shamdasani (1990) noted 6–12 as a common practice. Fern (2001) offered a range of 8–12 either as a single whole heterogeneous session or three small homogeneous groups. It should be noted that all these numbers are suggested within a particular research setting. In gifted program evaluation, we typically plan for 8–12 stakeholders in a focus group session. For adult stakeholder groups, we consider the representation of grade and teaching experiences in regular and gifted teachers and school representation for the building and program personnel. In addition, evaluators need to consider the possible absence of some anticipated participants due to various reasons.

Developing Focus Group Questions

When we design the stakeholder focus group protocol, we need to keep four elements in mind:

1. The questions are designed and tailored for different stakeholder groups, so they should be held for cross-group comparison in the process of analysis.

2. Wording changes may be needed. The way in which the questions are worded needs to be understandable to the stakeholders (this caution is particularly important for students at early grades).

3. The questions asked need to be relevant to stakeholders; the stakeholder should have at least some degree of involvement with the program.

4. The questions need to be designed to reflect sections in the survey questionnaire for data triangulation.

Stewart and Shamdasani (1990) suggested two general rules in developing focus group questions: "general-to-specific" and "the more-to-least-important." They suggested that placing the more general and unstructured question at the beginning will serve as the warming-up stage for participants. Meanwhile, such a question will not get participants' thinking primed toward a particular dimension. The latter rule specifies that the questions that address important issues need to be asked earlier than the less important ones. While we believe that all the questions in the focus group protocol we use in gifted program evaluations are equally important, we do have an order for them. Typically, a general question about the overall perception of the gifted program is the first question asked, and the perceived program strengths, weaknesses, and areas for improvement serves as the last question. Between the two questions, we ask participants' experiences and perceptions on identification, curricula and instruction, assessment, parental involvement and communication, and staff development in some adult stakeholder group sessions. These "between questions" reflect the question components in a typical stakeholder survey questionnaire (see Chapter 4).

In such a way, we not only get more insight into stakeholders' perceptions of particular program components through the source of the focus group, but we can also triangulate the findings with stakeholder survey findings. Table 6.1 illustrates the question probes we developed for focus group interviews in various gifted program evaluations. For a 1-hour focus group session, no more than six to eight questions can be managed.

Training for Focus Group Sessions

Another important element in the focus group planning stage in a gifted program evaluation is the training of team members. The contract

Table 6.1

Questions Developed for Focus Group Interviews

Program Dimensions	Question Probes
General perception	What are your perceptions of the current gifted program at your site?
Program effectiveness	a. What are the indicators that your gifted program is effective? b. How effective is your gifted program? What criteria did you use to determine this?
Identification	a. Do you understand how students are identified for the program? If yes, please describe. b. How effective is the identification procedure for the district program?
Curricula, instruction, and differentiation	a. What curricular areas does the program emphasize? How does instruction in these areas differ from that provided in the regular program? b. How differentiated is the curriculum for gifted learners? c. What are your perceptions of the quality of curricula and instruction?
Assessment	a. What assessment processes does the program use? How are students assessed? b. What approaches are used in assessing student performance? How effective are they?
Parental involvement	a. What kind of parental involvement model does the school system have? b. How effectively are parents involved? What opportunities exist for parent involvement?
Strengths, weaknesses, and improvement	What are the major strengths and weaknesses of the program? What do you see as priorities for improvement?

of a gifted program evaluation does not provide a budget to hire a professional moderator for the focus group sessions scheduled. Moreover, the
moderator is expected to have not only moderating skills, but also a good
background knowledge in gifted education and programming. Thus,
people in the gifted education field are the best candidates.

It is crucial that training is provided on how to facilitate a focus group
session, as well as on the consensus needed in the whole process.
Typically, the principal investigator provides a systematic in-house training on the rationale, format, procedures, and analysis and reporting of
focus group findings. Ongoing training is also in place for the novice during the on-site visitation. Novice team members are provided the opportunity of apprenticeship during their initial visits. They usually play the
role of note taker while an experienced researcher facilitator moderates a
focus group session, and then they facilitate a later session with the guidance of the mentor facilitator.

Focus Group Implementation

Procedures

In a typical 1-hour focus group session in gifted program evaluation,
the following steps are followed:

1. The facilitator briefly describes the purpose of the focus group
   and the manner in which the session will operate. The facilitator
   assures participants of the confidentiality of their remarks and
   stresses that the purpose of the focus group session is to get an
   overall picture of their gifted program with different perspectives.
   He or she also stresses that each participant is encouraged to contribute his or her experiences and ideas and that everyone's contribution is an important asset in the overall evaluation process.
2. The evaluation team members distribute two index cards and a
   pencil to each participant, which are used for recording their
   written responses to the focus group questions (participants can
   have more if they run out of cards).
3. The facilitator starts the session by reading each evaluation question one at a time and instructs participants to write down their
   responses on the index cards with the question number noted.

4. When most participants stop writing, it is a signal to the facilitator that it is time to engage participants in talking about their experiences and feelings about the questions. In the meanwhile, the note taker records key points from participants on the flip chart.

5. The facilitator moves to the next question in a similar fashion, keeping track of time. There should be no more than 7 minutes spent on a particular question in order to finish all questions within an hour's time. In addition, when repetitious responses occur on a particular topic, it signals the facilitator to move on to the next question.

6. Finally, the facilitator needs to debrief the session after all the questions have been asked, reiterating the purpose of the session and giving sincere thanks to all the participants for coming.

Analysis and Report of Focus Group Interview Data

Focus group researchers employ analytical methods typically used in other qualitative research methods, including conducting verbatim transcriptions, cutting and pasting under one theme, doing a word count for content analysis, and summarizing themes (Morgan, 1988; Stewart, & Shamdasani, 1990).

With focus groups that employ flip charts and index cards in lieu of audio or video recording, the data may be analyzed in a more flexible and efficient way because the discussion transcripts and participants' self-input are already available through flip chart notes and index cards, respectively. The focus group data analyses are typically organized into a summary chart, which is organized into three columns: focus group questions, key points from the group and individuals, and representative quotes from participants reflecting key points. In the process of conducting data analysis for focus group sessions, the following guidelines should be followed:

1. Include a chart of the total number of focus groups by category and the total number of participants by categories. Category specification will depend on the decision regarding analysis level.

2. Separate programs by program type (e.g., pull-out, self-contained, etc.) and by level (i.e., elementary, middle, and high school level).

3. On within-group summary charts, cite data that were expressed as themes (key points) by at least 50% of the group. Cite representative quotations reflecting these main ideas derived from the raw data. Review for accuracy in applying the rule.

4. Organize responses by questions within groups. Ensure that the narrative is supported by data in the charts. Support themes by using direct quotations where they can be extracted easily from the first stage of write-up. Start a question summary with a general statement of the main point, then provide elaboration or examples.

5. Use the same majority rule (50% or more) for composite charts dealing with themes across respondent groups. Indicate level of response in narrative and consensus or no consensus on a theme. Use examples or quotations to buttress major themes being extracted.

Table 6.2 is a cross-stakeholder focus group summary chart we derived from one local district gifted program evaluation. The example presents different stakeholders' perceptions of a question about the effectiveness of the identification procedure. The result from students and regular teachers is a summary of 16 sampled group interviews collected from the 16 sampled elementary schools for on-site visitation. The result from the parent focus group is a summary of three separate parent focus groups, including parents from each of the 16 sampled schools. Only one cross-building administrator focus group and one teacher of gifted students focus group were conducted; representation from each school was attained for each of these groups.

Based on this focus group summary chart, we conducted a content analysis to capture the prominent themes across stakeholder groups on the topic (identification). Following the rule of majority (50% and above), three themes were obtained. Table 6.3 illustrates both the themes and the groups that presented such views or comments during focus group sessions. Since these themes were derived from several different stakeholder groups, we were more confident in drawing conclusions on the effectiveness of the identification procedures and the related issues.

Triangulating Focus Group Findings
With Findings from Survey Questionnaires

As one independent evaluation component, focus groups not only empower the evaluator to derive findings by cross-group examinations, but also increase the validity of survey findings through a triangulation process.

First of all, focus group findings can be used to confirm survey findings. In the same evaluation, the stakeholder questionnaire for teachers, administrators, and parents had a parallel question on identification with regard to the fairness of the procedure and its congruity with the program services. The three themes derived from focus group interviews—the identification procedure has been improved (justifiable fairness), the procedure is problematic in missing particular populations (narrowness), and the broader identification procedure resulted in a mismatch with the current program services (broadness and incongruity)—concurred with the diversified distribution of survey respondents' opinions on the same issue (see Table 6.4).

Secondly, while the survey questionnaires anchored the magnitude of stakeholders' distribution of opinions on the two identification questions through the frequency of responses, the themes derived from focus group analyses explained why stakeholders viewed the procedures as broader or narrower and why there existed a mismatch between the services and the identification procedure. As one teacher noted,

> This procedure is effective in identifying a wider and larger population. What I see is that we are involving more nonverbal [students]. . . . I wonder if we need to vary our services more. [There is a] mismatch between who is identified and [the] services provided.

Thirdly, focus groups help the evaluator make judicious interpretations of data by providing salient situational factors and explaining conflicting results. For example, parents viewed the newer identification procedure as both negative and beneficial. Those who viewed it negatively had children who were already in the program, thus a broader inclusion of newly identified students in their children's classes resulted in a negative perception. Parents whose children were admitted to the program through retesting or new instruments certainly applauded the broadened identification. Thus, the insights obtained through on-site focus group interviews alerted the evaluators that results from both survey questionnaires and focus group sessions are a consequence of both personal experience and ideology. Subsequently, in suggesting plans of action, the evaluator was able to make a professional judgment in distin-

Table 6.2

An Example of Elementary Focus Group Summary Chart at One Local District Gifted Program Evaluation

	Questions	Key Responses	Quotes
Students Group = 16 Participants = 148	How effective is the identification procedure for the gifted program?	• Effective • More entry points needed	"Some other people should be in the program." "Some people need more chances to get in." "I think they do a good job of selecting people for the program."
Regular teachers Group = 16 N = 67	How effective is the identification procedure for the gifted program?	• Not sure about the ID process • Newer process was an improvement • Newer process too liberal • Not reaching the right students • Process should have more teacher input	"I think the way they got the students worked well because I don't think they let any students out that deserved to be in the program." "The new process is better than before because it's more encompassing." "Lots of students don't test well, but they're gifted."
Teachers of gifted students Group = 1 Participants = 25	How effective is the identification procedure for the gifted program?	• Same kids tested too many times; grouping too subjective • Not enough requirements at 5th grade (particularly use of GPA) • Mismatch between procedure and nature of programming • Using more than two criteria is recommended • Intended to admit more culturally diverse (minority, ESL, low SES), but not effective	"I think the identification process is effective in identifying a variety of giftedness but the problem arises when we try to serve all these students in one group." "This procedure is effective in identifying a wider and larger population. What I see is that we are involving more non-verbal students–some are very non-verbal. Because of this, I wonder if we need to vary our services more. Mismatch between who is identified and services provided. Some students are very lop-sided. It does not identify our ESL students very well."

		• Teacher input, GPA is not good substitute for level C performance-based assessment task	
Building Administrators Group = 1 Participants = 16	How effective is the identification procedure for the gifted program?	• ID procedure is more open • Too long of a time delay between testing and placement • ID is culturally bias • ID and program do not match	"The ID system is more flexible but dependent upon the school's population." "The ID system is not reaching minority groups or different kinds of giftedness." "The gifted program is enrichment-based and is not built upon the types of students it serves."
Parents Group = 3 Participants = 26	How effective is the identification procedure for the gifted program?	• Negative impact on students who don't test well on standardized testing procedures • Teachers need to know more about procedures • Improved over last year • Is effective – retesting is conducted to ensure access • Does not appear to be considerate of culturally diverse • Not responsive to twice exceptional students • Sometimes teacher is the "gatekeeper" determining whether students get in or not • Don't know much about process/not knowledgeable enough to comment • As effective as with any using standardized testing	"Has given child confidence." "Some very bright children not in program due to identification procedure."

Table 6.3
An Example of Content Analysis on Stakeholder Focus Group Results

Themes Derived	Group Representation*	N (%)**
The identification has been improved, where a larger population was identified as gifted students.	S, RT, GT, A, P	5 (100%)
The identification procedure is problematic in that certain populations are disadvantaged, including students who are not good test-takers but are very bright, ESL students, twice-exceptional students.	S, RT, A, P	4 (80%)
The broader inclusion of a diverse range of students makes the differentiation difficult, resulting in a mismatch between the students identified and the services provided.	RT, GT, A	3 (60%)

Note. * S = Student FG; RT = Regular Classroom Teacher FG; A = Administrator FG
GT = Teachers of Gifted Students FG; P = Parents FG.
** In a focus group design with five stakeholder groups, the consensus of at least three groups is needed for extracting a theme, following the minimum of 50% consensus rule.

guishing between grounded reasons and feelings, between consensus and split perspectives.

How Focus Group Data Informs Policymakers

Focus group data within the gifted evaluation process must be presented in a manner that is informative, balanced, and ultimately useful to decision and policy makers. This implies that the recommendations are solidly based on the data gathered and communicated in ways that makes sense to stakeholders, decision makers, and policymakers. Policymakers

Table 6.4
Triangulate With Elementary Stakeholder
Survey Results on Identification Questions

	RT	GT	Admin.	Parents
Fairness of the identification criteria	*N* = 115	*N* = 30	*N* = 40	*N* = 140
Fair	30.4%	63.3%	47.5%	52.1%
Too broad	49.6%	33.3%	27.5%	18.6%
Too narrow	12.2%	3.3%	22.5%	7.1%
Other	7.8%		2.5%	22.1%
Congruence with the services	*N* = 124	*N* = 30	*N* = 41	*N* = 140
Match the services	33.9%	76.7%	52.4%	57.9%
Do not match the services	15.3%	10.0%	33.3%	11.4%
Don't know	46.0%	10.0%	11.9%	30.7%
Other	4.8%	3.3%	2.4%	

Note. RT = Regular Teacher; GT = Gifted Teacher

respond to the needs that are demonstrated through the culminating evaluation from multiple sources of data. The focus group data need to be captured in such a way that the sum results represent the pulse of stakeholder responses so that policymakers can create a policy for the district (or school program) that is directly responsive to stakeholders' perceptions. In our evaluation experiences, some typical policy outcomes resulting from gifted program evaluations at the local level have included attention to the establishment of a policy on forms of acceleration and grouping, policies on curricular flexibility and course-taking access, policies on professional development, and others relative to data outcomes and recommendations (VanTassel-Baska, 2003).

Conclusion

Our evaluation experiences and the focus group research literature suggest that the use of focus group interviews can be an efficient and valuable data collection strategy in gifted program evaluation. Building upon its strength of group dynamism, as well as being an integral part of a comprehensive evaluation design, focus group findings provide the evaluation researcher an angle to understand program issues at a deeper level and brings forth stakeholders' perspectives in a lively contextual background. Despite the limitations of the method and caveats in the implementation process, the triangulation process of focus group data with other data sources is a valuable asset that an evaluator can count on when drawing conclusions and developing a strategic plan of action for gifted program improvement.

Practical Tips

Following are practical tips for effectively utilizing the focus group as a data collection strategy in gifted program evaluation:

1. Nest the focus group component in a comprehensive evaluation design, making it an integral part of other data collection strategies, which include stakeholder surveys, classroom observations, individual interviews, and document review.

2. Develop focus group questions that are parallel to components in stakeholder survey questionnaires.

3. Provide training to evaluation team members to reach maximum consistency in focus group implementation and analysis.

4. Conduct focus group sessions with different stakeholder groups (e.g., parents, students, teachers, administrators, etc.) in order to ensure that a full range of experiences are represented.

5. Remain neutral in the process of gathering responses so that participants own the process, not the evaluator.

6. Employ strategies that encourage all participants to share equally and restrain conversation monopolizers while encouraging reluctant speakers.

7. Content analyze major themes found across focus groups representing different stakeholders in order to identify valid findings.

8. Triangulate focus group findings with other data sources, especially surveys.

References

Avery, L. D., & VanTassel-Baska, J. (2001). Investigating the impact of gifted education evaluation at state and local levels: Problems with traction. *Journal for the Education of the Gifted, 25,* 153–176.

Berg, B. L. (1998). *Qualitative research methods for the social sciences* (3rd ed.). Boston: Allyn and Bacon.

Clark, B. (2002). *Growing up gifted* (6th ed.). Columbus, OH: Merrill/Prentice Hall.

Fern, E. F. (2001). *Advanced focus group research.* Thousand Oaks, CA: Sage.

Fullan, M. (2001). *The new meaning of educational change* (3rd ed). New York: Teachers College Press.

Gallagher, J. J. (1998). Accountability for gifted students. *Phi Delta Kappan, 79,* 739–742.

Greene, J. (2001). Evaluation extrapolations. *American Journal of Evaluation, 22,* 397–402.

Knodel, J. (1993). The design and analysis of focus group studies: A practical approach. In D. L. Morgan (Ed.), *Successful focus groups: Advancing the state of the art* (pp. 35–50). Newbury Park, CA: Sage.

Krueger, R. A. (1988). *Focus groups: A practical guide for applied research.* Newbury Park, CA: Sage.

Morgan, D. L. (1988). *Focus group qualitative research.* Newbury Park, CA: Sage.

Morgan, D. L., & Krueger, R. A. (1993). When to use focus groups and why. In D. L. Morgan (Ed.), *Successful focus groups: Advancing the state of the art* (pp. 3–19). Newbury Park, CA: Sage.

Shula, L. M., & Cousins, J. B. (1997). Evaluation use: Theory, research, and practice since 1986. *Evaluation Practice, 18,* 195–208.

Stake, R. E. (1995). *Program evaluation* (Occasional Paper Series). Kalamazoo: Evaluation Center, Western Michigan University.

Stewart, D. W., & Shamdasani, P. N. (1990). *Focus groups: Theory and practice.* Newbury Park, CA: Sage.

VanTassel-Baska, J. (2003). *Curriculum planning & instructional design for gifted learners.* Denver: Love

Wolff, B. F., Knodel, J., & Sittitrai, W. (1993). Focus groups and surveys as complementary research methods: A case example. In D. L. Morgan (Ed.), *Successful focus groups: Advancing the state of the art* (pp. 118–136). Newbury Park, CA: Sage.

 **7**

Collecting Student Impact Data in Gifted Programs: Problems and Processes

by Annie Xuemei Feng & Joyce VanTassel-Baska

The primary purpose of social programs is to improve the human condition . . . [and] one of the most important contributions of evaluators is to help determine whether the promised improvements of social programs are actually delivered, that is, to assess program effects.
　　　　　　　　　　　　　　—Mark W. Lipsey (2001, p. 325)

The crucial test of program effectiveness in any area of endeavor rests in the capacity to attribute special interventions with bringing about positive change in a target population. We want to know "what works" in education just as we want to know "what works" in the other areas of our lives. If we take a pill for arthritis, we want evidence of its effectiveness for the condition. If we engage in counseling, we want to know the likelihood of its working. If we buy a new computer, we want a "warranty" of its effectiveness in key areas of operation. As a consumer-oriented society, we view our world through the lens of effectiveness in products. Obviously, education is not immune to this orientation, even though it is slow to respond to the call from the public for this type of accountability.

Many educators decry the emphasis on standards and accountability measures in education because of their use as punishment for teachers, schools, and districts that don't measure up. But, the very real issues of individual student learning may still be swept under the rug through such large-scale efforts. It is especially difficult to track the learning pattern of our best learners in schools due to several issues.

Issues in Assessing Gifted Student Learning

One issue that makes it difficult to assess gifted student learning is the absence of appropriate standardized assessments for students who are already very advanced in a subject area. If students enter grade 4 already scoring at the 95th percentile on an in-grade language arts assessment, no matter how strong the teacher or the curriculum, the learning results on that same measure will reflect only minor if any growth gains at the end of the year. The problem rests with the assessment test, not the learner's growth pattern, because the assessment does not allow us to see the real growth that has occurred. If the same type of assessment tool were used off-level, at least we could assess how much more learning beyond grade-level expectations a gifted student had progressed. Thus, *off-level assessment* represents an important direction for consideration in understanding gifted students' learning.

A second issue in assessing gifted student learning is the nature of the assessment itself. Since programs for the gifted pride themselves on addressing higher level thinking, problem solving, and research in the curriculum, typical school assessments rarely address those areas. Thus, the use of other types of assessments to show growth is warranted. The most promising direction for such growth has been the employment of *performance-based measures* that demonstrate how advanced students are in these skill areas. Pre-post or time-series designs that can illustrate student change over time are the most helpful measurement approaches to be used for assessing specific gifted curricular outcomes.

A third issue to be aware of in assessing gifted student learning is the propensity of this population to do well on short-term content-based assessments, while demonstrating few important gains in higher level skills. Thus, assessment that only focuses on content learning to the exclusion of more transferable skills may also be limited in tapping into the nature and depth of gifted student learning. Thus, the use of *product assessment tools* may be important for purposes of demonstrating the depth of knowledge and skills attained at a given point in time. A drawback of this approach rests with the difficulty in determining good preassessment data within the same year. Rather than relying on a post-only analysis, researchers should plan to collect product assessment data over 2 or more years in order to record meaningful growth gains through this approach.

Assessing Learning Through Multiple Approaches

Just as the identification of gifted students requires multiple criteria for selection, so too judgment about the learning of gifted students must also employ multiple measures. Ideally, gifted programs would collect multiple types of assessment data on students annually, as shown in Table 7.1. Standardized achievement test data should be collected to demonstrate appropriate levels of mastery within the ceiling effect range of the test at the upper end or actual mastery using off-level advanced versions of the test. Performance-based assessment should be employed pre- and postintervention to demonstrate short-term gains on higher level task demands crafted for the gifted population. A multiyear design model should be employed to assess long-term gains on product-relevant skills such as problem solving and research. Finally, portfolio assessment should be employed to assess learning processes in key areas of work. For example, use of portfolios could show how and when the integration of specific scientific research processes began or how the writing process unfolded over a period of time.

There is a paucity of literature on the effectiveness of gifted programs as measured through student outcome data (see the review in Chapter 2). Thus, the need is great to see an emphasis in this area included in progress for the gifted at all levels.

Definitions of Outcome Assessment

Since there is much confusion about what outcome and impact assessments are, it is important to clarify these terms. Schalock (2001) defined outcomes "as personal or organizational changes or benefits that

Table 7.1

Types of Student Assessments for Gifted Programs

Type of Assessment	Application/ Purpose	Use in Gifted Program
Standardized achievement tests (on-level)	Mastery-oriented	To assess current levels of mastery and ensure reasonable growth
Standardized achievement tests (off-level)	Mastery-oriented	To assess "real" gifted student achievement in an area
Advanced Placement/ International Baccalaureate (Secondary)	Advanced mastery in subject areas	To assess levels of gifted students' advanced learning
Performance-based (all levels)	Pre-post or time series	To assess short-term growth in advanced skills and processes
Product-based (all levels)	Pre-post over multiple years	To assess enhancement of research and problem solving skills
Portfolios (all levels)	Evolving competencies-based	To assess the process of learning as it unfolds in key dimensions.

follow as a result or consequence of some activity, intervention, or service" (p. 7). Outcomes can be short, intermediate, or long term.

For example, a student who is identified and placed in a gifted program with a focus on math might feel more enjoyment in her classes and become more motivated to learn and work harder in her academics. By the end of one semester's program experiences, she might receive more challenging math in her gifted program and perform better in districtwide or statewide tests. She might participate in mathematics competitions and even win some medals. Many years later, her stimulated interest from the program might orient her to choose a mathematics major in college, and she might become a famous mathematician.

These are all possible outcomes from the gifted program for this individual student. Some outcomes are proximal or short term, while still others may be considered distal. This chain of potential outcomes of a gifted program may be applicable to all gifted students in district programs. Thus, the outcome assessment in gifted program evaluation tries to assess the extent to which proximal, distal, or both types of outcomes have been achieved.

Impact assessment detects the effect of a program on learners. It assesses "if a program made a difference compared to either an alternative program or no program." (Schalock, 2001, p. 7). Good questions to ask for an impact analysis are: "Does gifted program X produce better outcomes than gifted program Y?" or "Does gifted program X produce better student performance than would be the case if students were not in the program?" Therefore, an impact assessment depends on the analysis of learning outcome levels before and after a treatment by either comparing them with a comparable alternative program or counterfactual estimate, if the program were absent.

Scenarios in Gifted Program Evaluations

The lower ranking of U.S. students in the Third International Mathematics and Science Study (TIMSS; National Center for Educational Statistics, 1999) heightened parents', teachers', administrators', and policymakers' incremental concerns over student performance in academic areas such as mathematics and science. Such concerns also extend to gifted program stakeholders. In some of our gifted program evaluations, local educators asked us to conduct an impact analysis of their gifted program. However, in the absence of systematic pre-post assessment data on gifted learners, these analyses were difficult to conduct.

As the preceding discussion of outcome and impact assessment implies, clients need help in conducting outcome assessments of gifted programs. We could conduct such outcome analyses for districts that were interested in the cognitive, affective, and or behavioral outputs as a result of gifted program services and perform an impact analysis for districts who wanted to know the degree of effect their gifted program had on particular outcomes. Such analyses, however, take time that is frequently not budgeted in the scope of a typical evaluation.

The following section addresses the process of conducting outcome and impact assessment and reviews designs that help achieve outcome and impact assessment goals, citing illustrative examples available from the evaluations we have conducted.

Identifying Program Outcomes

Outcome Constructs, Variables, and Outcome Indicators

Before proceeding to the identification of program outcomes, we need to clarify the definitions of *outcome constructs*, *variables*, and *outcome indicators*.

A *construct* refers to "something that exists theoretically, but is not directly observable; a concept developed for describing relations among phenomena or for other research purposes, and a theoretical definition in which concepts are defined in terms of other concepts" (Vogt, 1999, p. 53). The outcome constructs of a gifted program, for example, might be academic achievement or self-concept.

A *variable* is "something that can take more than one value, and those values can be words or numbers. Variables are measured by their indicators, and indicators are defined by their values" (Bernard, 2000, p. 35). For example, gender, ethnicity, and grade-point average (GPA) are variables. Students' grade-point average scores are the indicators of the variable of GPA.

While an outcome variable denotes a construct, an outcome indicator specifies the measurement of the construct. *Outcome indicators* refer to variables employed to operationalize a construct. For example, high academic achievement is an expected outcome for intellectually gifted students; the outcome indicators of the academic achievement can be students' GPAs, standardized test scores, off-level test scores, and pre- and posttest scores.

Source of Outcome Input

To conduct an outcome assessment, first of all, we need to derive the outcome constructs and variables. We can identify outcome variables mainly from three sources: stakeholder input, the evaluator's analysis, and a review of the literature. A focus group session can be conducted with stakeholders to elicit their expectations for the program. We can also review the literature on salient outcomes of a particular model of gifted programs. Thirdly, the evaluator may conduct an outcome tracking analysis by examining the program documents, stakeholders' expectations, and the results of literature review in order to lay out both the short-term and long-term outcomes of the program.

In the process of identifying outcome constructs, the evaluator should also be aware of any unexpected outcomes, negative outcomes, and any other possible side effects. For example, it is not new to the gifted field that a pull-out model often entails a schedule conflict between students' classwork and their time in gifted program. For a program that is more enrichment-focused (particularly those with a lack of connection between the gifted curriculum and the regular curriculum), a student's participation might result in a decrease of performance on high-stakes tests. A program without an explicit exit policy might result in some students' containment in the program, which may demoralize other students in the program based on the retained students' nonperformance. All of these are examples of unexpected outcomes for the employment of particular program designs and procedures.

Proximal and Distal Outcomes

In identifying gifted program outcomes, one should be aware of distinguishing short-term, intermediate, and long-term outcomes. In an outcome assessment, it is important to inform clients that, while they may be expecting distal outcomes yet unachieved, some short-term and intermediate outcomes might have been met and can be assessed. These assessments of the more proximal variables, on the one hand, will reflect a more accurate picture of program effects at the moment, and it will also alleviate stakeholders' pressure of accountability by indicating some proximal program outcomes. Figure 7.1 is an illustration of both short-term and long-term outcomes. Such a graph will also help the evaluator determine the unit of analysis, type of data set to be requested, and the feasibility of various analyses. In a continuum from proximal to distal, local program educators often request the evaluator to measure the intermediate outcome, such as assessing students' progress from pre- to postassessment in targeted areas or, sometimes, with the suggestions of the evaluators, conducting a trend analysis of Advanced Placement data to

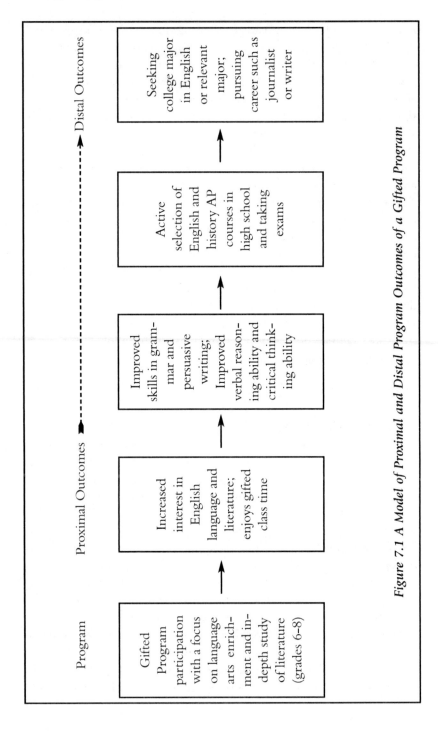

Figure 7.1 A Model of Proximal and Distal Program Outcomes of a Gifted Program

assess the distal outcomes of gifted program participation at earlier stages of schooling.

Criteria in Selecting Outcome Measures

Some criteria have been widely documented as important in selecting outcome measures (Harty, 1999; Schalock, 2001):

1. Be acceptable to stakeholders.
2. Conform to established psychometric standards (highly reliable and valid measures).
3. Be cost-effective in terms of both time and budget in obtaining the data.
4. Be relevant to the goals and objectives of the program.
5. Be relevant to the period of evaluation.
6. Have a logical connection to the program or intervention.
7. Have a longitudinal data component.
8. Be culturally sensitive.

In addition to the acceptability to stakeholders, the outcome measures should also be acceptable to the evaluator. Before the evaluator starts to conduct the analysis, he or she should consider the feasibility of the analysis that the client is requesting. If the evaluator determines that the analysis is not feasible, he or she should either convince the client that the analysis cannot be used to attribute any results to the program or inform the client that the proposed analysis might not answer a particular set of questions. In either case, the evaluator should refuse to perform the analysis.

Multiple Dimensions of Program Outcomes

It is also important to identify outcome constructs and variables with multiple dimensions. More often than not, a program outcome in an educational setting is construed as students' performance on a high-stakes test. However, as evaluators, we need to inform our clients that the outcomes of a program should include affective and behavioral results, as well as cognitive outcomes. The outcome assessment should include not only analysis of hard data as obtained through students' academic performance, but also a substantial examination of students' and other stakeholders' perceptions of dimensions of outcomes, such as students' motivation to learn and behavioral changes. Figure 7.2 is an example of an outcome design that tracks gifted program outcomes and outcome indicators across four dimensions of student learning.

It is true that many outcomes are involved in an assessment of the program. In reality, the client is not interested in nor is the evaluator able to cover all of these outcomes given time and budget constraints. What is important is the identification of the "inherently valued" outcome dimensions for the purpose of answering the proposed outcome questions that interest both the evaluator and the client. Particularly, if the local district is interested in discerning the program effect (or impact) on students' performance on standardized tests, the outcome measures will have to be confined mainly to testing data.

Basic Evaluation Designs for Outcome/Impact Analysis

A commonly accepted idea is that "one good design is worth 10 better measurements." In the quantitative realm, good research and evaluation designs are essential in making valid conclusions to track the causality of certain program outcomes and impact. Many modern research methods and relevant texts elaborate classic works such as Campbell and Stanley (1966) and Cook and Campbell (1979) and classify research and evaluation designs.

Mohr's (1995) further elaboration was clear in distinguishing designs into experimental, quasi-experimental, and ex post facto based on two criteria: manipulability of the intervention variable and the method of assignment to treatment and comparison group. In the true experiment, the researcher is able to manipulate the intervention variable and randomly assign subjects into treatment and control groups. If the researcher is able to manipulate the intervention variable, but cannot conduct a random assignment of the intervention or program, he is employing a quasi-experimental design. However, if neither the intervention is manipulable, nor a random selection process involved, yet the purpose of a research or evaluation is still to derive the causal inference of an intervention or program, an ex post facto design may be employed.

In order to distinguish the feasibility of implementation, as well as the degree of differences of the comparison group, we will discuss four types of basic evaluation designs that have been employed by evaluation

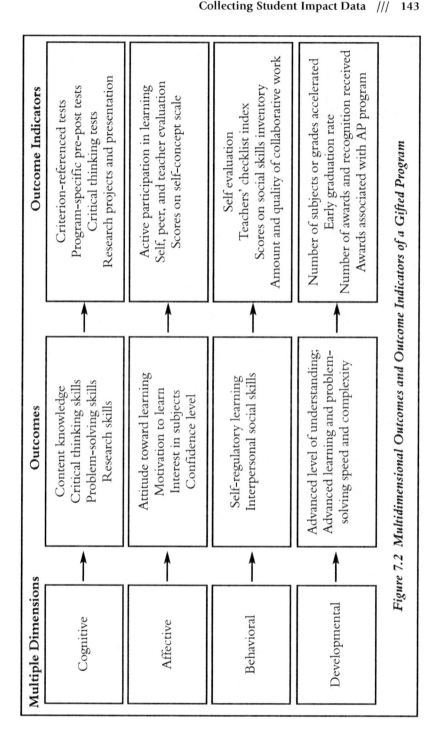

Figure 7.2 Multidimensional Outcomes and Outcome Indicators of a Gifted Program

researchers: experimental designs, quasi-experimental designs, time-series designs, and regression discontinuity designs (Table 7.2 summarizes the four basic types and their relative strengths and weaknesses).

Experimental Design

Experimental design, which is often called the "gold standard," is the most rigorous design employed to establish cause-and-effect relationships between program intervention and learning outcome. There are two main types of design under this category: random posttest design and random pre- and postdesign. By random assignment, equivalent groups are created; thus, various types of selection biases are eliminated. Although randomization makes the pretest of two groups not a necessary condition for a true experimental design, the latter design with a pretest will double warrant the equivalence of the two groups by a further check-up.

Despite being the most rigorous design for causal inference, it is difficult to implement a true experimental design in a real educational and social setting, thus it is a "gold standard" theoretically and laboratorily, but may not be highly feasible in the real world of schools. Current federal research has placed a premium on the use of this type of design for national educational experiments.

Quasi-Experimental Design

Quasi-experimental design is preferred by researchers and evaluators because it is easier to implement in schools. There are two main types of design under this category: posttest-only design and pre- and posttest quasi-experimental design. In the former design, although the researcher cannot randomly assign subjects to treatment and comparison groups, he or she is able to find two comparable groups and assign the treatment to one group. For the latter case, the researcher may not be able to find two similar groups, but is able to pretest both the treatment and comparison group using statistical techniques to control for the extraneous effects. By pretesting or carefully selecting two equivalent groups, this design allows the researcher to reach a causal inference in a more realistic setting.

However, the shortcoming of this design is its creating selection bias in the initial selection process of the comparison group. Since it is not a randomizing process, it increases the likelihood of subjective bias. In addition, possible contamination in the process of program intervention

Table 7.2

Basic Outcome/Impact Design in Gifted Program Evaluations

Design Name	Method and Mode of Selection	Strengths	Weaknesses
Experimental			
• Posttest only random design	manipulated	Creating equivalent comparison group, bias due to selection, history are eliminated	Difficult to implement; may not be practical
• Pre-post test random design	randomized		
Quasi-experimental			
• Posttest only	manipulated	More realistic to implement; statistical techniques can be applied to control extraneous effects	Selection bias
• Pre- and post Comparative (or non-equivalent group)	autonomous/ controlled		Possible contamination
Time Series			
• Interrupted time series	manipulated nonrandom	Off-set the selection bias; practical to be implemented; examine change longitudinally	History bias (Maturation bias; attrition)
• Comparative time series	manipulated nonrandom		
Regression			
• Discontinuity Design (or cutting point design)	Manipulated through cutoff score	The concept of counterfactual estimates; using the regression framework to analyze change	Contamination bias
	Quasi-randomized		

implementation is another threat to the internal validity of the design. In the field of gifted education, it has been employed often in examining the effects of curriculum and instruction in affecting students' competence in targeted areas (VanTassel-Baska, Bass, Ries, Poland, & Avery, 1998; VanTassel-Baska, Zuo, Avery, & Little, 2002).

Time-Series Design

Time-series design is a design of within-group comparison over time. It has been categorized as one type of quasi-experimental design (Cook & Campbell, 1979; Mohr, 1995). There are two major time-series designs: interrupted time series and comparative time series. In the former, only the treatment group data are available before and after the treatment. The latter design adds another similar comparable group whose data for the equivalent period of time are also available to offset the maturation bias that may occur frequently in the interrupted time-series design.

The time-series design focuses on examining change brought about by a program or intervention over time, thus it is practical and feasible in gifted program evaluation settings. Since program evaluation is a process to determine change, and this design is sensitive to change, it is a preferred design compared with the quasi-experimental design, where the measurement of changes often focuses on differences of estimates in outcomes between two points of short duration. The time-series design aims to examine change longitudinally. However, it is vulnerable to maturation or attrition bias.

Regression Discontinuity Design

Regression discontinuity design has also been categorized as a type of quasi-experimental method (Campbell, 1969; Trochim, 1984). It is similar to the pre-post quasi-experimental design in that it requires a preprogram measure (e.g., pretest), a postprogram measure (e.g., posttest), and a measure that denotes the assignment of the participants into either the program/intervention group or comparison group. While in the pre-post quasi-experimental design, the assignment variable might be a composite of demographic statistics expected to make the treatment and comparison groups as equivalent as possible, the assignment in regression discontinuity design is solely based on a cutoff score on a preprogram measure. Those who score above or below a certain cutoff score will be assigned to the program (e.g., gifted education or special education, respectively). The rest form the information source group whose testing scores will be used to derive the counterfactual estimates for program recipients, that is, the expected posttest scores had these program participants not received the program or intervention. By comparing the observed posttest scores and the expected posttest estimates for the program participants using regression analysis, the difference between the true score and counterfactual estimate is attributed to the effect of the program.

The regression discontinuity design has been most useful for studies examining the effect of a program that is need- or merit-based (Mohr, 1995; Trochim, 1984), and it has been largely employed in compensatory education. However, it deserves much greater application in evaluating gifted program impacts. Since the placement of gifted students in the program depends on rigorous cutoff scores or score ranges, if a district can provide the evaluators postprogram measures for both gifted students and nongifted students (e.g., criterion-referenced tests), we can detect the program impact on targeting domains using this design.

Qualitative Approaches to Impact Analysis

Despite the differences of the above designs in the method and mode of selection of participants and assignment to treatment, they are common in their quantitative orientation and positivist's reasoning about causal inferences.

However, it is increasingly common for qualitative approaches to be employed in program evaluation (Mohr, 1995; Stake, 1991; Yin, 1989). While such methods are not highly respected in the realm of outcome and impact analysis (Stake), some scholars have attempted to conduct outcome and impact assessment employing qualitative methods through the "signature" or "physical causality" inferencing process. Mohr (1999) delineated this causal inference in the following way:

> Y has occurred and the task is to demonstrate that the treatment T caused Y. This is done in part by the process of elimination. That is, there are several other possible causes of Y, such as U, V, and W, and these must be eliminated as contenders in order to settle on T. The process also depends critically on the idea that each possible cause has a known "signature," and if the signatures of U, V, and W can be shown to have been absent while that of T was present, then it may be concluded that T was the cause. (p. 72)

He argued that evaluators need to demonstrate that this signature of T itself was present and prove it to be the causal source. Just as a doctor diagnoses a woman's dying of a heart attack by examining tissues (the signature of heart attack) instead of proceeding to bring forth counterfactual evidence (i.e, estimate what if the woman had not died of heart attack). Mohr (1999) argued that, by using one qualitative case study, it is possible to derive the causal inferences by examining the signature of physiological reasons such as the presence of certain behaviors.

Seminal as the idea and rationale imbedded in conducting impact analysis using the one-case qualitative approach is, we should be cautious in employing such an approach in conducting outcome and impact assessment of gifted programs since the identification of signatures depends on a large amount of prior evaluation research, that is, the metaevaluation results for a targeted phenomenon. Unfortunately, the field of gifted program evaluation is still far from having such available metaevaluation results to document the patterns of signatures. Lipsey (2001) noted that "If we, as a field, have a deep understanding of how the changes that programs attempt to produce actually occur and the role of the program in creating them, we will also have a basis for new tools to assess program impact" (p. 328).

Examining Distal Program Outcomes

In our experience of examining program outcomes and impact for state and local school districts, we have found it is not unusual that program-relevant data (e.g., criterion-referenced tests, pre-post tests) are often unavailable. Not many gifted programs keep a systematic database of their gifted students starting from entry into the program. Yet, due to the accountability-driven reform movement, districts need such information desperately.

One method of analysis that we can present to local or state educators on program outcomes is multiyear Advanced Placement data because it is available in every school district. One advantage to using AP data is that the exams are psychometrically strong and highly accountable to various stakeholders. While the program evaluation levels are mainly elementary and middle school, AP results may be considered as a proxy for a distal or long-term outcome of a gifted program. We reason that, through years of participation in the gifted program, gifted students are expected to take more AP courses and exams than their regular class peers and perform at higher levels on the exams. Moreover, the elementary and middle school gifted program focus in targeting subject areas (e.g., language arts) may affect the pattern of distribution of AP exams taken by gifted students.

In evaluating the gifted program in one large metropolitan district, we offered to conduct a trend analysis of the Advanced Placement data of junior high and senior high students from 1999 to 2001. Comparative analyses were conducted between gifted students and regular students to explore the pattern of their participation in AP classes and performance on AP exams. Overall, there were more gifted students than regular students who took AP exams from 1999 to 2001 (681 vs. 491). While there was a higher percentage of regular than gifted students who took one to two AP exams (75.4% vs. 62.8%), a greater percentage of gifted students took more than three (37.2% vs. 24.6%).

We compared the distribution of the types of AP exams that gifted students and regular students took and found that higher percentages of gifted students took exams in five out of seven academic grouping subjects (history, English, foreign languages, science, and mathematics), the exceptions being art and music and government, politics, and economics. Moreover, we found a significantly higher percentage of gifted program students taking AP English (71%) than their peers (41%). This result documented the sustaining effect of the gifted programs in this district, particularly at the middle school level, where language arts was the main subject of enrichment and in-depth study. We inferred from these data that program students' participation in language arts likely seeded their inclination and confidence in taking AP exams in English. However, 9% more regular students took AP exams in art and music, which might indicate a weaker dimension of the gifted program in this district.

As expected, the gifted students, on average, scored higher than regular students in all academic grouping subjects except for foreign languages. These results indicated that gifted students not only participated in AP exams at a higher percentage in a majority of the subject areas, but also performed better in most of these domains, as well. Thus, by examining the pattern of AP data, we concluded that gifted students' participation in the program at the K–8 level in this district might have increased the likelihood of their selection of AP courses, the type and quantity of AP exams taken, and the performance on the exams.

We must admit that a causal link is not rigorously established through such an analysis. However, we believe that it is one approach to inferring program outcomes in a realistic setting. We also believe that, with more accumulated evidence of linking gifted program intervention to distal outcomes, we might be able to find the "signatures" of effective gifted programs, which will provide more flexible alternatives in conducting outcome and impact analysis in gifted programs.

Examining Off-Level Testing Participation

Another way of examining gifted program outcomes is to investigate patterns of students' participation in a variety of university-sponsored summer programs for intellectually and academically gifted students. The selection criteria for such programs are often off-level testing results. With an examination of the trend of students' participation in off-level tests, we are able to infer the pattern of real growth, avoiding the ceiling effects embedded in many standardized tests.

In an evaluation of the gifted program of a Midwestern state, we conducted a trend analysis of middle school students' participation in the Midwest Talent Search across a 4-year span. Comparative analyses were also made between students in this state and the level of participation and program enrollment by students in seven other Midwestern states.

The Midwest Talent Search is based on the premise that early and accurate assessment of students showing evidence of advanced academic abilities or achievement through off-level testing is useful in designing and obtaining more appropriate academic programs suited to their needs. Students in grade 6 who score at the 97th percentile on nationally standardized tests (such as the California Achievement Test or Iowa Test of Basic Skills) or students in grades 7 and 8 who score at the 95th percentile or higher in math, verbal, or composite scores are eligible to participate. The ACT or SAT I are administered to these middle school students, and results are shared with students and parents in a format that helps in planning the high school course sequence. For students scoring at a particular threshold on these off-level experiences, eligibility is established for special university-based academic programs. Top scorers are invited to attend an awards ceremony at the university, and the highest scoring students on each exam receive scholarships for the on-site summer program.

We examined the distribution trend of middle school students who took these off-level tests (SAT/ACT) in the evaluated state from 1993 to 1996 and compared it with that of the other seven participating states during the same period of time. Indeed, this state's 1996 level of participation was 12.9% higher than the 1993 level. Such an overall increase is notable in and of itself; participation alone reflects both the distribution of high-performing students and their motivation in taking challenging off-level tests. The results demonstrated the increasing interest of program students in seeking academic challenges and opportunities over the years, an expected situation for gifted students. Moreover, the overall increase takes on added significance in light of the decrease in the size of the baseline population of middle school students in this state.

We then examined the number and percentages of students who qualified for special summer academic programs by passing a particular threshold score and compared them with those of the other seven states. The results indicated that, in all 4 years examined, the high-achieving middle school students in the testing exceeded that of the combined performance of students in the other seven participating states, suggesting a consistent pattern among highly gifted students in this particular state.

Like the examination of multiyear AP data as a distal outcome index, the analysis of students' participation in off-level testing serves as another tool in determining both the proximal and distal program outcomes. Moreover, since ceiling effect can often be avoided in an off-level test, it becomes a crucial source of data to delve into the actual level of student functioning in key domains, an important factor to be addressed in the evaluation of program effectiveness in respect to curricular suitability.

Conclusion

Under the current call for accountability in education, gifted program administrators are facing new challenges. These challenges rest in demonstrating the effectiveness of gifted programs with respect to student learning. The scarcity of available student learning outcome data, particularly that which is psychometrically sound and appropriate, creates a special challenge for evaluators in planning and improving gifted programs by assessing student learning.

Practical Tips

1. Collect annual assessment data on gifted students in the program.

2. Use a mix of assessment approaches to ascertain student learning: mastery-oriented, performance-based, and portfolio.

3. Clarify the purpose of analysis.

4. Analyze both short-term and long-term gifted program outcomes.
5. Analyze gifted program outcomes and impacts multidimensionally.

6. Request psychometrically strong data sets (reliable, valid, sensitive to change).

7. Document the process of each outcome and impact evaluation in detail.

8. Employ metaevaluation results on gifted program outcomes for identifying program "signature" and utilize a qualitative approach to impact analysis.

References

Bernard, H. R. (2000). *Social research methods: Qualitative and quantitative approaches*. Thousand Oaks, CA: Sage.

Campbell, D. T. (1969). Reforms as experiments. *American Psychologists, 24*, 409–429.

Campbell, D. T., & Stanley, J. C. (1966). *Experimental and quasi-experimental design for research*. Chicago: Rand McNally.

Cook, T. D., & Campbell, D. T. (1979). *Quasi-experimentation design and analysis issues for field settings*. Skokie, IL: Rand McNally.

Harty, H. P. (1999). *Performance measurement: Getting results*. Washington, DC: Urban Institute.

Lipsey, M. W. (2001). Re: Unsolved problems and unfinished business. *American Journal of Evaluation, 22*(3), 325–328.

Mohr, L. B. (1995). *Impact analysis for program evaluation* (2nd ed.). Thousand Oaks, CA: Sage.

Mohr, L. B. (1999). The qualitative method of impact analysis. *American Journal of Evaluation, 20*(1), 69–84.

National Center for Educational Statistics. (1999). *Highlight from TIMSS* (Publication #1999081). Washington DC: U.S. Government Printing Office.

Schalock, R. L. (2001). *Outcome-based evaluation* (2nd ed.). New York: Kluwer Academic/Plenum.

Stake, R. E. (1991). Retrospective on "The Countenance of Educational Evaluation." In M. W. McLaughlin & D. C. Philips (Eds.), *Evaluation and education: At quarter century* (pp. 67–88). Chicago: University of Chicago Press.

Trochim, W. M. K. (1984). *Research design for program evaluation: The regression-discontinuity approach.* Beverly Hills, CA: Sage.

Vogt, W. P. (1999). *Dictionary of statistics & methodology* (2nd ed.). Thousand Oaks, CA: Sage.

VanTassel-Baska, J., Bass, G. M., Ries, R. R., Poland, D. L., & Avery, L. D. (1998). A national pilot study of science curriculum effectiveness for high ability students. *Gifted Child Quarterly, 42,* 200–211

VanTassel-Baska, J., Zuo, L., Avery, L. D., & Little, C. A. (2002). A curriculum study of gifted student learning in the language arts. *Gifted Child Quarterly, 46,* 30–44

Yin, R. (1989). *Case study research: Design and methods.* Newbury Park, CA: Sage.

Metafindings
on the Utilization
of Evaluations

by Joyce VanTassel-Baska

Evaluation has moved from being primarily a reservoir of methods for eval-
uation to now also becoming and being a reservoir for knowledge about
generic patterns of program effectiveness.
— Michael Quinn Patton (2001, p. 334)

P rogram evaluation utilization is a critical issue in the field of general education (Weiss, 1998) and gifted education (Callahan, 1995;
Tomlinson, Bland, & Moon, 1993). Yet, evaluation of gifted programs in general suffers from a lack of attention.

In a survey of all states with legislation regarding the provision of
services to gifted and talented students (Council of State Directors of
Programs for the Gifted, 1998), only eight states had conducted a
statewide evaluation of gifted programs in the previous 7 years. The
actual frequency with which local district gifted program evaluations are
undertaken is not known, although word of mouth would suggest that
such occurrences are somewhat rare, and the few evaluation reports that

are generated rarely get disseminated beyond the district of origin. Johnsen (2000) found only 15 evaluation reports in the gifted literature base during the previous 10 years that included program findings and results. Such paucity is particularly surprising in an era that has emphasized educational accountability.

Purpose

The purposes of this metaevaluation, then, were to describe some of the parallel findings from seven gifted program evaluations, one conducted statewide and six in a local school district, and to highlight through survey and interview findings how evaluation data were or were not acted upon. In this era of data-driven decision making, how do administrators use the findings and recommendations from gifted program evaluation studies, and what factors promote or impede evaluation utilization? This metaevaluation investigated the relationship between having and using information in order to understand better how to improve both the evaluation and the utilization process. The state- and the local-level studies have been collapsed because the researcher found important similarities of issues and needs across both levels. Rather than being idiosyncratic of the programs reviewed, these problems may be representative of the state of the art of gifted education as a whole.

Review of the Literature

The national priorities established by the *National Excellence* report (U.S. Department of Education, 1993) set the stage for program improvements envisioned over the last decade by calling for a broadened definition of talent, diversification in the populations identified, higher standards of learning, and curriculum differentiation strategies that work across different organizational and grouping models. Shifts in the nomenclature of the field from *gifted education* to *talent development* also emerged in the literature, further evidence that the field was in transition (VanTassel-Baska, 1998). Treffinger (1998) has described the situation as one in which "we wish to have a cure, but we are not certain at all about the medicine" (p. 753).

Against this backdrop of complex expectations and epistemological discourse, policymakers and program administrators must make choices that carry consequences. Some turn to external evaluators to help them collect data that will inform their decision making. There are two strands in the literature that contribute to making this process effective. The first strand focuses on practices in conducting gifted program evaluations; the second offers insights on the follow-up use of evaluation data in gifted and general education programs.

The Literature on Gifted Program Evaluation

According to Johnsen (2000), the literature on gifted program evaluations is indeed limited. A similar conclusion was drawn by Tomlinson and Callahan (1994), who stated that "educational accountability is a popular topic in political circles, but in practice, effective evaluation in school programs is sporadic at best" (p. 46). In spite of this limitation, some knowledge can be culled regarding gifted evaluation practice. For instance, Hunsaker and Callahan (1993) studied practices in gifted program evaluation and noted three trends related to "promising practices:" 1) an emphasis on formative data related to program improvement, 2) the targeting of specific areas of interest or concern, and 3) the articulation of specific recommendations.

Part of the difficulty in evaluating gifted programs lies with the selection of an appropriate evaluation methodology. One approach to designing evaluation studies for the gifted was delineated by Carter (1992), who used an ex-post-facto design to offset for the lack of experimental conditions. Farrell (1992) advocated a process for analyzing lesson plans as a way to assess the micro-level of curriculum efficiency. House and Lappan (1994) provided useful ideas for evaluating programs for disadvantaged learners, recommending multiple approaches, including authentic assessment.

The central focus of gifted program evaluation has also received some attention, with researchers suggesting that student performance is a critical and nonnegotiable dimension (VanTassel-Baska & Avery, 1997). Coleman (1995) called for examining both cognitive outcomes and "insider qualities" such as a change in the students' sense of who they are and what they might be capable of doing, their ability to interact more effectively with others, and their satisfaction in finding intellectual peers. Coleman and Cross (1993) were able to link program changes to students' ratings of internal satisfaction.

In her recent review of published gifted evaluation studies over the last decade, Johnsen (2000) summarized recommendations for practitioners and evaluators:

1. Select a trained evaluator.
2. Define clearly program outcomes and degrees of implementation.
3. Use evaluation for not only examining the program's effectiveness, but also for improving it.
4. Use contrast groups in designing an evaluation.
5. Use multiple data-gathering methods, formats, and techniques.
6. Select quality instruments.
7. Allow diverse opinions to emerge.
8. Collect data over time.
9. Provide the necessary time needed for evaluation among administrators and faculty.

These recommendations speak to the purposes, strategies employed, and political dimensions of effective evaluation practice.

The Literature on Evaluation Utilization

Part of what makes an evaluation effective is that the findings and recommendations from the evaluation report support program development. Even so, there is a specific body of literature on evaluation utilization. Tomlinson, Bland, and Moon (1993) and Callahan (1995) identified practices related to the effective utilization of evaluation findings in gifted education including appropriateness of design, availability of funding to support recommendations, factors related to message content and message source, and the multiplicity of data-gathering methods. Avery, VanTassel-Baska, and O'Neill (1997) generated additional factors that contributed to the success of a local district evaluation conducted in Greenwich, CT. These factors included 1) linking the evaluation to practical, rather than ideal, program development needs; 2) creating forums for processing divergent, even hostile, opinions and perspectives; and 3) offering flexibility in the recommendations. VanTassel-Baska and Avery (2001) found that, after 6 months, the evaluation had raised consciousness, been used as a tool for gifted program planning, and was seen as an agent of change in one state and one local district.

Research drawn from general education provides additional insights into the utilization process. In a review of the literature, Shulha and

Cousins (1997) noted that "the emergence of a conception of evaluation as a continuous information dialogue began to lead to more frequent occurrences of evaluators and program stakeholders' sharing responsibility for generating, transmitting, and consuming evaluation information" (p. 197). Specific trends cited in their review of the literature included: 1) the rise of considerations of context as critical to understanding and explaining use, 2) identification of process use as a significant consequence of evaluation activity, 3) expansions of conception of use from the individual to the organizational level, and 4) diversification of the role of the evaluator to facilitator, planner, and educator/trainer. They also acknowledged that understanding misutilization has become an additional focus for theory and research in this area.

The survey of current and developing conceptions of use carried out by Preskill and Caracelli (1997) amplified the notion of *process use* as distinct from *use of findings* and the importance of organizational learning. They defined process use as occurring "when those involved in the evaluation learn from the evaluation process itself" (p. 217) and reported that 90% of survey respondents believed it to be a valuable distinction. In exploring the relationship between evaluation use and organizational learning, they reported that 72% believed evaluation contributes to an organization's ability to learn from its experiences, but only 26% expected evaluation findings to result in fundamental changes in how organizations achieve their goals.

Collaboration between evaluators and program staff has been found to enhance local use of findings. Evaluation findings are more likely to be implemented if they (a) are instrumental, (b) mobilize support for change, (c) are conceptual, and (d) influence other institutions or events (Shadish, 1997, as cited in Weiss, 1998). Evaluation provides an aura of substance and legitimacy, as well as signaling potential problems. Thus, evaluators need to assume broader roles as consultants and advisors to organizations and programs. Although there is a constructivist press for thinking and acting locally, generalizability is a reasonable and necessary pursuit for evaluation work.

Lipsey (2001) noted the need for more connected use of evaluation findings, calling for metaevaluations and greater sharing of findings across evaluation projects. Having consistent information across programs would lead to the design of better programs and to the conduct of better evaluations.

Scriven (2001) ascribed to a view of evaluation as an act capable of creating, not just describing, the future. He saw an increasing need for evaluations to educate politicians, program managers, and the public about what we cannot know.

Weiss (1998) identified barriers to implementing evaluation findings as: (a) staff lack of consensus on issues, (b) staff turnover that occurs post-evaluation, (c) rigidity of organizational procedures, (d) changes in the political climate, and (e) budget cuts. Because of such barriers, contemporary evaluator skills that are needed for assisting school districts include:

- performing timely analysis and making reports useful;
- developing strategies for capitalizing on politics;
- promoting organizational learning, such as group process, collaboration, and interpersonal communication;
- partnering with stakeholders as coach, facilitator, and critical friend;
- · cultural sensitivity and dealing with conflict resolution; and
- strategic planning and goal development.

Evaluation has become methodologically ecumenical, the field accepting the idea that evaluation studies could be conducted in different ways (Reinhardt & Rallis, 1994). House and Howe (1999) suggested the use of deliberative democratic evaluation that follows the principles of inclusion of all relevant stakeholder perspectives, values, and interests; extensive dialogue between evaluators and stakeholders; and extensive deliberation to reach valid conclusions.

The evaluation process requires the integration of both objective and subjective data. Such chemistry is not formulaic. The biases of the evaluators influence the distillation of meaning from the data, and the very act of conducting an evaluation study mobilizes political constituencies. Assessing the value or worth of an enterprise creates opportunities for competing viewpoints and interests to emerge. How this conflict is processed can impede or enhance the use of evaluation findings. In this way, evaluating gifted education programs is a microcosm of the issues of educational accountability in general.

Methodology

All seven evaluations were grounded in the William and Mary Eclectic Model of Evaluation and drew on multiple data sources, perceptual and empirical, to produce results. Quantitative data were collected through educator and parent surveys and classroom observations; qualitative data were collected through document review, individual interviews, and focus groups convened at selected sites.

Evaluations were launched with the drafting of a proposed evaluation design to respond to a Request for Proposal (RFP). Upon award of the contracts, the evaluators met with key stakeholders to explicate the design and negotiate changes based on feedback. During these initial conversations, the context for the evaluation was established and expectations clarified. Of particular concern for the state evaluation was modifying expectations regarding student impact data. The evaluators stated that they would pull data from extant sources, but were at the mercy of data collection efforts employed by local district personnel. They further emphasized that it was unlikely that "hard data" sources, such as student learning gains on standardized measures, could be secured.

Comparable methods were employed across studies. The state studies surveyed gifted program coordinators and teachers using similar questionnaires. At one state site, 12 districts were selected for in-depth case studies based on a stratified sample representing urban and rural settings drawn from different regions of the state based on socioeconomic status and size. These case studies employed coordinator interviews; document reviews; focus groups of students, parents, teachers, and administrators; and classroom observation. The same methods were used for separate local district evaluations. Focus group questions were structured; classroom observations involved an observation form used in previous gifted program evaluations that focused on good teaching practice, differentiation for gifted learners, and elements of instructional reform. Student performance measures were not included in the local district evaluation, but student perceptions of the effectiveness of the gifted program on specific behaviors or characteristics were collected from random samples of identified gifted students across grades 3–8. Several evaluations included the preparation of a trend analysis of test scores on Advanced Placement for participating high school students. The state evaluation also included a fiscal analysis. These analyses served as the basis for the "hard data" the leadership of the organizations were seeking.

Findings Across Seven Evaluations

Findings were reported for each component of the seven evaluation designs. For the state study, this involved a report of the findings from surveys, student performance data (AP trend lines), fiscal comparisons, and 12 case studies. The local evaluations reported findings across four components of the design: classroom observations, focus groups, educator and parent surveys, and student impact questionnaires. Selected findings were found to be similar across all seven evaluations in the areas of student learning data needs and issues of program growth, staff development, and parent involvement.

Student Learning Data Needs

One of the key findings across all evaluations was the absence of data on student learning, particularly from a systemic perspective. Program effectiveness, while rated quite highly by most stakeholders interviewed in focus groups, was almost universally judged on the basis of perceptions about the program.

In the state study, the local districts were invited to submit copies of their evaluation reports or studies over the previous 3 years. Also, the state was asked to send copies of a sample of annual reports submitted by local districts. In no reports was there any focus on measuring student learning gains. This held true for the site visits, as well. Even in districts that had self-contained classrooms at elementary and middle school levels, there was no attempt to use off-level tests to see what gains were actually occurring.

Program Expansion and Depth Issues

Survey data and onsite case studies from the statewide evaluation showed that services were fragmented and inconsistent across both subject matter areas and grade levels in most schools. The pull-out model, which is extremely popular at the elementary level, appeared to be enrichment-focused and was described as interdisciplinary in nature. Language arts and math were the predominant subject matter foci at the middle and high school levels. Of particular concern was the lack of articulation, the systematic design of services across building levels that allowed for a curricular scope and sequence tied to stated goals. Of additional concern were the limited high school options, even though the increase in the use of Advanced Placement courses was seen as very positive in several locations.

Related to the concern about inconsistent implementation was the limited use of acceleration. Dual enrollment and Advanced Placement were the most pervasive acceleration options. Few districts used early enrollment or grade skipping, nor was content-based acceleration routinely practiced.

Local evaluations reflected much the same picture. The pull-out model at the elementary level was enrichment-focused, yet disconnected from the regular classroom. Moreover, there was little evidence of differentiation in the regular classrooms observed. Middle school programs were limited to honors offerings at the seventh- and eighth-grade levels, and there was little articulation between grades 9 and 10 and Advanced Placement offerings at grades 11 and 12.

Staff Development Issues

In the statewide study, it was shown that most districts provided two or fewer staff development activities a year for teachers, and the most frequently used vehicle for staff development was summer institute attendance. In local-level evaluations, this issue was examined through questionnaires to relevant groups. There was some confusion among groups as to the goals and philosophy of the program and the meaning of differentiation. These misunderstandings suggested that staff development for high-ability learners had not been adequately addressed in most of the districts. Furthermore, classroom observations suggested a need for staff development in differentiated practices. Questionnaire data suggested the need for greater frequency of staff development sessions in gifted education for specialists and regular classroom teachers.

Parent Involvement Issues

In spite of the strong emphasis in educational reform on the role of parents in strengthening educational services, there was limited evidence of parent involvement in gifted programs in any of the evaluations. Few districts in the state study reported the use of parent advisory councils or parent groups. The local district evaluations showed that parents, like educators, were uncertain about the philosophy of the gifted program, but parents were more vocal about program limitations in regard to level of challenge and extent of differentiation. Even in districts with strong parent support for the gifted program, parents expressed a need for more communication and understanding about the program.

Recommendations Made Regarding the Findings

In both the state and local reports, a recommendation was made to develop an evaluation plan that would track student performance annually and use trend analysis to decipher patterns. These data would be more cogent if they were linked to students who had progressed through gifted programs, a linkage that has implications for the design of tracking systems. Similarly, local districts were advised to think through what measures of student learning would show that their interventions were making a difference.

The lack of a solid student impact database for the gifted programs was somewhat explained by the fragmentation of services across the system. If a district sees a program as a smattering of services, rather than a cohesive, integrated whole, there is little recognition of the importance of measuring impact beyond stakeholder perception. This problem with service gaps was first cited in the Marland report (1971), and it appears that it continues to plague the field. One of the recommendations regarding this issue focused on the need to create a plan of action that would move programs toward greater levels of articulation. A second recommendation targeted to the local districts encouraged a realignment and increase of staffing in the central office to provide greater coordination of services across schools.

The concerns with staff development and parent involvement were also handled by advising that more attention be accorded these aspects of the program. In the case of teacher training, the emphasis was on creating a staff development plan. The focus in this plan needed to be on linking content and instructional pedagogy so that teachers had strategies for differentiation that could be implemented in their organizational settings. This recommendation was as viable for the state organization as it was for the local district. In the case of parent involvement, the emphasis was on creating more forums for parents to get information and training. In order to build this constituency, more attention had to be placed on meeting their needs.

Evaluation Reporting and Follow-Up

Both the state and local evaluations included written and oral reporting processes. Draft reports preceded final reports, and executive summaries were prepared to enhance distribution of the information. For the state evaluation, a half-day planning session was conducted for the state advisory council comprised of the state superintendent, legislators, parents, and educators. For the local evaluations, individual oral reports were

Table 8.1

Dissemination and Utilization Map

Group	Immediate Use	Future Use
Public groups (community, participants, parents)	Press releases Abstract of findings for all publics	Suggestions for how to improve programs used as a planning tool
Policy makers (school board)	Report of major findings for relevant audiences	Suggestions for change incorporated into action plan
Practitioners (teachers)		
Program administrators (coordinators of gifted programs, specialists)		Use of evaluation to build a case for future findings
Other administrators (principals, curriculum coordinators)		
Other (researchers)		

made to internal administration, in some cases the district gifted advisory council and the local school board.

Table 8.1 illustrates a way to think through dissemination and utilization procedures for a district evaluation. Considerations include identifying the group or audience for whom the evaluation information is relevant, assessing the immediate uses of the findings, and considering future uses.

Utilization Evaluation

The evaluator next solicited feedback from two key stakeholders at each site regarding the utilization of the evaluation findings and the outcome of the process at least 6 months after the evaluation study had been completed and disseminated to key publics. Twelve structured survey questionnaires solicited the nature and degree of use made of evaluation findings. Open-ended questions probed the overall impact that the evaluation had on the gifted program (positive, negative, or unintended) and factors that facilitated or impeded the implementation of evaluation recommendations.

Quantitative data were analyzed through descriptive statistics. Qualitative data were analyzed by content analysis, leading to the identification of key themes.

Response to Quantitative Survey Questions

All districts and states that contracted for an evaluation developed a follow-up plan. One did so in concert with the head evaluator and the associate superintendent in the school district. Five of the school organizations reported that they had implemented the evaluation recommendations. Two indicated that such an implementation was in process.

The survey also probed the extent to which the evaluation report was well received by relevant stakeholders. On a scale of 1 (low) to 5 (very well), the mean response was a 4.7, indicating that the report had been well received by both gifted and general education staff. The specific changes enacted in the gifted program as a result of the evaluation are included in Table 8.2.

Respondents were also asked to rate the relative helpfulness of the data sources employed in the evaluation. All school agencies (100%) reported the classroom observation data as helpful, while 83% cited the questionnaire data as helpful, and 71.4% found the focus groups to be a useful source of data. Two districts reported that the individual interviews were helpful. Only one district found the document critique to be of use.

For school agencies that received secondary data analyses, such as Advanced Placement trend lines for gifted students in course taking and performance or fiscal analyses, two-thirds (67%) of the clients found these to be helpful for future planning purposes.

Themes Derived From Qualitative Analysis of Survey Responses

One theme that emerged from the content analysis of the open-ended questions to decision makers in the districts was the role of evaluation in

Table 8.2
Nature and Frequency of Gifted Program Changes Enacted

Change	No. of Districts
Planning for the future of gifted education in the district	7
Assessment and evaluation of student learning	5
Interactions with general education staff	5
Program implementation strategies	4
Interaction with gifted staff	4
Interactions with parents	3

confirming or disconfirming preexisting perceptions about the program. One coordinator noted "[the evaluation] confirms our observational feedback of the unevenness in program implementation across schools and subjects," while another stated, "I knew that differences existed in curriculum implementation and delivery, but this evaluation pointed out where teachers were in their attempts to deliver curriculum and services." Another commented that the evaluation illustrated how "the program was moving in the right direction." A third observation related to this theme was "The overall excellence of my teachers was confirmed, as were the strengths and weaknesses of the curriculum and level of parental support."

Another theme emerging from the analysis was the *positive impact it had on program status and importance in the school district*. One coordinator commented,

> The results of this evaluation have created an increased sense of awareness about our gifted program. Some general staff members are now viewing the program in a different light. For the first time in a very long time, lots of positive interest has been focused on our gifted program. This increased positive awareness has opened the possibility of funding some aspects of gifted education through the general fund . . . not a current practice!

Another key decision maker noted, "[The evaluators] forced the program administrator to be more proactive about making the changes to the program, in tandem with changes that have been taking place in education, society, and the world." Another coordinator also echoed the access to money not available before the evaluation and the increased respect for the program and its personnel.

The theme of *self-assessment and reflection about best practices with gifted students* also emerged from the utilization data. One senior official noted that "the evaluation made us more conscious of best practices, and to think through why we do not wish to adopt some of these best practices, and where to find research evidence to back our decisions." A coordinator cited greater staff engagement with the program: "Since the evaluation, some staff members have become more serious about their work; therefore, they are more receptive to my direction within the gifted program." Another commented on "common dialogue among program staff and stakeholders regarding mission, goals, and elements of the model, [leading to] a push forward in program initiatives."

Moreover, the theme of *gifted program improvement* permeated the follow-up utilization responses. One official noted that the report would lead to a "reconceptualization of our approach to affective education." Several districts commented on the need for enhancement of staff development services through targeted emphases, especially to regular classroom teachers, as a result of the report. Two districts planned to focus on establishing a longitudinal database for gifted learners with an eye to collecting uniform assessment data. The state coordinator cited the need to develop a state scope and sequence of curricula for gifted learners. Most districts also cited the need to improve and refine current curricular efforts.

While the themes just enumerated reflect on the positive aspects of evaluation utilization, the agencies also reported on unintended consequences of the evaluation, not all of which were positive. One coordinator cited the "time-consuming and labor-intensive" aspect of the evaluation for those in the evaluated district. Another noted that the evaluation heightened expectations for identification and service among parents that could not be met in the short run.

Yet, positive unintended consequences also occurred. In one district, there was a discussion by the superintendent and school board to develop a school for the gifted in grades 3–8 in the district to serve as a model for differentiated practice by using an alternative service-delivery model. The evaluation process and findings were highly instrumental in effecting this change.

Discussion

The evidence from these seven evaluations showing evaluation utilization within 6 months of the conclusion of the evaluation effort may confirm the importance of seeing evaluation of gifted programs as a formative exercise, indeed useful in catalyzing program improvement and elevating various publics' awareness of the legitimacy of the enterprise of gifted education.

Weiss (1998) has written about various types of uses for evaluation. One such use is as a tool where program administrators decide what to do next based on findings. They might extend a program, modify its curriculum, or change the training of its staff. If the program changes are relatively small-scale and cost-effective and serve a school district's larger agenda, instrumental use of evaluation findings is likely. This situation clearly emerged in all seven of the postevaluation analyses.

Another use for an evaluation might be for demonstrating the program director's rationality and good management techniques. The existence of an evaluation adds to the perception of program accountability. Thus, stakeholders' awareness of the district going through the process enhances program credibility. This use of evaluation was also observed in most sites during the evaluation, as well as through follow-up analysis.

Finally, the fact that an evaluator is willing to study a program speaks to the seriousness of the program enterprise itself. The program is worth devoting time and resources to, suggesting legitimacy in the eyes of relevant stakeholders. Again, evidence exists from the postevaluation data that legitimacy of the program in these locations was heightened as a result of the evaluation experience.

Persistent Problems

While utilization of results is a positive sign for gifted program evaluation, there are less-healthy signs observed within these evaluation contexts that question the extent to which long-term program improvement is likely to occur.

One major problem appears to be the persistent lack of resources to move gifted program agendas forward. Regardless of the grouping model or program services approach employed, districts are not funding programs adequately at the personnel level in order to accommodate the need for change. As some districts move from a pull-out to a resource model, for example, there are serious resource consequences. While special education resource teachers have student caseload upper limits (typically in the range of 75), teachers of the gifted are expected to staff classrooms where target gifted students may number up to 300. In addition, they are expected to collaborate with regular classroom teachers while doing demonstration lessons, creating classroom differentiated centers, and working with cluster groups of students. The expectation is well beyond the reasonable capability of most educators, yet, in many districts, gifted program progress depends on these individuals' skills in negotiating these multiple tasks. Program services to gifted students are thus diffused, with little gain in regular classroom teacher involvement and commitment to compensate for this loss in direct service. Without greater personnel support at the building and central office level, most programs cannot effectively implement evaluation findings that suggest the need for deeper program development. Resources are already stretched too thin.

A second problem is the leadership expertise available in school districts to administer gifted programs. Because gifted educators lack a mandate and certification requirements in most states, educators occupying leadership positions in the field lack deep knowledge about gifted education, as well as about educational leadership. Either gap is problematic for advancing a gifted program agenda. Without a firm grounding in gifted education, the commitment and advocacy necessary to withstand political pressures and to advance some gifted program policies in the agency is missing. Without administrative knowledge and skills, the program becomes subject to the thinking of other administrators more skilled in implementing educational agendas, with the result being a reactive, rather than a proactive, program. Moreover, many educators in leadership positions in the field may understand one aspect of the field very well, but do not have the capacity to see the program as a total entity that requires development on several fronts simultaneously. Thus, gifted program leadership requires setting a proactive agenda annually to focus on the interrelated components of identification, curricula, instruction, staff development, student assessment, and evaluation.

A third problem that may limit the utility of evaluation findings in many contexts is the lack of sophistication in viewing it as a fundamental part of the program development process itself. There is a sense that evaluation findings can either be used or not, depending on how people respond to them, as opposed to viewing such findings as critical to advancing the program. The political process has become more invasive in educational practice than ever before, and it has proven to be an addi-

Table 8.3
A Stage Model for Evaluating Gifted Programs
to Enhance Utilization

Stage I Analysis of purpose and use(s) of the evaluation	Stage II Design of the evaluation based on the purposes/key questions	Stage III Collection of data, analysis of data, and interpretation of findings in concert with coordinator, et al.	Stage IV Dissemination of findings and facilitated plan of action developed
Determine primary intended users	Make design methods and measurement decisions	Collect data	Disseminate findings to potential users
Negotiate a process to involve primary intended users in evaluation decisions		Analyze data	Facilitate 3–5-year plan based on recommendations
Determine the primary purposes and intended uses of the evaluation		Organize data to be understandable to users	Evaluate the evaluation after 6 months
		Actively involve users in interpreting findings	

tional burden at the postevaluation phase. The assumptions for conducting an evaluation in the first place are violated when those findings are not used to move programs to the next level of excellence. The expense of program evaluation in money and time on the part of all stakeholders and evaluators behooves the need for it to be a catalytic force for program improvement. When that does not happen in a context, a key lever for positive program change has been squandered.

The Utilization Process

Enhancing utilization of findings requires viewing the evaluation as a four-stage process. It begins with a thorough analysis of purpose, audience, and uses for the evaluation (Stage I), then moves on to the design process (Stage II), then to the data collection and analysis process (Stage III), and finally to the dissemination and action plan process (Stage IV). Table 8.3 on page 171 characterizes each of these stages.

Conclusion

The future of meaningful program development for the gifted rests on a recognition of the need for dynamism in the program. Just as programs are planned and implemented, they also need to be studied and corrected in course as a part of the process. Use of evaluation findings then becomes a natural part of program development and implies positive change. In the absence of this dynamism, programs will only stagnate and eventually die. Educators must recognize the importance of evaluation in the continued life of a gifted program and do all that is possible to promote growth and renewal.

Practical Tips

1. Develop a 3-year action plan based on evaluation findings within 6 weeks of the report to decision makers.

2. Involve all relevant stakeholders in crafting the plan.

3. Include accountability for implementing the plan by vesting key individuals with the responsibility for implementation of certain aspects of it.

4. Monitor the implementation of the plan at 6-month intervals.

5. Address findings that are most doable first; save difficult ones for the second and third years.

6. Tackle recommendations for systems building right away. It will take time to get these in place.

7. Praise all staff for their support during the evaluation.

8. Remember that utilization concerns must be addressed at all stages of the evaluation process, beginning with planning.

References

Avery, L. D., VanTassel-Baska, & O'Neill, B. (1997). Making evaluation work: One school district's experience. *Gifted Child Quarterly, 41*, 124–132.

Callahan, C. M. (1995). Using evaluation to improve programs for the gifted. *The School Administrator, 52*, 22–24.

Carter, K. R. (1992). A model for evaluating programs for the gifted under non-experimental conditions. *Journal for the Education of the Gifted, 15*, 266–283.

Coleman, L. (1995). The power of specialized educational environments in the development of giftedness: The need for research on social context. *Gifted Child Quarterly, 39*, 171–176.

Coleman, L. J., & Cross, T. L. (1993). Relationships between programming practices and outcomes in a summer residential school for gifted adolescents. *Journal for the Education of the Gifted, 16*, 420–441.

Council of State Directors of Programs for the Gifted. (1998). *The 1998 state of the states gifted and talented education report.* Denver: Author.

Farrell, B. G. (1992). Lesson plan analysis as a program evaluation tool. *Gifted Child Quarterly, 36*, 23–26.

House, E. R., & Howe, K. R. (1999). *Values in evaluation and social research.* Thousand Oaks, CA: Sage.

House, E. R., & Lappan, S. (1994). Evaluation of programs for disadvantaged gifted students. *Journal for the Education of the Gifted, 17*, 441–466.

Hunsaker, S. L., & Callahan, C. M. (1993). Evaluation of gifted programs: Current practices. *Journal for the Education of the Gifted, 16*, 190–200.

Johnsen, S. K. (2000, Fall). What the research says about accountability and program evaluation. *Tempo*, 23–30.

Lipsey, M. W. (2001). Re: Unsolved problems and unfinished business. *American Journal of Evaluation, 22*, 325–328.

Marland, S. P., Jr. (1971). *Education of the gifted and talented: Report to the Congress of the United States by the U.S. Commissioner of Education*, 2 vols. Washington, DC: U.S. Government Printing Office (Government Documents, Y4.L 11/2: G36).

Patton, M. Q. (1997). *Utilization-focused evaluation: The new century text*. Thousand Oaks, CA: Sage.

Preskill, H., & Caracelli, V. (1997). Current and developing conceptions of evaluation use: Results from a study of evaluation use TIG members. *Evaluation Practice, 18*, 209–225.

Reinhardt, C. S., & Rallis, S. F. (Eds.). (1994). *The qualitative-quantitative debate: New perspectives*. San Francisco: Jossey-Bass.

Scriven, M. (2001). Evaluation: Future tense. *American Journal of Evaluation, 22*, 301–307.

Shulha, L. M., & Cousins, J. B. (1997). Evaluation use: Theory, research, and practice since 1986. *Evaluation Practice, 18*, 195–208.

Tomlinson, C. A., & Callahan, C. M. (1994). Planning effective evaluations for programs for the gifted. *Roeper Review, 17*, 45–54.

Tomlinson, C., Bland, L., & Moon, T. (1993). Evaluation utilization: A review of the literature with implications for gifted education. *Journal for the Education of the Gifted, 16*, 171–189.

Treffinger, D. J. (1998). From gifted education to programming for talent development. *Phi Delta Kappan, 79*, 752–755.

U.S. Department of Education, Office of Educational Research and Improvement. (1993). *National excellence: A case for developing America's talent*. Washington, DC: U.S. Government Printing Office.

VanTassel-Baska, J. (1998). The development of academic talent: A mandate for educational best practice. *Phi Delta Kappan, 79*, 760–763.

VanTassel-Baska, J. (Ed.). (1998). *Excellence in educating gifted and talented learners* (3rd ed.). Denver: Love.

VanTassel-Baska, J., & Avery, L. D. (1997). Perspectives on evaluation: Local considerations. *Research Briefs, 11*, 118–128.

'VanTassel-Baska, J., & Avery, L. D. (2001). Investigating the impact of gifted education evaluation at state and local levels: Problems with traction. *Journal for the Education of the Gifted, 25*, 153–176.

Weiss, C. (1998). Have we learned anything new about the use of evaluation? *American Journal of Evaluation, 19*, 21–3

9

Knowledge Utilization:
One School District's Experience

by Julie Long

Evaluation will be a collaboration between/among citizens, funders, program staff, participants, and evaluators. The mission will be to improve the social condition, to do good through evaluation.
                                        —David Fetterman (2001, p. 384)

The purpose of this chapter is to describe the experiences of one local school district that undertook a total gifted program evaluation. The district places a high value on excellence and has a number of special programs that were developed to implement choice options. Each year, the school board asks the district to evaluate several special programs. In 2000–2001, the program of choice was the gifted program.

Description of the District

The district under consideration is a medium-sized southeastern suburban district with approximately 17,500 students. Of these, about one-fourth qualify for gifted services. The district is about half-minority and half-majority students, with students coming from many parts of the world. There are 11 elementary schools and 4 middle schools, all of which house gifted programs. The high school components of the gifted program are not under the aegis of gifted services and, therefore, were not evaluated.

Approximately 20% of the students in the district qualify for free or reduced lunch. Five of the 11 elementary schools and 2 of the middle schools have been designated as Title I schools. In addition to areas of poverty, there are also neighborhoods of great wealth and a growing middle class.

The school district has a strong tradition of excellence and has responded rapidly to the challenge of changing demographics. It is the second fastest growing school district in the state and, therefore, faces the challenges posed by rapid growth. The district's gifted program is located in all of the elementary and middle schools. The teachers of the gifted are part of the school faculties and are extensively involved in general school activities, as well as the activities of the gifted program.

The district's gifted program is one of the oldest in the state, having been in existence for 27 years. The program had been evaluated 15 years earlier, but had had no formal outside evaluation since that time. The program coordinator had evaluated informally various aspects of the program during the intervening years, but these efforts had not produced a total picture of the program's strengths and areas that need attention.

Unique to this program is the fact that it has its own foundation to assist with various activities. The foundation raises money each year, primarily through a mail-out inviting parents to join various levels of contributions; the year before the evaluation took place, the foundation raised about $20,000 in program funds. A board of directors, made up of parents, governs the foundation. The coordinator is an ad hoc member. Funds are used to provide scholarships for field studies to needy students. The foundation has also sponsored teachers to attend conferences and other staff development opportunities and has purchased equipment for the gifted classes, including computers, printers, digital cameras, and camcorders. In the early years of the foundation, it provided classroom basics such as dictionaries and other resource books when other funding sources were limited.

General Information About the Program

Program goals and objectives are absolutely essential for evaluation, as they establish the focus and direction for the program. This particular program has seven goals with accompanying objectives and action plans for achieving them. These goals had recently been updated during a strategic planning process.

In grades 2–5, a full-day pull-out model is used for gifted services, while grades 6–8 employ a social studies content-based model. The middle school program model was changed from a pull-out model 11 years earlier. There are 29 teachers of the gifted, serving students in grades 2–8. The elementary staff is full-time, while the middle school teachers work 20–40% of their time in the gifted program.

At all grade levels, students study three in-depth units each year. Some of the William and Mary science and language arts units are used with the elementary students, while the middle school students employ teacher-developed social studies units. The elementary curriculum has a 2-year cycle, with second and third graders studying a predetermined set of units and fourth and fifth graders doing the same. This enables some flexibility in placing students to meet the state-mandated pupil-teacher ratios of 15:1. At all grade levels, there are five skill areas that are stressed: creative thinking, critical thinking, research, social/emotional development, and technology.

Importance of External Evaluations

Even though informal evaluations had been conducted, it was important to have an outside perspective to gain a better picture of the gifted program. External evaluators can come into a district without the biases that a coordinator might have. They can see the program through fresh eyes.

Moreover, most middle-sized and small school districts do not have the resources to conduct a full-scale evaluation of their programs. Large research departments virtually do not exist. Even with district research personnel available, there is great competition for their time and expertise, and often gifted programs are not given priority in accessing these resources. In addition, these research personnel usually do not have expertise in gifted education. Therefore, an external evaluator with a background in gifted education can bring a thoroughness to the task that a district cannot otherwise provide. They can gather, analyze, and interpret large amounts of data that would be difficult for a district to process in a timely manner.

Another issue is of that of the expertise of the program coordinator. Many coordinators of gifted programs do not have a background in gifted education. Many come from special education, and they often have responsibility for the gifted program along with many other aspects of curriculum and instruction. He or she may lack an understanding of gifted program development and how various aspects of a program fit together. In these cases, it is especially important to secure the services of external evaluators with expertise in both gifted education and research methodology to assess the quality of a program.

It is also important to make clear that the purpose of the evaluation is to help improve the program, rather than to threaten it or lead it to its dissolution. All gifted programs can improve, even the most outstanding ones. If the district is committed to its program and if the evaluators are committed to its improvement, evaluations become positive tools for change. The coordinator's attitude toward the evaluation is also important, as the teachers take their cues from him or her.

In the district being evaluated, there had been a history of program evaluation, and the coordinator saw the evaluation of the gifted program as an opportunity to obtain data and information that would otherwise not be available. These data could be used to bring about program improvement, as well as celebrate program strengths.

Choosing an Evaluator

For a large-scale evaluation, fiscal policy will probably dictate the use of a Request for Proposals (RFP) procedure. When writing the RFP, a district can shape the evaluation questions and establish the intent of the evaluation. The RFP process enables a district to see which evaluators can really meet its needs.

It is important to choose an evaluator who has knowledge of the specialized aspects of gifted programming. This should be specified in the RFP, and the evaluator's credentials should be carefully scrutinized.

Another way to assess the qualification of an external evaluator is to ask for his or her past evaluation reports. These will provide information on the thoroughness, scope, and tone of an evaluator's work. It will help a district ascertain whether or not an evaluator can provide the kinds of information it is seeking.

Coordinating the Data Collection Process

The role of the district coordinator is to ensure that the whole data collection process and beyond goes smoothly and to provide necessary support and coordination at each stage (see Table 9.1).

In this particular evaluation, data were gathered from a number of sources. Questionnaires were used to collect information from different stakeholder groups. The evaluator had sample questionnaires that were modified to meet the needs of the school district. Based on the informal evaluation done the previous year in the district, questions were added relating to the level of challenge found in the regular classroom, amount of time spent on homework at various grade levels, and needed staff development activities.

All students in the program in grades 2–8 completed a student questionnaire. This involved approximately 2,700 program students; random samples of student questionnaires were drawn to represent the demographics of the school district.

All parents were sent questionnaires through the mail. Some parents received multiple questionnaires if they had more than one child in the program. Self-addressed, stamped return envelopes were included to encourage response. The response rate from parent questionnaires was 35%.

At school faculty meetings, all classroom teachers, teachers of the gifted, and school administrators were asked to complete an educator questionnaire. At some schools, the return rate was low because personnel were asked to complete the questionnaires and return them later. These schools were asked to repeat the process. Ninety-eight additional surveys were returned from educators. To be certain that these surveys did not skew the data, analyses were run with these added data and without. No substantive differences were found between the two data sets.

Document review was another source of data for the evaluations. Curricular units from each grade or planning level were evaluated. Other

Table 9.1

District Coordinator's Involvement in the External Evaluation

Phase	Tasks	Procedures/Standards
Before Evaluation	• Identify district needs	Program needs, fiscal capacity
	• Send RFP (Request for proposal)	Specify questions, requirement for the bidder, time frame for evaluation
	• Select an external evaluator	Examine credentials, evaluate former reports by prospective external evaluators, and interview potential evaluators
During Evaluation	• Coordinate data collection on behalf of the district	Coordinate with schools to identify stakeholder samples according to provided sampling plan for different components of data collection; schedule on-site visits
	• Provide support to external evaluators	Provide needed help during on-site visits (e.g., transportation to schools, supplies)
	• Be involved directly in selected components of the evaluation	Team with external evaluators to collect data for selected evaluation components as needed; receive training as needed; experience the whole evaluation process with the

	• Increase program visibility through frequent contact with building administrators and teachers	external evaluator, (Increase self-repertoire of skills for internal evaluation) Assert leadership as the program coordinator through effective and efficient organization, coordination, and communication among building administrators, teachers, and external evaluators, increasing stakeholders' awareness and concerns about the program
After Evaluation	• Develop a 3–5-year plan of action • Implement selected recommendations according to schedule	Discuss with relevant personnel the feasibility of implementing each recommendation; develop short term and long term action plan; implement short term plan immediately
	• Seek more funds for programs	Seek more funds from district using well-developed plan based on evaluation recommendations
	• Establish long-term consultation relationship with the external evaluator	Secure long-term consultation relationship with the external evaluator and invite continuous advice for the program

program documents reviewed included the technology plan, strategic plan, staff manual, policy manual, and the evaluation/placement team policies. The document review process provided information on the level of sophistication of the curricula. The policy manuals gave insight into the level of institutionalization of various policies and procedures. The strategic plan provided guiding information for the evaluation because it included the operationalization of the goals and objectives of the program. The technology plan provided evidence of individualized staff development in this area. In addition, because the program coordinator evaluates the teachers annually, samples of these evaluations were also submitted.

During on-site visits, focus groups were conducted with various stakeholders in the program. Initially, the principal evaluator met with a group of parents from the foundation's board of directors, a group of teachers of the gifted, and various district-level administrators, including the superintendent, the chief academic officer, the program coordinator, and others. This initial visit helped give the evaluator a picture of the district, its organization, and its climate. During a later site visit, the evaluation team met with groups of classroom teachers selected from each school, elementary and middle school principals or their designees, teachers of the gifted, gifted students, and a group of parents representing all schools. This visit allowed the evaluators to collect additional information on various aspects of the program from different stakeholders' perspectives.

Classroom observations were conducted in all elementary and selected middle school gifted classrooms. The evaluator trained local personnel in this process. The evaluator and the trained district personnel worked as a team, observing sampled gifted classes for 40 to 50 minutes using a structured observation form developed by the evaluator (see Chapter 5 for a discussion of the Classroom Observation Form). This process helped to provide information on the level of instructional expertise of the staff and the extent to which program goals were being implemented in the classrooms.

The entire evaluation process spanned 2 school years. It began in the spring of one year and concluded in the fall of the next. It was important to keep the teachers of the gifted informed about each step of the evaluation process, and this proved to be a challenge. District growth had necessitated the hiring of a number of new teachers in previous years, and the close nature of the staff was not as strong as it once was when there were fewer teachers. Even outstanding and experienced teachers had levels of anxiety. Because the coordinator understood the tradition of evaluation of special programs in the district, she was able to alleviate many of the concerns, but this process would have been easier with better and more frequent communication.

Presentation of Results

Following the collection and analysis of all the data, an extensive evaluation report was prepared. Prior to the presentation of the report to the district school board, it was sent to the chief academic officer to verify the factual content. The coordinator also reviewed the report and found no errors.

In many ways, the report confirmed what was known about the gifted program in the district. The outstanding abilities of the teachers were noted. Praise for and appreciation of excellent, dedicated teachers came through in the questionnaires, observations of classes, and focus groups. A key ingredient of any program is the quality of its teachers, and the high quality of these teachers was obvious from all data sources. This was a great morale boost for the staff.

The early and ongoing nature of the identification process was also commended. Although this is a time-consuming process, the district believes that it is important to place students in the program as soon as possible. Because there is an Army installation in the district, it seems even more important to place students as soon as they qualify.

The data showed that the school district implemented the pull-out program model well and that the model was supported by all segments of the community. Although this was not new knowledge, it was nice to have it confirmed by an external evaluation. This, too, was a tribute to the skills of the teachers in the program. They constantly engaged in public relations with their communities and schools.

The evaluation also confirmed the need to refine and improve the curricula and the need for more differentiation for gifted students both within the program and in regular classes. Although it was believed that differentiation was occurring within the gifted program, data sources suggested that it was more limited than educators thought. Upon reflection, it was decided that this area needed more concentrated work.

Another excellent recommendation was that of establishing a student database to follow students from entrance to the gifted program through high school and beyond. The district had not previously done this. But, as a result of the evaluation, the school district made a commitment to establishing such a database, even though its lack of research personnel had been a hindering factor in setting one up and maintaining it in the past. It recognized the importance of following high-ability students to ascertain whether they are receiving the proper kinds of opportunities and experiences. It is believed that information from this database can also help to shape new directions for the gifted program in grades 2–8. It might also reflect the need for more specialized guidance services or curricular modifications to ensure that students succeed in high school and beyond. Included in this database would be such variables as test scores, grades, levels of high school courses taken, Advanced Placement (AP) courses taken and student performance on AP exams, college admissions, and scholarships earned. These data should enable the gifted program to provide better guidance services to gifted students and their parents over time.

Direct Positive Consequences From the Evaluation

As a result of this evaluation, the gifted program and its personnel are being seen in a new light by the rest of the district. Although individual principals appreciated the quality of the staff in their schools, they did not have knowledge of the outstanding nature of the teachers in other schools. The evaluation gave them that information. They also gained a deeper appreciation of the quality of the program in general, and they concurred with the recommendations.

District Responses to Recommendations

In retrospect, the main benefit of having a thorough evaluation of a program is obtaining information on the strengths and needs of the program. A secondary benefit is getting access to additional school district resources to follow up on the recommendations.

As soon as the evaluation report was presented to the school board, the program coordinator was asked to develop an anticipated action plan to outline the implementation of the recommendations. For each recommendation, a set of anticipated action steps was written. For example, one recommendation was to continue differentiation of curricular and instructional processes for gifted learners in both the gifted and regular classrooms. Among the anticipated action steps was to provide more staff development for classroom teachers. This was included in the district's staff development plan that is required by the State Department of Education each year. Continuing to revise the curricula in the gifted program to accommodate various levels of giftedness and learning styles (verbal, visual/spatial, etc.) was a need clearly identified by the evaluation. As a result, the teachers of the gifted were included in the district's summer staff development plan and were paid for working on this aspect of the program during the summer.

A need that was identified in both the evaluation report and the program's strategic plan was that of having training in a new critical thinking model. As a result, all teachers of the gifted received a 2-day training session during the summer. Prior to the evaluation, there had never been money available to pay all the teachers in the gifted program for summer staff development. Now there *is,* and it is hoped that this trend will continue.

In addition to refining the curricula in the gifted program, a unit from each planning level will be evaluated yearly using the William and Mary Composite Evaluation Form for Curriculum Units for Gifted Learners and a unit evaluation form that was developed during the program's strategic planning process. The unit evaluation will be conducted jointly by the coordinator, lead teachers, and a professional within the state with knowledge of gifted curricula. After 3 years, all of the units will have been evaluated by this rigorous process, and the review cycle will begin again, thus ensuring continuous attention to evolving, quality curricula.

A third recommendation for the evaluation was to continue to articulate the gifted program within the regular classroom. This is a perennial problem for pull-out programs. Several steps are planned to improve communication with regular classroom teachers and principals. The teachers of the gifted provide extension activities to the classroom teachers weekly. They also establish a mechanism for keeping classroom teachers informed about how the gifted program is helping to develop proficiency on the state curriculum standards. The program's Web site will also be used more extensively as a communications tool.

The coordinator developed and presented an information session on the gifted program to the district and school administrators at their summer in-service program. Historically, this time has been devoted to disseminating information about new state mandates and policies, and this was the first time the gifted program was included. The efficacy of other communication tools will also be investigated. The evaluation report helped focus attention on this communication problem, which has probably been complicated by the rapid growth of the district.

It was further recommended that the district develop a more comprehensive program for gifted learners such that students in grades K–1 receive systematic services and middle school and high school students receive multiple options and opportunities under the umbrella of the district gifted program. Although multiple opportunities are in place for older students, they have never been consolidated under the gifted umbrella. Plans to revise the coordinator's job description have been developed, and the various components of services for gifted students were consolidated in order to provide a more comprehensive and understandable set of gifted services for students of all ages.

Because of the diversity of the district, some students at the Title I schools were not succeeding as well as their counterparts at the more affluent schools. To help improve this situation, plans for a special mentorship program are being developed. High school students who were part of the gifted program will become mentors to fourth and fifth graders who may not have the home support and early experiences needed to develop their potential fully. High school students were chosen as the mentors because the younger students look up to them, allowing them to serve as role models for high academic achievement.

In addition to the summer curriculum development, a committee of primary, elementary, and middle school teachers met with the coordinator during the summer to write a staff development plan for the teachers in the program. Student diversity, follow-up on the summer critical thinking model, technology, scope and sequence update, and the incorporation of the evaluation results were among the topics discussed. The teachers will be surveyed to determine additional staff development needs. By developing this plan, it is anticipated that the program will have greater access to district staff development funds.

Another need the evaluation helped identify was that of additional parent education. A group of teachers and parents met with the coordinator during the subsequent summer to develop a parent education plan. State identification regulations, student diversity, underachievement, motivation, working with gifted children at home, and collaborating successfully with teachers are among the topics being considered for inclusion. A brief parent survey requesting suggestions for additional topics will also be employed.

The teacher evaluation instrument used by the district will be modified or replaced by the William and Mary Classroom Observation Form. A self-evaluation component will be added, and more follow-up observations will be scheduled. Information from this more precise evaluation will be incorporated with data from unit evaluations to develop further and refine the program's staff development plan and curricula.

A final major plan that will be developed is a schedule for evaluating various components of the program on a more regular basis. Although the district cannot mount annually the kind of effort that was used for the evaluation reported here, a plan to look at various components of the program each year can be devised. This should help with subsequent major evaluations, which should take place every 5 years, as well as with overall program improvement.

Conclusion

A thorough program evaluation by an outside evaluator can be of great benefit to a school district's gifted program. If done well, it can identify the strengths and needs of the program. An outside evaluator can see the program through unbiased eyes and offer helpful suggestions for improvement. Information about the state of gifted programs across the country can also be shared. Such an evaluation can enhance the perceptions of the gifted program. Recommendations can also give the program greater access to district resources, both personnel and fiscal.

Practical Tips to Districts Considering External Evaluations

1. Program coordinators can help an evaluation's usefulness by doing their homework on district gifted program problems and issues and key people to be involved, and by gathering basic demographic data on the program and the district.

2. View an outside evaluation as an opportunity to help a program improve and grow.

3. Work with staff to explain how the evaluation will work and allay concerns. Consider drafting a plan of action as a part of the evaluation effort while findings and recommendations are fresh in everyone's minds.

4. Think through the feasibility of all recommendations. Review all findings and sift out what can be done from what cannot.

References

Fetterman, D. (2001). Evaluation, knowledge management, best practices, and high quality lessons learned. *American Journal of Evaluation, 22,* 329–336.

 **10**

The Hunter School Evaluation Experience: A Special School's Journey

by Rena F. Subotnik, Janet F. Soller, & Sarah K. Hood

Making value judgments about the educational import of what has been seen and rendered is one of the critical features of educational criticism, as it also must be in the conduct of conventional educational research.
—Elliot W. Eisner (1991, p. 176)

The purpose of this chapter is to describe and assess the experience of evaluating the internationally recognized Hunter College Campus Schools from the beginning of the process to the final report. What the evaluation team learned can be applied to any publicly funded program for gifted students. Accountability for public funding provides an opportunity to demonstrate excellent educational practice.

Located in the heart of Manhattan, Hunter College Campus Schools (HCCS) are publicly funded schools for intellectually gifted students, grades pre-K through 12. Hunter College High School (HCHS), which currently encompasses grades 7–12, was founded in 1869 as a Female Normal and High School. In 1902, the normal school component evolved into Hunter College, and, in 1955, HCHS became a laboratory secondary school for intellectually gifted girls. By 1974, in response to legal challenge, Hunter College High School began admitting boys.

The Hunter College Elementary School (HCES) was established in 1870 as a model demonstration school for the Hunter College teacher education program. In 1940, Hunter College reorganized the school as an experimental center for intellectually gifted students, grades pre-K to 6.

> The goal of HCES [from 1940 to the present] is to teach students to think critically and creatively, to appreciate the diversity of this educational environment, to develop the skills needed to further one's knowledge base in areas of individual interest and to prepare students to be leaders, thinkers, and doers of the future. (Hunter College Elementary School, 2001, p. 2)

Selection Criteria

Selection Criteria for the High School

In order to be admitted to Hunter College High School, one must be a resident of New York City. The process begins each year in September, when school principals throughout the five boroughs are asked to identify sixth-grade students who are eligible to take the Hunter College High School (HCHS) entrance exam, as determined by students' performance on fifth-grade standardized tests. A percentile cutoff on standardized tests of reading and mathematics is determined each year that will yield 3,000 to 4,000 test takers. The HCHS entrance exam, developed by the mathematics and English departments of the school, is then administered each year in January. In order to be accepted to Hunter College High School, a student must earn a score at or above a designated cutoff on the objective section of the exam and write a passing essay. Approximately, 170 top scorers on the entrance exam who also wrote a passing essay are offered admission. The top 30 economically disadvantaged students, ranked by objective score, who wrote a passing essay, are also offered admission. Students from the elementary school enter the high school automatically.

Selection Criteria for the Elementary School

The elementary school admission procedure is different from that of the high school. In response to written requests, application packets are mailed to the primary residence of custodial parents/legal guardians. Candidates for admission must reside in Manhattan and be between the ages of 3 and 5. In the first round of testing, after receiving an appointment card from the admissions office, parents arrange for their child to be tested by an approved private psychologist using the most recent edition of the Stanford-Binet individual IQ test. Children testing at or above the cutoff score (usually 97th percentile and above) are invited to "Round 2." During this next phase of the admissions process, children are observed negotiating individual and group tasks while interacting with peers and teachers. A school faculty committee reviews applications, test scores, and Round 2 data without access to candidates' names. Based on the faculty reviews, the director of admissions offers 50 placements per year and maintains a waiting list.

An Invitation for Evaluation

When Jennifer Raab became president of Hunter College in 2000, she was returning home. A graduate of Hunter College High School, President Raab invited an evaluation team of national experts in gifted education to conduct a review of HCCS. The goal for the evaluation was to provide concrete recommendations for fostering HCCS's role as a model of gifted education and talent development.

The evaluation team was selected according to the following criteria. One member was deeply familiar with the schools by way of a 15-year career in the Hunter College School of Education. Her area of scholarship was gifted education and talent development, and in that capacity she had served as curriculum and research consultant to the schools. The second member of the team was selected for his experience as director of a selective high school and scholar in the area of the social and emotional needs of gifted students. The third member of the team brought expertise in the area of curricula for the gifted, as well as a broad understanding of applying gifted education to various settings. All three of the team members were experienced evaluators.

The evaluation team designed the following objectives for the evaluation process and completion of the report:

- Collect information from all relevant constituencies, including teachers, parents, administrators, students, representatives from Hunter College's School of Education, and the president's office.
- Develop a data-driven report that includes recommendations for policy implementation that will aid the HCCS community in generating a strategic plan.
- Design recommendations in the form of desired outcomes that can be reviewed annually.

Data Collection

Data were collected by way of mailed questionnaires and from a variety of activities during a site visit. Surveys were distributed in two waves a month apart to students, parents, and teachers. The second wave was instituted to elicit additional responses.

Surveys

The surveys consisted of 14 items about admissions, curricula and instruction, assessment of learning, special student services (including talent development), counseling and other support services, and collaboration with the Hunter College School of Education. Respondents were instructed to answer items 1–12 using a Likert Scale (1 = Strongly Agree, through 5 = Strongly Disagree). For each question, respondents were also provided with space to write comments. Questions 13 and 14 were open-ended items (see Figure 1). Question 13 addressed ideas for a successful collaboration between HCCS and the Hunter College School of Education. Question 14 asked respondents to list what skills, knowledge, and attitudes students should have at various points in their career at Hunter Campus Schools and whether those aspired outcomes are appropriate to a gifted education. A total of 499 surveys out of 1,200 (42%) were returned: 23 from HCES students, 118 from HCES parents, 8 from HCES teachers, 153 from HCHS students, 168 from HCHS parents, and 29 from HCHS teachers (see Appendix C for a copy of the survey).

Site Visit

The 3-day site visit began in the president's office with the president, provost, the president's liaison to HCCS, the dean of the School of Education, faculty from the School of Education, and the evaluation team. At this meeting, President Raab gave the evaluation team its charge and, during the next 3 days, the team toured the site, attended classes, and met individually and in focus groups with all constituencies of HCCS.

Focus groups were comprised of students, parents, faculty, and administration from HCES, HCHS, and the Hunter College School of Education. From HCES, the team met with 60 parents, 20 faculty and staff, 16 selected fifth and sixth graders, and the principal. From the high school, the team met with four administrators and the director of admissions, all HCHS seventh and eighth graders, eight selected juniors and seniors, 30 parents, three staff from the guidance office, and all the department chairs. Four administrators from the Hunter College School of Education conferred with the team, as well. Notes from all the focus group interactions were recorded, and index card responses were collected from 84 HCES parents, 16 HCES students, 64 HCHS parents, and eight HCHS students. In addition to the survey and focus group responses, the team received 18 highly detailed comments from HCES parents.

During the focus group meetings, the team requested and enforced constructive responses from the participants. Focus group participants also recorded their comments and responses on index cards. Each group was asked the following questions, tailored to the specific audience:

1. What is best about HCCS? What would you not want changed?
2. What support is available to students who need help? What support is available for those students who have already demonstrated mastery of classroom requirements?
3. What classroom/instructional strategies best help the gifted child?
4. If you could change only one thing about HCCS, what would it be?

Document Requests

The evaluation team requested access to archived and public documents available to outside educators or the general public. Appendix D lists the documents and other materials that HCHS was asked to submit to the evaluation team for review.

Data Collection Experiences

The site visit was organized and facilitated through the efforts of the president's office and administrators of HCCS. Students led the team on a building tour. Evaluators observed a seventh-grade music class, a French 6 AP class, an eighth-grade social studies class, a high school physics class, a pre-K and a kindergarten/first-grade class, fifth-grade mathematics and language classes, a fourth-grade mathematics class, and an elementary science class. The majority of the visit was devoted to daytime and evening meetings with the HCCS community, including the administration, faculty, staff, students, and parents.

Translating Analysis Into Specific Recommendations

In order to present the data in the most useful form, the report followed a three-part format. The first portion of the evaluation report summarized the evaluation team's activities from the site visit and a review of available materials. The second part provided an analysis of the data in the following areas: 1) admissions, 2) communications, 3) curricula and instruction, 4) assessment of learning, 5) special student services, 6) counseling and other support services, and 7) collaboration with the Hunter College School of Education.[1] The final section of the report translated the results across all data collection methods into specific recommendations. The team's recommendations were premised on the strengths of the school and were designed to inform the strategic planning process encouraged by President Raab.

Writing and Presenting the Report

Toward the end of the site visit, the consultants convened for several hours to review and synthesize the data. They found that the results were consistent across all the data sources available on site in a number of areas. All stakeholders agreed that the students were outstanding. In addition,

---

[1.] This chapter does not include discussion of data under the categories of School Organization and Structure. Nor are the recommendations under other categories reported comprehensively in order to protect the privacy of the school and to honor the client-evaluation team relationship.

parents, teachers, and HCCS administrators clearly wanted to make HCCS the most exemplary schools for the gifted possible. Everyone wanted a strong partnership with Hunter College.

The evaluation team developed a set of overheads to address each of the categories of analysis for the president, provost, dean of education, and HCCS administrators. The discussion helped to clarify the task and organize the report into sections that would be public and those that would serve as a reference only for the president and her cabinet.

After the site visit, the team then set about the task of entering and analyzing survey data and focus group cards and writing the report. The evaluators were geographically distant from one another; therefore, follow-up report writing took place electronically. Because all the data were housed at one location, referring back to particular documents was sometimes difficult for the evaluators at the other locations. Nevertheless, the team was able to produce a finished document for Hunter within 3 months.

Recommendations to the Campus Schools From the Evaluation Team

The following recommendations offered by the evaluation team could be applied to any publicly funded gifted program. Schools that function optimally to serve gifted students integrate their admission criteria, curricula, support services, ongoing assessment, and desired outcomes at graduation. An institution's true mission is reflected in its selected population. For this reason, the evaluation team began by asking the HCCS community to answer with clarity, "Whom do the Hunter Campus Schools serve?" In the course of deciding whom to serve, a school for the gifted can select:

- The most brilliant young people from among those who apply. This arrangement is what most closely describes the current admissions process.
- The most brilliant young people in New York City. In order to carry out this mission, outreach must be strenuous and the school must be prepared to accept a more economically and ethnically homogeneous student body due to variations in the quality of schooling and extracurricular opportunities available around the city.

- The most brilliant from among those whose families have the fewest educational options because they are too poor or too uninformed to be "in the loop" for private education or other selective schools. Embracing such a mission would provide a unifying ideal and a unique niche in the specialized school community. However, taxpayers whose children would then be excluded from the admissions process would feel disenfranchised, ultimately undermining support for the school.

- Those most accomplished or brilliant young people in at least one academic area. The focus of the school would be to develop the specific talent areas of students while providing a rigorous college-bound course of study to all. This solution may provide a more diverse population and one more closely aligned with the adolescent profiles of adults who have transformed our society.

Each of the above listed missions has attractive qualities and serious constraints. The evaluation team strongly urged the HCCS community to select a mission (population to serve) or devise one of its own. A clear mission allows a school for the gifted to offer a cohesive curriculum and set of support services, making it even more likely that students will receive the special kind of education they should expect from a selective school for gifted students.

Once HCCS decides which students they wish to serve, the evaluation team recommended that the community delineate desired outcomes for these students at the end of their HCCS career. Although the most commonly reported desired outcome on the part of parents and students was admission to the most reputable postsecondary institutions, the team thought this short-term goal was too limited. From the perspective of talent development, the schools should also aim for generating transformational leaders in scholarship, the professions, business, and the public sector.

The evaluation team presented recommendations in the hope that HCCS would embrace long-term goals that integrated admission criteria, curricula, support services, ongoing assessment, and desired outcomes at graduation. Wherever possible, the evaluation team built on suggestions offered by previous evaluation reports conducted at the school that still required attention and framed the recommendations in a way that could be useful for the school's upcoming strategic planning process.

Admissions

In general, the evaluation team commended the HCCS faculty committees and the director of admissions for their continuing efforts to improve the quality of the admissions process. In addition, the evaluation team recommended the following:

- The process should continue to be guided by best practice in gifted education, including the use of multiple criteria for selection and an optimal match between program delivered and student population selected.
- Admissions criteria for HCES and HCHS should be aligned as closely as possible to address desired outcomes for the end of 12th grade.
- Admissions decisions should remain data-driven.
- The process should ensure that all New York City elementary schools—public, private, and parochial—have equal access to admissions information.
- The admissions director should design and implement an aggressive yearlong preparation program for underrepresented groups prior to each entry point.
- Because of the central role of admissions in carrying out the mission of the school, the director of admissions should also serve as an advisor in other matters central to the mission of the schools (organization, curricula and instruction, etc.).

Curricula and Instruction

HCCS has many outstanding teachers whose professional skills are channeled into curriculum development. Because of the uniqueness associated with each classroom, the curriculum is not as aligned as it might be across grades and from grade to grade. If gifted programs are to serve as purveyors of excellence in the public domain, they need curricular frameworks. These documents should address, in a sequential manner, expected goals and outcomes for students in each grade. Along with the statement of goals and outcomes, the document should delineate how the goals and outcomes meet and exceed those expected for students in New York State.

- Each subject area in the elementary school should have a faculty member whose special responsibility lies in curriculum development, coordination, mentoring, and monitoring.
- Each department chair should work collaboratively with the other chairs in order to synchronize the sequence of topics and skills taught to students so that the curriculum makes sense as a whole. Hunter College School of Education and School of Liberal Arts faculty should be available to collaborate in the curriculum development process.

In order to carry out these recommendations, the evaluation team suggested the following to the president of Hunter College:

- released time for faculty to write curricula and plan cross-disciplinary units/projects;
- ongoing staff development differentiated by teacher expertise and experience, with a special focus on teaching gifted students;
- development of materials for external audiences that document and describe the schools' curricula and projects;
- competitive funding, perhaps generated by parents, to support teacher presentations at national and local conferences;
- a program of electives for all students at all grade levels based on interest, a specific talent, or both;
- a scope and sequence guide to pre-K–6 curricula; and
- development of a mechanism for compacting the curriculum in basic verbal and quantitative skills for exceptionally talented pre-K–6 students.

Assessment of Learning

Gifted education is a form of special education. Therefore, a system needs to be in place whereby each student's academic profile is easily accessible and reviewed regularly. The evaluation team recommended:

- a long-term (3 years) and short-term (coming academic year) staff development plan;
- for secondary-level programs, an evaluation design that focuses annually on (a) student awards and distinctions, Advanced Placement examination performance, PSAT/SAT scores, and

college acceptance data; (b) perceptual data from students and parents on program effectiveness; and (c) self-assessment by faculty and staff; and

- for elementary-level programs, an evaluation design that focuses annually on (a) standardized test scores, (b) student distinctions, (c) secondary school acceptance data, (d) perceptual data from students and parents on program effectiveness, and (e) self-assessment by faculty and staff.

Talent Development

Within the gifted student population are those with exceptional abilities in particular subject areas or domains. Learning services should include a purposefully designed program for the talent development of specific academic talents. These services may come in three forms: acceleration, electives, and extracurricular activities. Recommendations included:

- Provide access to acceleration into more advanced classes.
- Offer electives for students in all grades in order to maintain special interests that help students prepare for competitions and other extracurricular experiences that require portfolios or research experiences.
- Create an activities director position. This person would guide especially talented students to extracurricular classes, mentorships, internships, and experiences before the senior year and serve as a liaison for parents.
- Create a program in coordination with counselors and the activities director to help highly talented students develop the social and practical intelligence needed to open doors for them in their areas of deep interest.

Counseling/Guidance Program

High-quality counseling is essential to the success of a gifted program. Students, their families, visitors, and potential funding organizations should be able to ascertain from the materials presented to them by the counseling staff what services are being offered and how they are uniquely suited to the gifted students. In that light we recommended the following to the school's counseling department:

- Identify the goals of the counseling program in the elementary school and the high school and make them explicit and well known to the school communities.
- Delineate and publicize how the social, emotional, and college and career guidance needs of each gifted student are being addressed.
- Indicate to the HCCS community how the special needs of students in grades 7, 8, and 9 are being addressed in the context of a 7th–12th-grade school environment.
- Institutionalize ways to plan together and solve problems with classroom faculty.
- Delineate and publicize how the counselors collaborate with special service agents (e.g., learning specialist in the elementary school and advisor to high school seniors conducting special projects) and throughout the city.

These suggestions could be developed into a brochure or guidebook that could be made available to all members of the HCCS community, Hunter College, and to school visitors. The brochure should be periodically revised and reevaluated in light of changes in program or goals at the Campus Schools.

Relationship With the Hunter College School of Education

Association with a university or school of education can be extremely fruitful. The evaluation team suggested some of the following ways in which such collaboration would benefit the Hunter community:

- clinical placement of undergraduate and graduate students in relevant HCCS contexts, including, but not limited to, counseling, classrooms, and administrative internships;
- School of Education faculty consultation on special-needs students, beginning with observation and assessment and leading to prescribed interventions;
- establishing a gifted education program in the School of Education; and
- research conducted on gifted learners, their families, and effective school interventions used with them. Some ideas for potential research include:

Table 10.1

Data Needing to be Examined in a Gifted Program Evaluation

Type	Data to be Examined
Curricula	• a curricular framework and scope and sequence of curricula for each grade in each subject.
Services	• services available to students with special learning needs and to those with exceptional ability in a given subject • admissions criteria
Staffing	• faculty accomplishments, including published research • criteria for selecting teachers
Outcome/ Impact data	• longitudinal and other study data on the school • data on alumni accomplishments • number of Advanced Placement courses available, taken, and annual performance data from AP exams • number of students taking college-level courses (beyond AP) • awards and recognition received by students • mean Scholastic Aptitude Test (SAT) and PSAT scores

1. case study research on twice-exceptional children, and
2. collaborative action research and publication about what works in the classroom with gifted children at different levels of development and in different content areas.

Communication

Communication with the outside world about the Campus Schools and its role in gifted education needed to be enhanced. The team urged the president of Hunter College to provide resources that could be applied to broadcasting the special features and accomplishments of the schools. All publicly funded schools for the gifted should have the data about curricula, services, staffing, and outcome/impact data available for visitors (see Table 10.1).

Practical Tips

The Hunter College Campus Schools evaluation experience provided lessons for both evaluators and personnel of gifted schools.

Tips for Evaluators

1. *Make your life as an evaluator easier.* A well-designed evaluation plan will ensure that your clients are satisfied. Some rules of thumb:

    - Include clients' goals as central to the evaluation objectives. You may want to negotiate presenting a report that comes in both public and private formats so that the clients may find out what they need even if it does not reflect directly on improving the school.
    - Triangulate data by asking similar written and focus group questions to each group of stakeholders.
    - Generate questions that elicit positive, solution-oriented responses from focus group participants. This helps to reduce the amount of nonproductive complaining or defensiveness that may come from stakeholders.

2. *Learn from mistakes.* The evaluation team's experience in data collection led them to a number of conclusions about how to collect data more efficiently. Sometimes, focus group sessions may be too large or too small, which calls for adjustments. Second-round mail-outs to survey participants may prove cumbersome and impractical, thus necessitating that the evaluators settle for a lower rate of return. Report writing is difficult to effect once the team disperses. Thus, there are real advantages to finishing a draft report on site.

Tips for Specialized Schools

1. *Publicly funded schools for gifted students need to be held accountable.* Publicly funded schools for gifted students have a special responsibility to demonstrate to the public that they are fulfilling a need that cannot be met as well in a regular setting. Without clear indication that this is the case, our field can be accused of elitism and depleting the pub-

lic coffers to "cream" students who might otherwise boost the quality and test scores of their home school and classroom. This means that mechanisms for monitoring student growth and achievement must be employed unhindered by ceiling effects.

2. *Schools need to reflect on definitions of success.* Schools that are successful at getting their graduates into excellent schools at the next level may be reluctant to change. Gifted education programs should certainly provide the best possible opportunities for its students, but the school community needs to discuss whether that is a sufficient goal to rationalize the use of public funds.

3. *There is a need for clarity and consistency in outcome measures used to assess the effectiveness of gifted programs.* Perhaps the best way to determine whether a school is contributing to the growth of individual students, no matter where they started, is to use a value-added model (Sanders & Rivers, 1996; Wright, Horn, & Sanders, 1997). Such a model shows how much each year of instruction contributes to the academic development of each student. In order to implement such a plan, however, a program of consistent and well-organized on-level and off-level testing and record keeping needs to be in place.

4. *Gifted schools need to demonstrate alignment of mission, admissions, curricular goals and outcomes, and assessment.* There are two kinds of problems that can plague institutions that serve gifted students. One kind is specific to the personalities, locale, and financial status of the stakeholders. Another kind of problem, misalignment, is common to many gifted programs. Unless the key factors of mission, admission, curricula, assessment, and outcomes are aligned, there will be uneven quality of services, claims of inequities, and a climate of stress on the part of stakeholders.

References

Eisner, E. W. (1991). Taking a second look: Educational connoisseurship revisited. In M. W. McLaughlin & D. C. Philips (Eds.), *Evaluation and education: At quarter century* (pp. 169–187). Chicago: University of Chicago Press.

Hunter College Elementary School. (2001) *HCES: An introduction, 2001–2002* [Brochure]. New York: Author.

Sanders, W. L., & Rivers, J. C. (1996). *Cumulative and residual effects of teachers on future academic achievement.* Knoxville: University of Tennessee Value-Added Research and Assessment Center.

Wright, S. P., Horn, S. P., & Sanders, W. L. (1997). Teacher and classroom context effects on student achievement: Implications for teacher evaluation. *Journal of Personnel Evaluation in Education, 11,* 57–67.

The Singapore Evaluation Experience: One Country's Progress in Gifted Program Development

by Chwee Quek

Evaluators have a role to play in ensuring that the interests of all individuals and groups in society are served both locally and globally.
—Rodney Hopson (2002, p. 384)

The purpose of this chapter is to share Singapore's experience in monitoring and evaluating their gifted education program. Using the most recent evaluation team findings from 2002, it describes the evaluation approaches adopted and the ways in which evaluation data were utilized to inform decision making about program development.

The Gifted Education Program (GEP) was introduced in Singapore in 1984 for intellectually gifted children, in line with the philosophy of ability-based streaming to allow each pupil to learn at his or her own pace. Students are identified through tests in linguistic, mathematical, and general ability in a two-stage screening/identification process. The program caters to students from Primary 4 to Secondary 4 (grades 4–10). It was a deliberate decision not to adopt the acceleration model of grade skipping, as the aim was to enrich the students' overall intellectual and creative development and not push them ahead in subject learning. It was important to ensure that students develop socially and emotionally with age peers. The enriched curriculum is anchored in the regular curriculum and extended in breadth and depth. Such a model is necessary because GEP students take the national examinations at two key branching points: the Primary School Leaving Examination (PSLE) and the General Certificate Examination at "Ordinary" Level (GCE "O") at Primary 6 and Secondary 4, respectively. It would also facilitate a transfer to the mainstream should a student withdraw from the program.

History of Evaluation of the Program

As for all new programs, it is important to have an evaluation to ascertain if the program is doing what it has been established to do (Rossi & Freeman, 1993). When the GEP was in its incipient stage, an external evaluator assessed whether it had been built on a strong foundation and if it were progressing in the right direction and determined areas for further development. The major recommendation from this evaluation was the need to step up staff development efforts by inviting gifted education experts from the United States to train Ministry of Education personnel in the Gifted Education Branch (GEB), who would, in turn, train GEP teachers. Trained GEB personnel should then work out the scope and sequence for all enriched subjects. In terms of curricular content, though reliance on U.S. materials was understandable while the program was still new, it was advised that efforts should be made in the long run to develop more locally relevant enrichment materials to give the program a distinctively Singaporean flavor. On the issue of national examinations (which were not based on the enriched curricula), it was suggested that the GEB look into making what was taught in the program "count for something." It was noted that the definition of giftedness as general intellectual ability could pose difficulty at the secondary level when students' abilities differentiate and patterns of strengths and weaknesses became more apparent. To keep classes homogeneous, it might be necessary to modify the concept of giftedness at the secondary level. Although the program was only in its second year, it was felt that a plan for evaluating it and its pupils should be instituted as a way of monitoring progress and determining its efficiency.

In 1989, a second external consultant was invited to help the GEB establish a comprehensive plan to evaluate the impact of the GEP. One major recommendation was that key personnel should be given opportunities to pursue graduate studies in gifted education, to groom a "cadre of specialist-educators for gifted education" and expand the pool of qualified teachers of the gifted. It was also suggested that GEP students' advanced work be taken into consideration for progression to high school or admission to the university. It was felt that services could be extended to younger children, but provisions for the higher levels should only be made when GEB personnel were ready to design and develop curricula for high schools. The same observation that the conception of giftedness needed modification at the secondary level was made in this report, as well.

Use of External Evaluation Data

The data from both evaluations guided the GEB in adopting initiatives to address the areas highlighted by the consultants. Experts from overseas were invited to provide intensive training for GEB personnel and, in later years, for GEP teachers and administrators, as well. Both GEB officers and gifted education teachers were sent for overseas conferences on gifted education, summer institutes, and visits to gifted programs in other countries. Scholarships were given for eligible staff to pursue graduate degrees in gifted education. There were regular in-service courses on gifted education, content, and pedagogy for gifted education teachers. The main priority was to build an adequately trained staff to develop the curricular and instructional materials and monitor the implementation of the program before considering the other recommendations. On the conception of giftedness, no changes were made, as the Ministry believed that the program should not emphasize specialization before Secondary 4. Some of the other recommendations that were not immediately accepted did, however, guide thinking about future developments for the program, what Rossi and Freeman (1993) termed "conceptual utilization of evaluation data."

Internal Program Monitoring and Evaluation

In addition to these two external evaluations, the Gifted Education Branch of the ministry has been conducting internal evaluations of the program on an annual basis through program monitoring, which is another basic form of evaluation (Royse, Tyler, Padgett & Logan 2001). Needs assessments of teachers are carried out to establish the extent and distribution of areas of concern to be addressed. Parents of gifted program pupils at critical levels (Primary 6 and Secondary 4, end of primary and secondary GEP, respectively) are surveyed to gather feedback on the extent to which they feel the program has met its goals,[1] and their perceptions on how the program has contributed to their child's development. In terms of curricular evaluation, subject specialists in the Gifted Education Branch of the ministry meet with teachers to discuss the enriched curriculum during biennial curricular meetings, as well as an annual weeklong conference. Curricular modifications are regularly made based on feedback and discussion with teachers implementing the curriculum. Feedback on in-service courses is used to guide the conceptualization and modification of staff development programs. Students are surveyed on a needs basis, as in instances when a new syllabus is introduced or new strategies are tried out.

The summative evaluation to ascertain the outcomes of the gifted program takes the form of comparison of GEP and top non-GEP students' performance in national examinations at Primary 6, Secondary 4, and Junior College 2 (grade 12). Data on participation and prizes won in high-level academic competitions like the International Olympiads for Math, Science, and Technology, as well as winners of prestigious scholarships, are also collected to track GEP pupils' academic achievements. In terms of affective outcomes, GEP pupils' participation in cocurricular and community service activities, leadership roles, and, for the males, ranks in national service also serve as measures. A longitudinal study of GEP graduates has also been undertaken to track these students through their school careers and beyond to see the impact the program has made in their lives. Without equivalent comparison groups, it is difficult to prove that the GEP *caused* these outcomes. To quote Rossi and Freeman (1993), "When there are preexisting differences between those who enroll in a program and otherwise eligible persons who do not enroll, the outcomes of the program may be accounted for by selection and not be attributed to the intervention" (p. 223).

[1.] The GEP meets the cognitive needs of gifted students by developing intellectual depth, nurturing creative productivity, and developing attitudes for self-directed lifelong learning. Affective needs of students are met by enhancing aspirations for individual excellence and fulfillment, developing a strong sense of social conscience and commitment to serve society and nation, and developing moral values and qualities for responsible leadership.

Need for Another Comprehensive Evaluation

With changes evolving in the education system, many new initiatives have been introduced that have made it possible to replicate in mainstream classes what is being done in the gifted education program. In the current ability-driven phase of education in Singapore, curricula have been revised to emphasize skills for thinking and independent learning. Content is reduced to free time for learning activities that foster critical and creative thinking. Project work and interdisciplinary curricula are routinely intro-duced in schools. Modes of assessment are expanded to elicit problem-solving behavior and promote teamwork and effective communication. Against this backdrop, the inevitable question has arisen: Is there still a need for the program? If so, what should be its key distinguishing features? To what extent has the gifted program attained its goals, and should its goals be modified? With new skills, competencies, and talents needed for the new economy, is the definition of giftedness still valid, and should its target group remain the same? With the expansion of the program over the years, should it retain its current structure, or has the time come to set up a school for the gifted? With the current size of the program, is the cur-rent structure that was set up two decades ago still the best for the pro-gram? Is the program preparing its students for the new knowledge-based and technology-oriented economy? If not, how should it be repositioned to do so? To find the answers to these questions, it was felt that another comprehensive evaluation of the program was due.

The Review Structure

A review committee was formed to undertake the task. In determin-ing the composition, conscious effort was made to include members from diverse backgrounds and disciplines, including GEP and non-GEP administrators and an educational psychologist (a psychometrician) to guard against the bias of internal evaluations (Joint Committee on Standards and Educational Evaluation, as cited by Nielson & Buchanan, 1991, pp. 281–282), as well as to ensure that issues were deliberated from multiple perspectives. In accordance with best evaluation practices (Landrum, Callahan, & Shaklee, 2001), experts in various facets of gifted education were appointed to assist and advise the review committee. This international advisory panel (IAP) comprised two scholars from the U.S.

and one from Taiwan. The involvement of personnel not related to the GEP, as well as non-Singaporean gifted education experts, minimized the chances that the authenticity of the findings might be questioned (Nielson & Buchanan, 1991).

To facilitate the evaluation design, the review committee proposed a framework detailing the terms of reference, as well as sources of information and indicators/measures of outcomes. It carried out what Wholey (as cited by Rossi & Freeman, 1993) termed an "evaluatability assessment." A program description was prepared based on written documents like a concept paper on the program, publicity materials, administrative regulations, and previous evaluation reports to give committee members a sense of what constituted the GEP's intent and the implementation and management of it. Data were collected through successive rounds of questions addressed to ministry personnel and other stakeholders. Based on the information collected, the committee decided on the evaluation tasks, explicated the objectives, and modified the terms of reference.

The Role of the International Advisory Panel (IAP) as Evaluators

The role of the IAP was spelled out in an agreement, which, among other things, specified the purpose and focus of the evaluation, the beginning and end dates of the panel's commitment, and the ownership of the data. Materials on the education system and the program were sent to members ahead of time. This served three purposes: to familiarize them with the educational environment in Singapore, to give them an understanding of the circumstances surrounding the inception of the gifted program and its development since then, and to provide a context for them to define their charge. On the first morning of their week on-site, the team attended presentations on the general education system and special components of the gifted program. This gave them the opportunity to request further data and also to validate the information and insights gleaned from the documents that had been sent to them earlier. Lesson observations were scheduled in three primary and three secondary schools across all the enriched subject areas. Additionally, the team observed a Junior College class (grade 11) comprising mainly former gifted program students. All lesson observations were supplemented by written lesson plans. During the school visits, lunchtime and tea meetings were arranged for team members to interact with both GEP and non-GEP teachers and school administrators. The team had two separate dinner meetings with the principals and heads of the gifted program departments. Time was also allotted for the team to formulate their findings, as they had to make an oral presentation of their draft report to ministry officials on the final day of their visit. This not only gave ministry officials the opportunity to seek clarification, but also provided the IAP with new perspectives to consider in interpreting their data and to refine their final written report (Royse et al., 2001).

The terms of reference and documents analyzed were used by the IAP to conceptualize guiding themes to inform their work. As new insights emerged in the course of the evaluation process, new themes were added. The terms of reference and the guiding questions may be found in Table 11.1.

The Review Process

As far as possible, and within the constraints of resources, the evaluation methodology and process was designed in accordance with recommended evaluation procedures: clearly spelling out the role of the evaluation team, using evaluation goals to guide the collection of data, surveying all critical stakeholders, and using multiple instruments to gather information, among other approaches. Documents were analyzed to check for coherence between program objectives and program implementation and to assess the extent to which program goals were met. Key stakeholders, such as GEP students, parents, and teachers, were surveyed to determine the effectiveness and impact of the program. Feedback was also sought from former GEP students, GEP school administrators, and GEB personnel. An independent research company was engaged to conduct the surveys and focus group discussions. In total, three quantitative surveys were administered in all nine primary and seven GEP centers. Questionnaires were distributed to all Primary 6 and Secondary 3 (grade 8) students and their parents. All GEP teachers and GEB personnel not in the review committee were also included in the surveys. One thousand questionnaires were mailed to former GEP students. A copy was also posted on the GEP Web site.

Four focus group discussions were held with principals of the GEP centers, GEP heads of department and teachers, non–GEP teachers, and former GEP students on issues listed in the terms of reference. That these focus group discussions were facilitated by an independent research

Table 11.1
Congruence of Themes Between Review Committee and IAP

Review Committee's Terms of Reference	IAP's Guiding Questions
Assess extent to which GEP has attained its objectives in terms of intellectual achievement, transmission of values, and GEP graduates' contribution as citizens.	To what extent are the cognitive and affective goals of the program addressed and attained?
Revisit the fundamental objectives of the GEP in the context of ability-driven education, addressing questions like the rationale for the GEP, its distinguishing features, the definition of giftedness, its target group, selection criteria, and methods.	How effective are the identification processes for the program?
Review the curriculum and special programs and assess how content and delivery can be enhanced to strengthen core values and develop students' EQ.	How effective are the processes promoting curricular design, development, and differentiation?
Review the staffing and resource needs and look into the issues of teacher recruitment, training, and deployment.	How effective are the teacher selection, training, and development mechanisms for the program?
Review the entry and exit points, progression paths, transition to postsecondary, degree of segregation from non-GEP students, roles of school and ministry administrators in program administration, and examining structures that could best enable GEP to meet its objectives.	What program organizational structures may best benefit the gifted students? To what extent does the program utilize partnerships and collaboration with the larger community (universities, businesses and parents) to address its goals, issues, and concerns?

firm reduced the chances of bias inherent in sessions led by facilitators who had a stake in the program being evaluated (Rossi & Freeman 1993). It was also in line with the recommended practice that focus group participants be grouped with peers to ensure that they are more forthcoming with their views (Royse et al., 2001). Results of the survey and focus group phase of the evaluation are incorporated into the commentary that follows.

IAP Findings and Recommendations

The findings and recommendations of the IAP were organized according to six questions.

To What Extent Are the Cognitive and Affective Goals of the GEP Addressed and Attained?

Findings and Recommendations. The IAP evaluated this against the two-fold mission of the GEP: to meet the needs of students who can exceed the standards of the prescribed curriculum and to foster the development of Singapore's future leaders and thinkers. The IAP observed that, while the GEP provided challenge for the GEP students who comprised the top 1% of their age cohort (based on tests used to predict their academic potential), there were also GEP students who were not sufficiently stretched even by the gifted program curriculum. This appeared to be true especially in the area of mathematics, an academic domain that has a tradition of prodigies (Feldman, 1985). Based on national examination scores, teacher anecdotes, and data gathered from surveys, the IAP also believed that there were non–GEP students who needed more challenge than they were receiving in the mainstream classes. The panel felt that the GEP emphasis on general ability and philosophical press for well-roundedness made it difficult for students with uneven abilities to plumb their strengths. They recommended that the program offer a continuum of services from selective accelerative programs, to broad-based enrichment activities. For instance, specific aptitude options in selected schools providing advanced instruction (e.g., in math) could cater to both identified students and non–GEP students with special aptitudes.

Findings revealed that the program had been effective in raising students' intellectual achievement. Most former GEP students attributed intellectual and personal development to the impact of the GEP. However, findings also showed that the program had contributed more to pupils' intellectual development than their moral development. In fact, from their interactions with teachers, the IAP surmised that gifted program students did not demonstrate strong evidence of empathy, motivation, or persistence. This was also supported by the surveys of GEP students who requested to have less homework, fewer projects, and lower teacher expectations. Non-GEP teachers also felt that gifted program students were reluctant to socialize with their nonidentified peers.

The IAP recommended addressing this issue through multiple lenses. Pupils entering the program should be informed that they will encounter higher expectations, greater competition, and more work and understand that those who are reluctant to undertake the rigorous course of study and exhibit poor performance in spite of sustained assistance will lose their eligibility to participate in the program. At the same time, GEP students who exhibit desired behaviors should be rewarded with incentives. Student growth in the affective dimensions could be assessed through writing and other products, as well as behavioral or attitude scales. These assessments could be used to supplement performance on national examinations when determining progression. To promote socialization of GEP and non-GEP students, it was recommended that more integrated, nonacademic events and activities be planned in schools where these integration problems were most evident.

Review Committee's Response. At the primary level, the review committee felt that GEP services should continue to be confined to the top 1% of GEP students, given the current level of resources and expertise. However, within-program modifications could be made to create advanced learning opportunities for GEP students who show exceptional talent in mathematics. At the secondary level, the extension of GEP services to a broader band of learners could probably be accommodated in the context of changes at the upper secondary/junior college level. For instance, the secondary schools that would be implementing the Integrated Program and offering an integrated curriculum from Secondary 3 to Junior College 2 (grades 9–12) are GEP schools. Accelerative options in math could be offered to both GEP and non-GEP students on a case-by-case basis. The committee also suggested that these schools negotiate with the local universities to allow accelerated students to enroll in university-level classes and earn credits for admission. This would also encourage bright students to apply to the local universities.

Parents would be asked to sign an undertaking that they subscribe to the goals and will work with the teachers to help develop their children's potential. Students would also be reminded that eligibility to stay in the program is dependent on performance, as well as motivation and a desirable learning attitude.

The review committee fully concurred with the IAP to encourage schools to be more proactive in facilitating socialization of GEP and non-GEP students. Cocurricular programs seemed to be the best avenue. At a minimum, GEP students should participate with non-GEP students in activities designed for character building and promoting a sense of national identity. Schools should also monitor GEP students' participation in cocurricular activities to ensure that they have ample opportunity to interact with non-GEP peers.

How Effective Are the Identification Processes for the Program?

Findings and Recommendations. The IAP felt that, in using the special education approach to meeting the needs of students, the GEP should make provisions for all students who are two standard deviations above the mean.[2] Therefore, non-GEP students who score at the 97th percentile of the national examinations and are two standard deviations above the mean would benefit from GEP services, especially in domains of their special aptitudes. Citing research-based best practice, the team recommended that high-stakes decision making be based on multiple measures (American Educational Research Association, American Psychological Association, & National Council on Measurement in Education, 1999; Landrum, Callahan, & Shaklee, 2001). At least three measures should be included, and they should be relevant to program emphasis and ensure equitable processes for selection and placement. Ideally, there should be different identification procedures for each level of programming, and identification procedures should be ongoing. The team therefore recommended that selection criteria for the GEP be expanded to include identification for specific aptitude based on teacher recommendation and demonstrated achievement in line with the talent

[2] In the disabilities field, a student who is two standard deviations below the mean qualifies for special services due to that exceptionality.

development approach. This would expand the GEP student population, with some students participating only in subject-specific classes for which they have special aptitudes.

Review Committee's Response. The review committee was not in favor of increasing the intake to include all students who are two standard deviations above the mean. Primary and secondary teachers have observed a greater diversity of abilities in the present cohorts of GEP students compared to the earlier years when the cohort was smaller. Teachers have also expressed the view that greater heterogeneity has made it more difficult to implement the enriched curriculum.

As for the use of multiple measures to identify students for the GEP, the review committee felt that these were not that critical in Singapore's context, where a two-stage screening/identification process is used and every Primary 3 student in the education system has a chance to sit for the screening exam. Additionally, in accordance with the educational philosophy of nurturing well-rounded students, it was decided that the operational definition of giftedness as general intellectual ability should be retained. The IAP's recommendation to use multiple measures, however, would be adopted when selecting students for mentorship programs and advanced math classes when they were offered. At the primary level, teacher recommendation and student demonstration of high ability would be criteria for participation in advanced classes. In the secondary schools offering the Integrated Program, teachers could nominate students who excelled in a specific domain for more advanced instruction, research work, or both in that domain, and identification for this purpose would probably be done on an ongoing basis.

How Effective Are the Processes Promoting Curricular Design, Development, and Differentiation?

Findings and Recommendations. Based on document analysis, the IAP found strong congruence of key variables. The program of studies appeared to be attaining curricular objectives, particularly in the cognitive domain. While program goals were being addressed in the realm of practice, it was not always done in an integrated fashion. Lesson plans given during classroom visits were clearly aligned to content guides prepared by the ministry. Pedagogy was strong in mathematics and science classes, but was more uneven in humanities and English classes. The implementation of cognitive and affective goals was found to be uneven, with mathematics and science classes focusing entirely on cognitive goals, mixed emphasis in English and humanities classes, and exclusive emphasis on the affective in Civics and Moral Education (CME) classes. The IAP recommended that the ministry revisit the rationale for separate classes for affective development that are neither linked to content nor assessed for student learning. They felt it was desirable to consider a greater integration of cognitive and affective goals across all content areas. It was suggested that classroom-based practice could be enhanced with more emphasis on evaluative thinking. Teaching students to use criteria to support arguments would reduce the amount of relativistic thinking. Civics education, it was felt, could be presented in a sophisticated fashion to engage students' intellect and stir their desire to contribute to the nation's future. For example, the use of primary documents and multiple sources of evidence might be used to deepen historical analysis, encourage multiple perspectives, and enhance understanding of the complexities of the nation's past and potential future. Getting students to engage in problem solving on global issues and those of local concern and inviting experts to evaluate their solutions could make them treat the enterprise with greater seriousness. Biographies of people who have contributed to the nation's development might also serve as role models and engage students' interest.

In the cognitive arena, it was felt that varying levels of student competence warranted greater differentiation of tasks and materials. More personalized options that could be offered via existing programs like the Individualized Research Study, mentorship programs, and competitions should be expanded at the secondary level. The GEB was encouraged to consider the benefits of greater flexibility of program implementation that recognizes individual school differences and needs. Stronger use of acceleration practices should also be explored.

In the area of assessments, it was recommended that instruments that are better matched to program and curricular outcomes be developed since national examinations, though useful as baselines, have, because of their ceiling effects, provided insufficient evidence to judge the impact of the program on students. Research-based best practice recommends that assessments be multidimensional and require students to demonstrate advanced learning. The IAP further added that content-based performance measures that are off-level should be developed for use at critical grade levels and systematic analysis of student outcomes should be done every 3 years. While the IAP noted that data collection was closely connected to decision making and used for future planning, they advised that an evaluation framework be formulated, as carefully collected information about all aspects of the program would be necessary for the most robust provisions for gifted learners to evolve.

Review Committee's Response. The review committee agreed that full integration of the cognitive and affective goals should be a guiding principle in the design of the GEP curriculum and, within the academic curriculum, cognitive and affective domains should be enmeshed across the subjects. A working committee set up to look into strengthening the affective development of GEP students proposed that citizenship and service learning be integral components of the curriculum. Further research would be undertaken on effective ways to teach civics education to gifted students to inform curriculum development and instruction. As for greater personalization of curricular opportunities, especially for students with exceptional ability in a specific subject, this would probably be best implemented in the context of the Integrated Program. Alternative assessments would be developed to supplement national examinations (PSLE), and these could include academic performance, independent work (Individualized Research Study), portfolios, and fulfillment of community service obligations. The GEB would also look into an assessment framework to measure systematically student growth over the years.

How Effective Are the Teacher Selection, Training and Development Mechanisms for the Program?

Findings and Recommendations. The advisory panel commented that the Ministry of Education's support structure for assisting schools in teacher selection and preparation was a highly desirable facet of teacher development. In the selection of teachers, it is important to remember that different types of teachers are needed for the course of a gifted student's development. One type helps the student to fall in love with a domain of study or performance. A second type provides the skills, knowledge, and rules a student needs to develop his or her expertise (Bloom, 1985). A third type provides the guidance and tacit knowledge needed to socialize a student successfully into a field (Sternberg, Grigorenko, & Bundy, 2001).

While the IAP found the overall quality of teaching to be high, they pointed to areas of need for further attention in teacher development. In-service courses for teachers should be targeted to content-relevant pedagogy, using strengths and weaknesses as a basis for planning. It was also necessary to differentiate the training based on teacher needs. More resources should be provided to assist in differentiating the more difficult areas of the program (e.g., moral education). Besides the continued practice of mentoring new teachers, the ministry should provide incentives for new teachers to remain in the program. They also advised that the target group of teachers for training in gifted education strategies be expanded; this would not only upgrade the overall education program in Singapore, but also serve as a base for selecting GEP teachers of promise. Moreover, it would pave the way for cultivating a broader band of learners who could benefit from GEP services.

Review Committee's Response. These recommendations would guide the selection of teachers, teacher deployment, and future staff development efforts. Of priority would be training for teachers to upgrade classroom practices and to deliver the more integrated curriculum. The GEB could organize talks and sessions that would expose teachers to issues of currency and help them engage students in meaningful discussions of a broader range of issues, including social and moral issues. Learning circles could be formed for teachers to share their experiences, challenges, and successes in teaching gifted students. The training of non–GEP teachers would be done when the GEB provided consultancy and training services to schools, including non–GEP schools, on a request basis.

What Program Organizational Structures May Best Benefit Singapore's Gifted Students?

Findings and Recommendations. The GEP is implemented from Primary 4 to Secondary 4, a duration of 7 years, which panel members deemed to be shorter than most programs in other countries. While acknowledging that the survey findings concluded that the program should not be extended to the lower levels, the IAP nevertheless urged the ministry to consider starting the program at least a year earlier, based on the principle of early identification and early enrichment. For both primary and secondary grades, they recommended scheduling classes[3] that would enable

---

3. The Joplin Plan was cited as an example. Students in heterogeneous classes most of the day are regrouped for reading or mathematics instruction.

advanced students to attend lessons for the next grade level. They concurred with the survey findings that the program should be extended beyond Secondary 4. They suggested that existing programs for Junior College students that addressed specific aptitudes should be provided in a more systematic way with a more differentiated curriculum for qualified students, including those who were not previously in the program.[4] If a special school was being considered, they recommended that two considerations be borne in mind. One recommendation was that secondary schools hosting the GEP be designated as gifted schools if the entire population was in the top 3%. The second was that the new gifted schools should combine Secondary School and Junior College grade levels and focus on the arts, math, science, and technology. Regardless of the model, it was pointed out that it was important that the administrator have the requisite knowledge base and specific competencies to articulate to different audiences the rationale for the program and its attendant features.

Review Committee's Response. The review committee concluded that the program should continue to start at Primary 4 because test scores were more reliable and stable for children older than 8.[5] Selection at Primary 3 would also allow time for schooling to have its impact in bridging the experiential gap of children from professional homes and those from less-advantaged homes (Phua, 1983). The recommendation that services be extended to students at the Junior College level would be considered in the context of reform efforts to restructure the upper secondary and Junior College education system. GEP schools offer an integrated secondary-Junior College curriculum to high-ability learners, and it was likely that subject-specific accelerative options would be extended to outstanding students whose needs were not sufficiently addressed by the enriched program. It would be instructive to heed the IAP's advice that mentors not be overtaxed and mentorships be open only to students who were ready to go beyond what the school/college offered.

The review committee weighed the pros and cons of a school for the gifted. At the primary level, it was decided that the current practice of self-

---

4. From document analysis, the IAP noted that almost 50% of Junior College students who represented Singapore in International Olympiads and participated in International Science Programs were non-GEP students.

5. Sternberg, Grigorenko, & Bundy (2001) noted that the predictive power of IQ increased yearly with the child's age.

contained classes in regular schools could be retained, as guidelines to optimize the mix of GEP and non-GEP students have been effective in ensuring ample opportunities for socialization between the two groups. As for the secondary level, the implementation of the Integrated Program would blur the divide between students in the program and the mainstream. In the context of the review of upper secondary/Junior College education, the committee felt it was opportune to introduce yet another option. A specialized school of math and science, set up in collaboration with a partner agency like a local university, could offer instruction to students who have the aptitude and interest to pursue advanced courses in math and science.

To What Extent Does the Program Utilize Partnerships and Collaboration With the Larger Community (Universities, Businesses, and Parents) to Address Its Goals, Issues, and Concerns?

Findings and Recommendations. The GEB offers 13 special programs to nurture students interested in creativity and innovation in math, science, humanities, information technology, and leadership. The GEB taps the resources of institutions of higher learning and professional agencies to run these programs. The IAP was impressed with the high-level quality of students' products. As part of extending services to the Junior College level, panel members suggested that mentorship programs at the university level could focus on specialized projects. This would mean further strengthening ties with the universities. It was also recommended that the GEB find opportunities to increase collaboration with the National Institute of Education (NIE).[6] NIE faculty could not only expand the pool of mentors for special programs, but they could also provide GEP teacher training and parent education programs and conduct GEP-related research, data analysis, and program evaluation. Collaboration with other professional groups in education and psychology was also encouraged.

Review Committee's Response. The review committee agreed that the gifted program could initiate ties with more partner agencies, strengthen those with existing collaborating institutions of higher learning, and tap other community resources. They could assist in multiple ways, not only

---

[6.] This is the only School of Education in Singapore, and it is part of the Nanyang Technological University.

in the provision of new program initiatives, such as holiday enrichment camps, but also in teacher training and parent education, as well as research and evaluation efforts to be undertaken by the GEB.

Discussion

On balance, the review committee accepted most of the international panel's recommendations, with the exception of those pertaining to identification processes, and this was mainly due to unique circumstances in the local context. It was felt that multiple instruments for identification were not critical since every child in the education system had an equal chance to be selected for placement in the program. Since not all children came from English-speaking homes, it was thought that the selection should not be done too early, since time was needed for differences to level out. Finally, the recommendation that the tests ought to identify students with special talents was not consonant with the ministry's general philosophy of a broad-based general education.

The panel's recommendations were timely when seen against the context of changes that were taking place in the upper secondary/Junior College sector. A bigger group of students could be served, and talented GEP and non-GEP students could be further stretched through acceleration in the Integrated Program. A specialized, combined secondary school-Junior College for students with special aptitudes for math and science would add to the plethora of options for students. In selecting students for all these new programs, multiple criteria would probably be used. The GEB has already commenced work on the recommendations pertaining to curriculum, instruction, assessment, evaluation, and staff development. Some of these can be implemented with immediate effect, while others will take more time and planning to effect.

Features That Characterized the Involvement of External (Foreign) Evaluators

The goals for the evaluation were clear to all involved in the exercise and were explicitly communicated to relevant stakeholders, as well as to others who might be indirectly involved in the evaluation process. The potential threat that such an exercise could pose to personnel responsible for the program was alleviated by ensuring that all concerned understood why this evaluation was necessary and that findings would be used to inform decision making and policy formulation that would help improve the program design and implementation and develop it to a higher level.

When foreign consultants were engaged, efforts were made to acquaint them with the local educational (and social/cultural) environment so that their charge could be set in proper context. To ensure that the evaluation exercise could be as comprehensive as possible and oriented to the objectives of the exercise, consultants never had to negotiate access to program information (Patton, 1987). They were given full access to information, data, and existing documents. Time was built in for consultants to discuss preliminary impressions with GEP personnel or, in the most recent exercise, the local review committee. This was valuable because clarification and dialogue gave the consultants additional insights, which, in turn, led them to reframe some of their questions and refine their approaches. Meal times also helped to build rapport between the local and external teams and contributed to the nonthreatening and pleasant circumstances in which the exercise was carried out. This model of a local review committee working alongside an external (foreign) team of evaluators was effective on at least two counts. First, the preliminary work done by the local committee (collection of relevant data, preparation of documents, discussion of issues) enabled the team to provide the external evaluators rich information efficiently and effectively. Secondly, the different perspectives and the expertise of the external team led the local team to recast challenges in a new light and helped them to explore solutions and new initiatives, bearing in mind best practices supported by research findings.

Another noteworthy feature was that the local review committee deliberated the recommendations of the external team against the context of past policies, current practices, and impending changes in the local education scene and, in turn, decided on which recommendations to accept for immediate implementation, which to consider for possible implementation in the near future, and which would be useful to guide thinking about future developments. Three reports emerged from this exercise: The external team presented their final written report to the local committee, the local committee then presented their response to this report to senior officials at the Ministry of Education, and, after further discussion of major issues, the local committee submitted a written report of its findings and recommendations, incorporating those of the external team, as well.

Conclusion

The value of the evaluation process is often overlooked once the exercise is completed. It is not uncommon to find many evaluations falling short of the final step: utilizing the process and the findings for program development and improvement. Evaluation findings can alert personnel who are closely linked to the program to "blind spots." While strengths of the program are validated, areas for improvement of which staff are not aware are also highlighted.

In the evaluation described in this chapter, the thorough probing and rich evidence surfaced during the process served to help administrators determine the critical aspects of the program that needed more immediate attention and plan the timeframe for further action. Involvement of a team of independent, foreign experts lent credibility to the findings, and the different perspectives worked to prompt local staff to challenge existing practices and assumptions. The process also contributed to new knowledge about effective practices and helped build a shared understanding among all who were involved in the enterprise. Finally, program personnel made a concerted effort to utilize knowledge and experience gained through the evaluation process itself. As Goethe once said, "Knowing is not enough; we must apply."

Practical Tips for Program Administrators

1. Be sincere about the evaluation effort. Do it with a view to finding better ways to do things. Remember that the evaluation outcomes are determined by the evaluation goals.

2. Be consistent in the collection of information. This determines to some extent how thorough the evaluation will be, and it will make the on-site evaluation more efficient.

3. When engaging external evaluators, be they external to the organization responsible for the program being evaluated or external to the country, provide every assistance to them to maximize their time and involvement.

4. Be open to best practices, but be sensitive to the local context. Best practices in general may not work in the local environment.

5. Document discussions and the rationale for accepting, storing, or rejecting recommendations. All evaluation documents could be useful for future evaluation efforts.

References

American Educational Research Association, American Psychological Association, & National Council on Measurement in Education. (1999). *Standards for educational and psychological testing.* Washington, DC: American Educational Research Association.

Bloom, B. S. (1985). *Developing talent in young people.* New York: Ballantine Books.

Feldman, D. H. (1985). *Nature's gambit.* New York: BasicBooks.

Hopson, R. (2001). Global and local conversation on culture, diversity, and social justice in evaluation: Issues to consider in a 9/11 era. *American Journal of Evaluation, 22,* 375–380.

Landrum, M. S., Callahan, C. M., & Shaklee, B. D. (Eds.). (2001). *Aiming for excellence: Annotations to the NAGC pre-K–grade 12 gifted program standards.* Waco, TX: Prufrock Press.

Nielson, M. E., & Buchanan, N. K. (1991). Evaluating gifted programs with locally constructed instruments. In N. K. Buchanan & J. F. Feldhusen (Eds.), *Conducting research and evaluation in gifted education: A handbook of methods and applications* (pp. 275–310). New York: Teachers' College Press.

Patton, M. Q. (1987). *How to use qualitative methods in evaluation.* Newbury Park, CA: Sage.

Phua, S. L. (1983). *The gifted project.* Singapore: Ministry of Education.

Rossi, P. H., & Freeman, H. E. (Eds.). (1993). *Evaluation: A systematic approach.* Newbury Park, CA: Sage.

Royse, D., Tyler, B. A., Padgett, D. K., & Logan, T. K. (2001). *Program evaluation: An introduction* (3rd ed.). Belmont, CA: Brooks/Cole.

Sternberg, R. J., Grigorenko, D., & Bundy, E. A. (2001). The predictive value of IQ. *Merrill-Palmer Quarterly, 47,* 1–41.

Metaevaluation Findings:
A Call for Gifted Program Quality

by Joyce VanTassel-Baska

There is no such thing as professionalism without a commitment to evaluation of whatever it is that one supervises or produces – and to self-evaluation as well.

—Michael Scriven (2000, p. 258)

Where are gifted programs going in the future? What are important trends and issues to consider? Our decade of evaluation research suggests that the field suffers from a series of interrelated problems.

First, there is a problem of credibility. Partially because of multiple conceptions of giftedness and multiple models with limited research behind them, we have failed to convince policymakers at all levels of the need to view gifted education as an important and serious concern for our society. Signs of this lack of credibility may be seen in the following: Fewer than 10% of our universities offer programs for gifted personnel preparation; our total funding is less than 1% of the federal education budget; more than 160 times more total dollars (state, local, and federal) go to support *other* exceptionalities; and less than half the states employ full-time coordinators of gifted programs.

A second problem is the political dynamics associated with operating gifted programs. Charges of elitism and perceived lack of sensitivity to those less fortunate plague program developers at all levels. The specter of the No Child Left Behind Act may serve to make gifted programming even more of a pariah as additional emphasis is placed on students not performing at adequate levels.

Given these two major problems, it is no surprise to find gifted programs in a stalemate based on lack of sufficient infrastructure. Because of the lack of resources, there is a widespread lack of deep program development and implementation. This program superficiality is most evident in 1) a lack of technical adequacy in identification tools, 2) a lack of understanding about how tools should be employed, 3) a lack of fidelity in translating program goals to classroom practice, and 4) a decided absence of program impact data.

The analysis of findings from multiple evaluations serves to substantiate the interwoven nature of problems in this field. We also must find ways to move beyond formative evaluation efforts that can only focus on improvement to summative evaluation that focuses on quality and value. In order to do that, we must create evaluation design as a part of nascent program development efforts that include well-designed, testable student assessment models. Such approaches then place a strong premium on effective planning as an antidote to sheer political response.

Methodology

When deriving findings from individual evaluation studies, our methods entailed two processes essential to demonstrating validity through verification procedures: member checks and triangulation (Creswell, 1998; Eisenhart & Howe, 1992). Each program coordinator reviewed a draft of the evaluation report and was engaged in a discussion of its accuracy and its consonance to the real world of what happened at school sites. Thus, there was an attempt to ascertain the truth of the findings through public disclosure (Shark, 2002). Each coordinator also completed a self-assessment of the program based on the National Association for Gifted Children standards as a cross-check to the report's findings.

This self-assessment also became part of the discussion regarding the report.

At a second level, all evaluation findings were cross-referenced to data sources to ensure that triangulation was occurring. Table 12.1 documents the triangulation process for one of the evaluation studies conducted.

The metaevaluation process was accomplished by applying a basic coding map to the seven sets of findings and recording the central ideas. Where two or more studies reflected a finding, it was coded into a relevant program development category. At Level 1 analysis, content categories were derived from multiple findings across studies on (a) identification, (b) curriculum, (c) staff development, (d) parental issues, (e) assessment and evaluation, (f) program design and development, and (g) program resource issues. The 1–5 designation indicates the number of findings within a given category. Once these findings were recorded, analysis was continued to derive themes. Finally, overarching general ideas emerged from the thematic analysis (Anfara, Brown, & Mangione, 2002). Table 12.2 demonstrates results of this process applied to the data sets. Through these techniques, then, we could make sense of what we had learned, paying attention to the practice and politics of interpretation (Denzin, 2000).

As we analyzed findings across the seven gifted program evaluations used as a data-base for this volume, it is striking how similar the findings were. While states and local school districts portray their educational context as unique, in reality, the problems of implementing gifted programs are very similar, even with variations in geography, district demographics, and philosophies regarding grouping.

Metafindings at Level 1

The majority of findings across evaluation reports using multiple data sources documented a set of persistent issues and problems encountered during the evaluation process.

Concerns About Identification Processes

In general, stakeholders found the identification process either too liberal or too strict, depending on their role and general perspective. In

Table 12.1

Sample Findings: Outcome and Process of Triangulation

Findings	Data Sources
There is a lack of equity and consistency in programs and services across buildings within one district as well as across districts within the state.	FG, I, DR, CO
The gifted identification process is not known by some student and adult stakeholders. It also relies too heavily on high achievement scores and teacher recommendations. No separate approach to identification is employed beyond elementary school in most districts.	FG, TH, DR
The identification process focuses on multiple categories in the majority of districts, but program services do not match up with the process.	I, DR, GPS
The identification process does not focus sufficiently on strategies to identify under-represented groups, including minority students (especially Hispanic), twice exceptional, ESL, and underachievers. Special program opportunities are not in place for these learners either.	DR, I, GPS
Gifted students are underidentified in the majority of school districts, given the national incidence rates (5–15%).	DR, I, FG
There appears to be an underutilization of flexible grouping approaches, with regular classroom placement and pull-out programs dominating.	FG, GPS, I
Contact time is more limited than the minimum necessary to provide a quality program, with almost 40% of programs meeting with gifted students less than two hours per week.	FG, GPS, FS
Curriculum emphases are derived from individual teacher preferences, with the majority emphasis areas being project work and critical or creative thinking.	GPS, CO, FG
Curriculum development for gifted students is needed at all levels of schooling, with a clear set of goals and outcomes specified. Differentiation of instruction is limited. Comprehensive articulation of curriculum offerings across domains is also currently lacking. Middle and high school options need to be increased, especially honors and Advanced Placement courses in multiple areas and technological/distance learning opportunities.	FG, TH, CO, DR

Pull-out programs dominate at the elementary level and are facilitator-driven with no set curriculum. While the program is perceived as challenging by students and parents, its fragmented nature creates a concern among stakeholders.	FG, DR, CO
Multiple instructional approaches are commonly employed with gifted students.	FS, GPS, CO, FG
The training grant was perceived as beneficial in that it provided a few teachers with opportunities for enhancing classroom practice. Many of the adults were unaware of it or felt it was "too little and too diffuse" to have a significant impact on programs. Major benefits of the training grant cited included raising teacher competency, meeting the needs of gifted students more effectively, and changing staff attitudes in a favorable way.	FG, I, GPS
Staff development opportunities in gifted education appear to be limited in number and focus. Over 70% of the districts noted that over half of their personnel still need training in gifted education.	GPS, FS, FG, I
Over half of the districts do not have a regular schedule for evaluation. Although self-report data suggest that gifted students are assessed on multiple measures, little evidence exists that such processes occur.	GPS, I, DR
Program management and appropriate supervision are hampered by most coordinators' having split positions and being untrained in gifted education.	GPS, FS, I
Communication with parents was found to be problematic on most gifted program issues. Very few formal parent education programs are available.	FG, TH, GPS
Lack of adequate staffing and resources to deliver the program at local sites was seen as a major barrier to program improvement by adult stakeholders. Lack of administrative leadership for the program was also perceived as a major problem.	FG, TH, CO, I, GPS
Provisions for improvement focused on curriculum development and articulation, more teacher training for regular classroom teachers, and more staffing.	FG, TH, FS, GPS

Note. CO = Classroom Observation; DR = Document Review; FG = Focus Groups; I = Interviews; GPS = Gifted Program Survey; FS = Facilitator Survey; TH = Town Hall Meeting

Table 12.2

Code Mapping: A Content Analysis of Findings
Across Seven Evaluation Studies

Level 1	A1	Identification system not well understood.
	A2	ID system not perceived to be effective.
	A3	ID system not sensitive enough to underrepresented populations.
	B1	Lack of strong differentiated practice in gifted programs.
	B2	Lack of differentiation in regular classrooms.
	B3	Lack of curriculum framework.
	B4	Lack of scope and sequence of curricula.
	B5	Use of multiple instructional approaches.
	C1	Staff development haphazard and teacher-driven.
	C2	Limited staff development opportunities.
	D1	Lack of effective parental communication.
	D2	Lack of strong parent involvement with the program.
	E1	Lack of evaluation as a part of program design.
	E2	Lack of gifted student assessment data, documenting learning in the program.
	F1	Lack of consistency of program implementation across schools.
	F2	Lack of scope and sequence of program from elementary to secondary levels.
	F3	Lack of comprehensiveness in talent area offerings.
	F4	High stakeholder satisfaction with student challenge and program benefits.
	F5	Availability of multiple program options.
	G1	Lack of human resources to implement the programs effectively.
	G2	Lack of full time coordination of the program.
	G3	Lack of funding to sustain and move the program forward.
	G4	High stakeholder satisfaction with program coordinators and selected teachers in the program.

Level 2	•	Dedicated personnel
	•	Perceived challenging opportunities
	•	Diversity of approaches and options
	•	Need for deeper personnel preparation to work with gifted learners
	•	Imperfect identification systems
	•	No evaluation design in place
	•	Underresourcing
	•	Need for program coherence in planning and implementation
	•	Need for evidence of student learning and program effectiveness

Level 3	•	Diffusion of gifted services by committed staff.
	•	Neglect of gifted program infrastructure.

several of the evaluations, there was no consensus on how to improve the process. Triangulation of data sources also suggested that disadvantaged gifted students, as represented by the population on free- or reduced-lunch status, may be underrepresented in gifted programs. Site visits confirmed that nonverbal measures of intelligence are not widely employed at the elementary level. While stakeholders expressed concern about the shortcomings of identification and curricular emphases for this population, they lacked a sense of how to respond proactively to the problem since, at many sites, the entire identification system was under siege.

Lack of Adequate Curricular Differentiation

A related concern was the lack of adequate curricular differentiation, given the needs of gifted learners. While gifted classrooms typically employed more strategies consonant with good teaching and differentiation, room for improvement in higher level thinking, problem solving, and accommodation to individual differences was noted. While not pervasive across all the classrooms observed during the on-site phase of the evaluation(s), there was evidence that the depth and rate of learning in some gifted classroom settings needed to be intensified. Moreover, differentiation in regular classrooms was significantly lacking when compared to gifted classrooms, suggesting that gifted practices have not impacted general teaching practice to the extent necessary for gifted students to profit from them.

Concerns About Staff Development

Concerns about the nature and quality of staff development for teachers of the gifted and regular classroom teachers were consistent across all relevant phases of the evaluations. Not only was the amount of in-service perceived to be inadequate, but there was no empirical framework for enhancing teacher competence tied to the goals of the program or its effectiveness with learners. The in-service that does occur is based predominantly on teacher interest or willingness to participate with no follow-up expectations regarding classroom implementation. Moreover, instead of strengthening staff development options for teachers of the gifted, most school districts expressed the desire to in-service the entire teaching population.

Lack of Active Parental Involvement

Multiple data sources suggested a lack of active parental involvement models at the program level. Data available from two states revealed that only one-third of the districts had parent groups. Furthermore, the heavy reliance on state dollars as the "bricks and mortar" in gifted program budgets speaks to the need to create strong parent networks to ensure advocacy efforts that will protect and expand these resources at the local level.

Little Emphasis on Program Evaluation

Local gifted programs put limited emphasis on the importance of program evaluation in terms of both the frequency of producing formal evaluation reports and the overreliance on perceptual data to demonstrate effectiveness. While community perceptions of gifted programs were perceived as high in the majority of districts surveyed, these ratings were not linked to student impact data even when databases such as Advanced Placement examination results were accessible to local administrators.

Lack of Minimum Expectations

While there was a lack of consistency across districts in relation to the nature and types of gifted programs, this mosaic also showed that there were significant gaps in subject matter categories, with programs in science, social studies, and foreign languages being particularly limited. While each district must certainly retain the latitude to "do its own thing," there is room for the field to come together around core elements or minimum expectations that would ensure some commonality of experience, which enhances program defensibility. The administrative alignment of the gifted coordinator position in several districts suggests that secondary program options need to be both expanded and more fully integrated into the menu of gifted program offerings.

What is the implication of a model of gifted services that stops at the middle school or early high school level? Regardless of the span of control of a coordinator's job, districts must embrace a gifted program model that extends throughout the gifted child's educational experience. Program articulation from elementary to middle school and from middle school to high school appears to be inadequate regardless of demography or organizational model. Stakeholders were uniformly vocal about this issue. In addition, the reliance on inclusion and cluster grouping by more than one-third of the elementary programs raises concerns about the quantity and intensity of curricular and instructional differentiation. The continued use of the pull-out model in 73% of elementary schools and 41% of middle schools makes articulation with the regular classroom of paramount importance. Consequently, because curricular differentiation and program articulation are typically complex issues, they may or may not be sufficiently addressed through the types of models observed in these evaluations.

Lack of Resources

In all of the districts and states studied, lack of resources at the teacher and coordinator level crippled the potential for program improvement. Many districts used teacher personnel to cover multiple schools and expected gifted specialists to be resources in the regular classroom and teach gifted students in a pull-out class, as well. Coordinators had many things assigned to them and multiple program responsibilities, with gifted education being but one. Funding was also found to be stagnant or cut for these programs.

Emerging Themes at Level 2

These findings also produced a set of common themes that affect gifted programs and their development.

Dedicated Personnel

The findings across evaluation sites suggested that, despite limited resources and support, gifted programs employ a strong cadre of teachers and program coordinators who perform particular tasks to keep gifted programs going. Many of these personnel also suffer verbal abuse and derision from colleagues because of their stance on program issues. They also tend to work hard and stay focused on the needs of gifted learners. Stakeholders hold them in high regard, frequently seeing them as "lifelines" to gifted students and families.

Perceived Challenging Student Opportunities

Stakeholders cling to the notion that gifted programs are highly beneficial to their targeted clientele, even in the absence of data to support this claim. In one community, for example, parents said they would do anything to keep the program intact as it was, even though classroom observations revealed poor teaching and no curricular base for these learners. The desire for these programs to work often overrides their obvious limitations in selected settings.

Diversity of Approaches and Options

An optimistic sign in many of these settings was the recognition of the need to create multiple options for gifted learners using diverse approaches. Some rural areas were quite sophisticated in their use of distance learning to serve the gifted, while urban areas established specialized magnet schools and International Baccalaureate sites at secondary levels. These options provided greater flexibility for gifted students in finding an optimal match to individual talent areas, as well as interests and predispositions.

Systematic Evaluation

If it is important for gifted programs to be accountable, then evaluation designs must be crafted and implemented in school districts to demonstrate both student learning and program effectiveness. Data collection is also necessary for effective planning and assessment of goal attainment. Repeatedly, gifted programs lack the expertise and resource power to institute such accountability measures. Moreover, documentation of student learning gains requires sufficient contact time with a differentiated curriculum in order to demonstrate positive results. Most settings lacked both of these requirements.

Imperfect Identification Systems

While there was evidence that districts were opening up their identification protocol to multiple criteria and multiple assessment measures, it was less clear that stakeholders understood either the process or the reasons behind it. Great skepticism persists over how gifted students are identified and the extent to which the process is equitable, especially for underrepresented minority groups and disabled populations. Ironically, more stakeholder satisfaction was apparent in districts using fewer criteria and serving fewer students in programs.

Program Incoherence

Evidence abounded that gifted program development has lain dormant for years or has failed to grow commensurate with the needs of students and schools. There was a decided lack of definition in the program structure beyond grouping practices that described the nature of the program, its philosophy and rationale, and its methods of operation. Curricular documents that could attest to the overall goals and outcomes of the program were frequently missing, as were scope and sequence documents necessary to demonstrate the vertical articulation of offerings to students. Lack of such documents impedes any degree of standardization across schools, a common flaw also found in programs. Moreover, many coordinators were new or overburdened with other responsibilities and lacked a background in gifted education. Most programs then were highly teacher-dependent in respect to curriculum, instruction, and assessment approaches employed.

Personnel Preparation Limitations

In most of the districts evaluated, personnel preparation was limited in respect to coursework in gifted education, as well as ongoing staff/professional development opportunities. Districts tended to hire teachers they could find, rather than examining the extent to which their background was solid in coursework in gifted education and evidence of teaching effectiveness with that population. They also were given little support for improving their practice once on the job, with the average number of staff development opportunities being two, sometimes limited to conference attendance. Little thought had been given to a staff development plan that was linked to program expectations.

Lack of Resources

At all levels, gifted programs suffered from a lack of adequate resources. The popularity of the resource consultation model leaves teachers of the gifted vulnerable to spreading their services too thin to benefit anyone.

While special education has a limited student caseload of no more than 60 students, gifted educators many times have responsibility for 300 gifted students in addition to working with all learners in the classroom, doing in-services, and consulting with the regular classroom teachers. This situation is a recipe for failure, based on the shackles it places on even the most energetic teachers. Delivery model features then complicate an already bleak fiscal picture at the local level. Gifted education does not have a sufficient nucleus of qualified personnel devoted to the program in either the schools or administrative roles. Lack of funding for professional development, materials, and program development work further impede the progress that gifted programs might make.

Central Ideas at Level 3

Finally, the analysis of these evaluation reports yielded a common core problem, perhaps not sufficiently acknowledged by the field: the neglect of gifted program infrastructure and direct service delivery to gifted students in favor of diffusion strategies to all teachers and all learners. While leaders in gifted education clearly support a multiple-level emphasis in gifted programming, underresourced districts are being forced to make untenable choices, usually opting for service to general, rather than gifted, education due to strong political pressures.

The field of gifted education may need to be clearer about its own priorities. We are a small field that has had a clear focus and mission. We exist to provide programs and services to students who deviate positively from the norms in general and specific areas of learning deemed important by school communities. Can we continue to improve these programs, which desperately need attention, at the same time we are working with all teachers and learners to promote differentiation?

I sense that at least a two-tiered approach to gifted education needs to emerge, one that is heavily invested in gifted program improvement and a second that capitalizes on opportunities to promote the reform agenda for all learners. In an ideal system, gifted education could be considered an equal collaborative partner in raising achievement for all. Given the lack of national policy and limited funding, this ideal cannot be easily realized in most school districts nationally. Thus, attention to the improvement of existing gifted programs and services needs to be a clear and unequivocal priority.

The findings from case study site visits were strongly congruent with survey report findings and program documents, in respect to both accuracy of reporting and amplification of central issues raised. Furthermore, the findings across all three program components support the need for an emphasis on comprehensive, continuous services for all gifted students. The only real answer to critics of gifted education lies with strong, effective programs and empirical data to show positive learning gains in student populations that are directly attributable to program impact. In the absence of such evidence, gifted programs will continue to be at the mercy of shifting public perceptions of worth and the vagaries of the state budget process.

Many of the findings that emerged through this evaluation process are complementary to needs identified in *National Excellence: A Case for Developing America's Talent* (U.S. Department of Education, 1993). This report also speaks to the importance of more rigorous standards for curricula, instruction, and assessment of gifted students; a stronger emphasis on teacher development; and greater outreach to disadvantaged and other underserved populations. In this respect, what is transpiring in these evaluations of local programs mirrors issues identified nationally that are of ongoing concern to advocates of gifted education programs.

The vulnerability of gifted education services at local levels makes continued vigilance urgent. From the findings in this metaevaluation study, there is persuasive evidence that only state-supported, guaranteed services will ensure appropriate and challenging learning opportunities for all gifted students.

Recommendations for Enhancing Gifted Program Quality

While the metaevaluation findings paint a somewhat bleak picture of current practice, there are specific measures that practitioners at state and local levels can take to elevate program quality. In an age of standards and accountability, gifted education programs and services must demonstrate excellence and practice ways to improve. The following recommendations represent important directions for the field to consider in answering the clarion call for quality in gifted education. Each categorical area of the metaevaluation findings is addressed. In addition, policy recommendations are cited for areas not receiving sufficient attention at the local level.

Policy Recommendations

- Develop local and state policies and procedures regarding acceleration, pacing, and continuous progress across the K–12 spectrum as
they would affect gifted program implementation. Since these
approaches to serving the gifted are very well documented in the
research literature and in the NAGC standards, more attention to
their effective implementation needs to occur.
- Develop counseling and guidance policies and procedures for all
gifted learners at elementary, middle, and high school levels. Lack of
evidence for a comprehensive model for addressing the affective and
future planning needs of the gifted suggests a deficit in local program
design. Using the NAGC standards on counseling and guidance as a
basis, programs should develop a strong focus in this area.

Identification Recommendations

- Identify and program for gifted populations by specific areas of talent,
as well as general intellectual giftedness. Appropriate services to intellectual, academic, creative, and artistic students should be thought-
fully developed. Program depth and articulation should not be
sacrificed to broad identification approaches that cannot be matched
to appropriate services.
- Continue to identify underrepresented groups for gifted programs,
including economically disadvantaged, twice-exceptional, second
language learners (ESL), and minority students.

Curricular Recommendations

- Address differential needs of gifted students through relevant experiences that are better tailored to their specific aptitudes and interests.
Many programs group gifted students together, but do not differentiate within special classes or programs.
- Develop curricular frameworks and scope and sequence documents
at each program level and across K–12 that demonstrate adaptations
in addressing the general education state standards for gifted learners.
Align all current and future gifted curricular work with the general
education state standards so that neither duplication of coverage nor
learning gaps occur.

- Develop statewide and local efforts to improve curriculum development for gifted learners, blending teacher-developed curricular approaches with extant exemplary curricula for gifted learners where available to form a richer base for differentiating instruction. Seek to adopt alternative texts and other materials appropriate for the population served.
- Because the nature of many gifted programs focuses on higher order process skills and products, it is essential that regular classroom teachers see the connection to their work and provide appropriate activities for gifted students in regular classroom settings. This recommendation springs from feedback from both principals and classroom teachers and suggests the need for joint planning and staff development sessions. More cohesion in curricular planning that bridges regular and gifted staff would increase awareness of the needs of gifted learners for differentiated instruction and contribute to the joint ownership of the responsibility to both serve these students and address state standards.

Professional Development Recommendations

- The need for staff development planning, perhaps at a statewide level, is an issue also brought to light by this metaevaluation. While the documentation shows that educators are involved annually in staff development, there are relatively limited opportunities for cohesive training that are directly related to delivering a quality program to gifted students. Expectations for teacher competency might be used as a basis for such planning, coupled with specific requirements for differences among local programs. Furthermore, there is a concern about tying staff development and training to hiring decisions to ensure that teachers of the gifted are adequately prepared to provide the level of differentiation of content and instruction that is essential to effective programming.
- More monitoring of classrooms by program coordinators using a standard classroom observation form, demonstration teaching, and videotape analyses of teaching might be employed to encourage the institutionalization of best instructional practice.
- Principals and other administrators should receive professional development in order to coordinate follow-up efforts and to socialize administrators to the educational needs of this population.

- Staff development sessions should be tied to areas of instructional need for differentiating for the gifted and should be open to both gifted and regular classroom teachers. Based on classroom observation data across studies, the main areas of focus would be in critical thinking, problem solving, and metacognition.

Parent Recommendations

- The issue of stronger parent involvement in local programming efforts is in need of serious consideration. Questions regarding the nature and extent of involvement have surfaced, given the limited picture of involvement delineated across studies. If both program improvement and program advocacy are long-term goals of local programs, then greater mobilization and education of parents is necessary.
- Develop parent education programs that focus on strengthening parent understanding of the gifted program via written materials and special workshops. Data across studies suggest that parents are dissatisfied with communication about the program. We recommend offering a series of parent workshops/seminars to provide a more formal forum for parent education and dialogue. These events could focus on specific program highlights, as well as general topics of interest to parents of gifted learners. They might highlight individual student work in addition to overall program performance results. This would elevate the understanding of what districts are already doing to meet the needs of gifted learners and provide positive channels for communication with parents.

Program Design and Development Recommendations

- Gifted program interventions need to be expanded in scope in order to respond to the variety of academic and artistic aptitudes gifted children possess. While opportunities in language arts and mathematics were prevalent across the districts studied, opportunities in science, social studies, and foreign languages were more limited. In an era of talent development based on domain, program opportunities in all subjects, including the arts, are clearly warranted. Consequently, these data pinpoint areas of needed expansion for many local programs.

- The issue of secondary programs, the nature and extent of offerings, and how they are perceived is another focus to consider for future development. The data indicate a sporadic approach to such programming, fragmented by grade level and subject area. Moreover, the national Advanced Placement program results suggest that gifted programs are producing a limited number of AP scholars (defined as scoring 3 or higher on three AP tests), even though AP was the most frequently cited program experience at secondary levels. This might suggest the need for greater attention to secondary programming, beginning no later than seventh grade and moving toward comprehensive advanced offerings in all areas of the secondary curriculum.
- Greater gifted program articulation is needed across building levels in local school systems. Many stakeholders recognized the lack of comprehensive programs from elementary to middle school and from middle to high school as a serious flaw in local program design that has serious consequences for the overall quality of the educational experience for gifted students.

Assessment and Evaluation Recommendations

- Valid and reliable data on program effectiveness are as critical at the local level as they are in statewide advocacy. An initiative should be supported that requires (or at least encourages) local districts to collect student impact data on those served in gifted programs. While perceptual data will continue to be important in ensuring that stakeholders are satisfied with local services, cognitive and performance data related to the services provided are more cogent indicators of program success and appear to be necessary in lobbying for additional resources.
- Develop a system of annual program evaluation that routinely collects evidence of student growth in gifted programs at each stage of development, possibly at the end of grades 3, 6, 8, and 12. Assessments of stakeholder perceptions should also be done biennially.
- Create and implement a system to collect trend data on graduating seniors as a basis for assessing the impact of the program over time. Track course-taking patterns in AP and dual enrollment for identified gifted students, as well as performance on high-stakes tests such as the PSAT.

Resource and Funding Recommendations

- Increase districtwide assistance in areas such as curriculum and staff development, expanding to incorporate areas like counseling and service articulation at early primary and secondary levels as important foci for increased attention and resources.
- Resource sharing among curriculum, technology, and staff development departments should be considered, allowing gifted education a "fair share" in order to upgrade curricula and professional development efforts.
- Provide full-time program leadership in all districts. Such coordination would require the program leader(s) to be endorsed in gifted education and highly conversant in gifted program options.
- Provide sufficient resources to carry out the program model successfully. If the resource collaboration model is to be successful, it must be properly staffed, with caseloads comparable to special education.

Conclusion

Gifted education as a basic provision in school districts is not a frill. Quality education for gifted students is a right, not a privilege. To overlook the obvious talents of all these students is to suggest that we care little about our collective future as a society. Lost in the mantra of "No child left behind" is the reality of gifted students daily losing their motivation to learn and perform at high levels in school. While we can help improve general education in a number of ways, perhaps the most powerful would be to construct quality gifted programs in every public school in this country so that there truly is a visible standard for excellence in schooling.

References

Anfara, V. A., Brown, K. M., & Mangione, T. L. (2002). Qualitative analysis on stage: Making the research process more public. *Educational Researcher, 31*(7), 28–38.

Creswell, J. (1998). *Qualitative inquiring and research design: Choosing many fine traditions.* Thousand Oaks, CA: Sage.

Denzin, N. K. (2000). The practices and politics of interpretation. In N. K. Denzin & Y. S. Lincoln (Eds.), *Handbook of qualitative research* (2nd ed., pp. 897–922). Thousand Oaks, CA: Sage.

Eisenhart, M. A., & Howe, K. R. (1992). Validity in qualitative research. In M. D. LeCompte, W. L. Millery, & J. Preissle (Eds.), *Handbook of qualitative research in education* (pp. 643–680). San Diego, CA: Academic Press.

Scriven, M. (2000). Evaluation ideologies. In D. L. Stufflebeam, G. E. Madaus, & T. Kellaghan (Eds.), *Evaluation models* (pp. 249-278). Boston: Kluwer Academic Publisher.

Shark, G. (2002). *Qualitative research: A personal skills approach.* Upper Saddle River, NJ: Merrill/Prentice Hall.

U.S. Department of Education, Office of Educational Research and Improvement. (1993). *National excellence: A case for developing America's talent.* Washington, DC: U.S. Government Printing Office.

■■■■ Appendix A
Summary of the Program Evaluation Standards

Utility

The utility standards are intended to ensure that an evaluation will serve the information needs of attended users.

U1 *Stakeholder Identification.* Persons involved in or affected by the evaluation should be identified, so that their needs can be addressed.

U2 *Evaluator Credibility.* The persons conducting the evaluation should be both trustworthy and competent to perform the evaluation, so that the evaluation findings achieve maximum credibility and acceptance.

U3 *Information Scope and Selection.* Information collected should be broadly selected to address pertinent questions about the program and be responsive to the needs and interests of clients and other specified stakeholders.

U4 *Values Identification.* The perspectives, procedures, and rationale used to interpret the findings should be carefully described, so that the bases for value judgements are clear.

U5 *Report Clarity.* The evaluation reports should clearly describe the program being evaluated, including its context, and the purposes, procedures, and findings of the evaluation, so that essential information is provided and easily understood.

U6 *Report Timeliness and Dissemination.* Significant interim findings and evaluation reports should be disseminated to intended users, so that they can be used in a timely fashion.

U7   *Evaluation Impact.* Evaluations should be planned, conducted, and reported in ways that encourage follow-through by stakeholders, so that the likelihood that the evaluations will be used is increased.

Feasibility

The feasibility standards are intended to ensure that an evaluation will be realistic, prudent, diplomatic, and frugal.

F1   *Practical Procedures.* The evaluation procedures should be practical, to keep disruption to a minimum while needed information is obtained.

F2   *Potential Viability.* The evaluation should be planned and conducted with anticipation of the different positions of various interest groups, so that their cooperation may be obtained and so that possible attempts by any of these groups to curtail evaluation operations or to bias or misapply the results can be averted or counteracted.

F3   *Cost Effectiveness.* The evaluation should be efficient and produce information of sufficient value, so that the resources expended can be justified.

Propriety

The propriety standards are intended to ensure that an evaluation will be conducted legally, ethically, and with due regard for the welfare of those involved in the evaluation, as well as those affected by its results.

P1   *Service Orientation.* Evaluations should be designed to assist organizations to address and effectively serve the needs of the full range of targeted participation.

P2   *Formal Obligations.* Obligations of the formal parties to an evaluation (what is to be done, how, by whom, when) should be agreed in writing, so that these parties are obliged to adhere to all conditions of the agreement or formally to renegotiate it.

P3   *Rights of Human Subjects.* Evaluations should be designed and conducted to respect and to protect the rights and welfare of human subjects.

P4   *Human Interactions*. Evaluators should respect human dignity and worth in their interactions with other persons associated with an evaluation, so that participants are not threatened or harmed.

P5   *Complete and Fair Assessment*. The evaluation should be complete and fair in its examination and recording of strengths and weaknesses of the program being evaluated, so that strengths can be built upon and problem areas addressed.

Accuracy Standards

The accuracy standards are intended to ensure that an evaluation will reveal and convey technically adequate information about the features that determine worth or merit of the program being evaluated.

A1   *Program Documentation*. The program being evaluated should be described and documented clearly and accurately, so that the program is clearly identified.

A2   *Context Analysis*. The context in which the program exists should be examined in enough detail, so that its likely influences on the program can be identified.

A3   *Described Purposes and Procedures*. The purposes and procedures of the evaluation should be monitored and described in enough detail, so that they can be identified and assessed.

A4   *Defensible Information Sources*. The sources of information used in a program evaluation should be described in enough detail, so that the adequacy of the information can be assessed.

A5   *Valid Information*. The information gathering procedures should be chosen or developed and then implemented so that they will assure that the interpretation arrived at is valid for the intended use.

A6   *Reliable Information*. The information gathering procedures should be chosen or developed and then implemented so that they will assure that the information obtained is sufficiently reliable for the intended use.

A7 *Systematic Information.* The information collected, processed, and reported in an evaluation should be systematically reviewed and any errors found should be corrected.

A8 *Analysis of Quantitative Information.* Quantitative information in an evaluation should be appropriately and systematically analyzed so that evaluation questions are effectively answered.

A9 *Analysis of Qualitative Information.* Qualitative information in an evaluation should be appropriately and systematically analyzed so that evaluation questions are effectively answered.

A10 *Justified Conclusions.* The conclusions reached in an evaluation should be explicitly justified, so that stakeholders can assess them.

A11 *Impartial Reporting.* Reporting procedures should guard against distortion caused by personal feelings and biases of any party to the evaluation, so that evaluation reports fairly reflect the evaluation findings.

A12 *Metaevaluation.* The evaluation itself should be formatively and summatively evaluated against these and other pertinent standards, so that its conduct is appropriately guided and, on completion, stakeholders can closely examine its strengths and weaknesses.

 # Appendix B
Classroom
Observation Form

 External Observer Form

Name of Observer: _____ Number of Students: _____
Date: _____ Grade: _____ Length of Observation (minutes): _____
Name of School: _____
Name of Teacher: _____
Course/Subject Observed: _____
Classroom Desk Arrangement: ☐ Desks in rows and columns ☐ Desks grouped
☐ Other (specify): _____
Please outline exactly what you are observing in the classroom with respect to curriculum and instruction.
Describe
     the specific lesson,   ___Regular   ___Cluster   ___Pull-out   ___Other
     the organization of the lesson,
     the texts and/or materials used,
     the methods used in communicating the lesson,
     characteristics of the learning experience and environment,
or any other observations and impressions which became the basis for completing the attached check-list. The
categories on the checklist are as follows:

Curriculum Planning	Expectations for Learning	Accom. for Indiv. Differences
Curric. Delivery Features	Gen. Teaching Strategies	Critical Thinking Strategies
Problem-solving Strategies	Metacognition	Classroom Extensions

Teacher Interview Questions
1 Do you have a written plan for this lesson?
2. What were your instructional objectives during the previous lesson with this class? What will you be
    covering in the subsequent lesson?
3. Are there any aspects of the lesson which you want to clarify with me before I finalize this observation form?
4.   Observer specified question: _____

_____

_____

Area	The Teacher...	Yes	No	Comments
Curriculum Planning	1. had a written lesson plan linked to course objectives.			
	2. communicated the purpose/objectives of the lesson to students.			
	3. adhered to the basic framework of the lesson as originally intended.			
Expectations for Learners	4. was clear in giving directions, and discussing activities and assignments.			
	5. sets high expectations for student performance in classroom.			
	6. provided clear and consistent feedback on student performance.			
Accommodation to Individual Differences	7. presented content which challenged students.			
	8. accommodated individual or subgroup differences through material selection or task assignments.			
	9. incorporated multicultural perspectives or knowledge, reflecting at least two cultures.			
	10. addressed at least 2 different modes of learning, e.g. visual, auditory, kinesthetic.			
	11. allowed students individually or in small groups to move through basic material more rapidly.			
Curriculum Delivery Features	12. emphasized depth in learning.			
	13. taught according to key concepts and ideas relevant to content area being addressed.			
	14. encouraged or indicated interdisciplinary connections.			
General Thinking Strategies	15. used flexible patterns of grouping to deliver the lesson.			
	16. used more than one instructional strategy to deliver the lesson.			
	17. provided activities in which students applied new learning.			
	18. provided the opportunity for the students to use technology.			
	19. kept all or most of the students on task.			
	20. used hands-on approaches including such things as journaling, manipulatives, experiments, etc.			
	21. used cooperative or collaborative learning strategies			
	22. allowed students to discover central ideas on their own through structured activities and/or questions.			
	23. emphasized higher level thinking strategies/skills.			
Critical Thinking Strategies	Used activities or questions which enabled students: 24. to make judgments or evaluate situations, problems, or issues.			
	25. to compare and contrast.			
	26. to generalize from specific data to the abstract.			
	27. to synthesize or summarize information within or across the disciplines.			
	28. to debate points of view or develop arguments to support ideas.			
Problem-solving Strategies	Used activities or questions which encouraged students: 29. to brainstorm ideas or alternatives.			
	30. to define problems (to go from a "mess" to a well-defined problem statement).			
	31. to select and implement solutions to problems.			
	32. to explore multiple interpretations.			
	33. allowed students to use alternative rather than single modes of expression for class/homework activities/products (e.g., charts, graphics, videos, journals, etc.).			
	34. allowed students to self-select topics for further investigation.			
Metacognition	35. modeled metacognitive strategies such as planning, monitoring, self-reflection or self-appraisal.			
	36. provided opportunities for students to think about their own thinking.			
	37. had students reflect on their own performance.			
Classroom Extensions	38. reinforced or expanded the lesson by assigning homework.			
	39. provided follow-up ideas of special projects for students to pursue.			
	40. identified people or materials which could be used to supplement student learning.			

 **Appendix C**

Sample Survey Questionnaire

Dear HCES Student,

Please respond to each question by circling the number that most closely reflects your thinking on the topic (1 = strongly disagree, 2 = disagree, 3 = neutral, 4 = agree, 5 = strongly agree). Room is provided for additional comments should you wish to make any. If you need more space for comments, you can attach additional sheets of paper. In order for the data to be most useful, questionnaires must be received by October 10 at the following address:

Rena F. Subotnik, Director
Center for Gifted Education Policy
Education Directorate
American Psychological Association
750 First St. NE
Washington, DC 20002-4242

> 1 = strongly disagree
> 2 = disagree
> 3 = neutral
> 4 = agree
> 5 = strongly agree

1. HCCS has been effective in developing the intellectual potential of its students.   1   2   3   4   5

_____
_____
_____

2. HCCS has been effective in developing students' ability to think critically.　　　1　2　3　4　5

_____

_____

_____

_____

3. HCCS has been effective in developing students' ability to think creatively.　　　1　2　3　4　5

_____

_____

_____

_____

4. HCCS has been effective in developing students' ability to think independently.　　　1　2　3　4　5

_____

_____

_____

_____

5. HCCS has contributed to students' moral development.
　　1　2　3　4　5

_____

_____

_____

_____

6. The method of gifted identification (i.e. admissions) is appropriate.
　　1　2　3　4　5

_____

_____

_____

_____

7. Performance should serve as an appropriate measure for continued participation.　　1　2　3　4　5

_____
_____
_____
_____

8. We need more opportunities for acceleration in math and other school subjects.　　1　2　3　4　5

_____
_____
_____
_____

9. Entry points (currently P–K, K, 7th grades) should be reconfigured.
　1　2　3　4　5

_____
_____
_____
_____

10. The faculty is well prepared to work with intellectually/academically gifted students.　　　　　1　2　3　4　5

_____
_____
_____
_____

11. The HCES library serves the students well.
　1　2　3　4　5

_____
_____
_____
_____

12. Students who have special talents and deep interests in specific sub-
    jects should be able focus on developing those talents, even at the
    expense of some well-roundedness.   1   2   3   4   5

    _____

    _____

    _____

    _____

13. What skills, knowledge, and attitudes should students have after early
    (P-K–1) grades? How do these outcomes jibe with the mission of a
    school for gifted students?

    _____

    _____

    _____

    _____

    _____

    _____

14. What skills, knowledge, and attitudes should students have after
    upper elementary (2–6) grades? How do these outcomes jibe with
    the mission of a school for gifted students?

    _____

    _____

    _____

    _____

    _____

    _____

Thank you for your contribution.

◾◾◾◾ Appendix D
Requested Documents

Area of Analysis	Document/Reports
School Organization/ Accountability	• Brochures, Hunter College High School and Hunter College Organizational chart • Descriptions of administrative responsibilities • Allocation of instructional budget beyond salaries • Criteria/process for selecting and hiring teachers • Criteria/process used for evaluating teachers for tenure • Institutionalized efforts to allow for teacher planning within/across disciplines/grades
Admissions	• The admissions process (description and sample applications) • Data collected on admissions in recent years
Curriculum & Instruction	• Curriculum, scope, and sequence pre-K–12 for all subjects • Statements describing the ways in which the curriculum addresses the needs of gifted students, with references to models or theories of gifted education • Documentation of action research projects pertaining to curriculum and instruction • Lists of research being conducted or recently conducted with name of principal investigator and university affiliation

Area of Analysis	Document/Reports
Assessment of Learning	• Standardized test scores for elementary students • Test scores of HCES students on HCHS exam • Listing of honors and awards • List of university college credit earned from courses taken at university • Standardized test scores for high school students (including SAT I, SAT II, ACT, and AP)
Counseling	• Counseling program description • Mechanisms for counseling underachieving/under-performing students • Mechanisms for counseling extraordinarily achieving students • Statistics (numbers and percentages) about (1) accelerated students by grade and subject, (2) identified LD students, (3) appropriate IEP and 504 statistics • List of colleges applied to and acceptance rates • Documented efforts to facilitate student transitions from elementary to middle to high school
Special Student Services, including Talent Development	• Number of accelerated math and foreign language students • Statements describing the ways in which the curriculum addresses the needs of gifted students, with references to models or theories of gifted education • Lists of student awards and competitions • Mechanisms for informing students about summer enrichment opportunities to parents/students • Complete documentation about the identification, records, and services provided to students with special needs, pre-K–12

 # About the Authors

Editors

Joyce VanTassel-Baska is the Jody and Layton Smith Professor of Education at the College of William and Mary in Virginia, where she has developed a graduate program and a research and development center in gifted education. Dr. VanTassel-Baska has published widely, including five recent books and over 260 monographs, book chapters, and articles in refereed journals. She also serves as the editor of *Gifted and Talented International*.

Annie Xuemei Feng is the research and evaluation coordinator of the Center for Gifted Education at the College of William and Mary. In addition to gifted program evaluation studies, her research interests also include gender-related studies and cross-cultural research, particularly focusing on highly gifted populations.

Contributors

Elissa Brown is the director of the Center for Gifted Education at the College of William and Mary. She also teaches graduate courses in gifted education. Prior to her work with the Center, she was director of the Chesapeake Bay Governor's School for Marine and Environmental Science. She has also been a gifted program coordinator and teacher. Elissa is the current president of the Virginia Association for the Gifted.

Chwee Quek was the deputy director of gifted education for Singapore. She is now a doctoral student at the College of William and Mary and the assistant editor of *Gifted and Talented International*.

Julie Long was the director of gifted programs for Richland Two School District in Columbia, SC, and a former professor of gifted education at Elon College in North Carolina. She retired in 2002.

Rena F. Subotnik is director for the Center for Gifted Education Policy at the American Psychological Association. Formerly, she was a professor in gifted education at Hunter College in New York City. She is widely published in the field of gifted education and talent development.

Janet F. Soller is the deputy director of the Center for Gifted Education Policy at the American Psychological Association. She also serves as the Center's online newsletter editor.

Sarah K. Hood works at the Center for Gifted Education Policy at the American Psychological Association, where she assists with program evaluation and research.